"BRAVO, BILL! You have given all of us educators a valuable gift by delineating your open humanitarian approach to teaching! You have passed on vital information that needs to be available for all new teachers of dance, as well as for long-time professionals who might not have re-looked at their own teaching lately!"

—Peggy Hackney, *author of Making Connections: Total Body Integration Through Bartenieff Fundamentals*

"An abundance of insight, gathered over a lifetime of teaching, choreographing, and performing. Evans provides a treasure trove of examples of incorporating effective practices and language, including that of images, prompts, anatomical clarity, all given to support deepening our students' experience of themselves dancing. Evans' personal journal through a long career of teaching dance while maintaining and generating enthusiasm and openness is an inspiration to fellow teachers to continue to grow and learn. His insights are specific, life affirming and useful. A rich resource for both new and experienced dance teachers. An inspiration. Wise and generous."

—Claire Porter, renowned choreographer, writer and performance artist

"*Teaching What You Want To Learn*, is a series of short, accessible and enlightening essays that celebrate the transformational power of critical thinking. Evans advocates for teaching the whole dancer by nurturing their intellect, emotions and physicality. A personal favorite are the *For Your Consideration* questions at the end of each essay that invite the reader to reflect on their own learning experience and how to enact change. A must read for anyone who values the learning process and is interested in teaching dance!"

—Edisa Weeks, Queens College, New York, USA

Teaching What You Want to Learn

Teaching What You Want to Learn distills the five decades that Bill Evans has spent immersed in teaching dance into an indispensable guide for today's dance instructor.

From devising specific pedagogical strategies and translating theory into action, to working with diverse bodies and embracing evolving value systems, Evans has considered every element of the teacher's role and provided 94 essential essays about becoming a more effective and satisfied educator. As well as setting out his own particular training methods and somatic practice as one of the world's leading dance teachers, he explores the huge range of challenges and rewards that a teacher will encounter across their career. These explorations equip the reader not only to enable and empower their students but also to get the most out of their own work so they are learning as they teach.

This is an essential book for anyone who wants to teach dance and movement, from professional and academic settings to amateur artists and trainee instructors.

(James William) Bill Evans is a Professor Emeritus at the University of New Mexico and a Visiting Professor Emeritus at the State University of New York College at Brockport. He is the founder of both the Somatic Dance Conference and Performance Festival and the Evans Somatic Dance Institute, now headquartered in Port Townsend, Washington.

Teaching What You Want to Learn

A Guidebook for Dance and Movement Teachers

Bill Evans

LONDON AND NEW YORK

Cover image: Illustration by Jude Clark Warnisher

First published 2023
by Routledge
4 Park Square, Milton Park, Abingdon, Oxon OX14 4RN

and by Routledge
605 Third Avenue, New York, NY 10158

Routledge is an imprint of the Taylor & Francis Group, an informa business

© 2023 Bill Evans

The right of Bill Evans to be identified as author of this work has been asserted in accordance with sections 77 and 78 of the Copyright, Designs and Patents Act 1988.

All rights reserved. No part of this book may be reprinted or reproduced or utilised in any form or by any electronic, mechanical, or other means, now known or hereafter invented, including photocopying and recording, or in any information storage or retrieval system, without permission in writing from the publishers.

Trademark notice: Product or corporate names may be trademarks or registered trademarks, and are used only for identification and explanation without intent to infringe.

British Library Cataloguing-in-Publication Data
A catalogue record for this book is available from the British Library

Library of Congress Cataloging-in-Publication Data
Names: Evans, Bill (James William), author.
Title: Teaching what you want to learn : a guidebook for dance and movement teachers / Bill Evans.
Description: Abingdon, Oxon ; New York, NY : Routledge, 2022. | Includes bibliographical references and index.
Identifiers: LCCN 2022001326 (print) | LCCN 2022001327 (ebook) | ISBN 9781032268491 (hardback) | ISBN 9781032228860 (paperback) | ISBN 9781003290209 (ebook)
Subjects: LCSH: Dance—Study and teaching. | Dance teachers—Training of. | Movement, Aesthetics of.
Classification: LCC GV1589 .E93 2022 (print) | LCC GV1589 (ebook) | DDC 792.8076—dc23
LC record available at https://lccn.loc.gov/2022001326
LC ebook record available at https://lccn.loc.gov/2022001327

ISBN: 9781032268491 (hbk)
ISBN: 9781032228860 (pbk)
ISBN: 9781003290209 (ebk)

DOI: 10.4324/9781003290209

Typeset in Sabon
by codeMantra

Dedicated with love, gratitude, respect and joy to Don Halquist, a superb teacher.

Contents

List of contributors   xv
Foreword   xvii
SELENE B. CARTER

INTRODUCTION   1
   1 *The Backstory* 1
   2 *Why This Title?* 6
   3 *Citing My Sources* 6

Chapter I. Notes to Self   10
   1 *Remind Yourself That You Love to Teach* 10
   2 *Embrace Evolving Values* 11
   3 *Teaching's Not Easy, But If It's Your Calling, Nothing Else Will Be As Satisfying* 12
   4 *You Always Have Something to Offer* 14
   5 *It's OK to Be Unpopular* 14
   6 *It's OK to Say You're Sorry* 16
   7 *Follow Your Personal Aliveness* 16

Chapter II. Underpinnings   19
   8 *Planting Seeds* 19
   9 *Crystallizing or Paralyzing Activities or Experiences* 20
   10 *All Students Are Smart* 21
   11 *Preparing Students for Their Future, Not Our Past* 22
   12 *Honoring Personal Uniqueness* 23
   13 *Knowing Themselves to Adapt to Different Styles* 24

14 Students Don't Need to Be Fixed 25
15 We Are All in This Together, But Each of Us Is Having a Different Class 26
16 Learning Is Active 28
17 Thought Creates Action 29
18 Inefficient Movement Patterns Are Not Moral Weaknesses 30
19 Replace. You Can't Just Erase 31

Chapter III. Cornerstones 34

20 Positive Self-Talk 34
21 Compete or Excel? 35
22 High Challenge But Low Threat 36
23 The Value of Refined Repetition 37
24 There Is No Meaning Without Context 38
25 Learning Can Be Serious Fun 40
26 Uncover to Discover 41
27 Never Work Harder Than Your Students 42
28 Teaching The People in The Room 43
29 Learning From The Living Body 45
30 The Mind-Body Organizing Power of Intent 46
31 Movement Occurs in Phrases 48
32 Neutral Alignment/A Change in The Part Creates a Change in The Whole 49
33 Brace, Collapse or Give and Take/Yield and Push to Reach and Pull 50

Chapter IV. Language 55

34 Words Matter 55
35 Invite 56
36 Allow 57
37 Reach and Other Integrative Verbs 58
38 We Are Not Objects 59

Chapter V. Guidelines and Strategies 61

39 Noticing Each Student in The Learning Circle 61
40 There Is No Front in Our Classroom 62

    41 *Wrapping Words Around Perceptions/*
       Pair and Share 63
    42 *Teaching Through Touch* 64
    43 *Balancing Portions of The Class* 65
    44 *Investigations Not Exercises* 67
    45 *Planning Backward* 68
    46 *Managing Time* 69
    47 *Previewing The Whole, Differentiating*
       The Parts and Integrating the Entire
       Investigation 70
    48 *Addressing The Cause, Not The Result* 71
    49 *Opening Rituals* 73
    50 *Closing Rituals* 74

Chapter VI. Body Specificity   76
    51 *Lung Respiration* 76
    52 *Cellular Respiration/We Are Mostly Water* 77
    53 *Breathdancing* 78
    54 *Dynamic Alignment/The Pathways Through* 79
    55 *Body-Part Phrasing* 80
    56 *Asymmetrical Body Sides* 81
    57 *Plié Is So Much More Than Bending*
       The Knees 83
    58 *Turn-Out Is Not All About The Feet* 84
    59 *Turn-In/Balancing Muscular Exertions* 87

Chapter VII. Anatomical Imagery   90
    60 *Allowing The Pelvic Outlet to Open* 90
    61 *The Pelvis Is Not Square* 92
    62 *Open-Chain Pelvic-Femoral Rhythm/*
       Thigh Lifts and Leg Swings 93
    63 *Pelvic Shift Happens* 97
    64 *Let's Liberate Our Elbows and Knees* 98
    65 *Walking Feet/Foundations and Levers* 100
    66 *The Feet Reorganize Continuously in*
       Each Plié 102
    67 *Tripods in The Feet and Near the Hip* 103
    68 *Honoring Spinal Curves* 106

69 Celebrating Spinal Possibilities 109
70 Successive Spinal Sequencing, With A Partner 111
71 Arm Circles/Scapulohumeral Rhythm 113
72 More Arm Circles/Gradated Humeral Rotation 116
73 Arm Circles With Shape Qualities 118
74 A Few Samples of Inner Speech 122
75 Axes of Rotation/Spreading The Workload 123

Chapter VIII. Converting Theory into Action   127
76 Riding The Dynamic Pelvis Through Space 127
77 Undercurves 128
78 Upper-Body Strengthening 129
79 Undercurve-Inversion Dance 130
80 Overcurves 134
81 Playing with Possibilities/Improvising to Learn Technique 135
82 Exploring Polar Opposites 137
83 Playing with Weight Centers 138
84 Shrinking Is As Important As Growing 139
85 The Interdependence of Mobility and Stability 140
86 Quantitative or Qualitative Strength and Flexibility 142
87 Recuperating Without Stopping 143
88 Spatial Imagery—Tensions, Pulls and Intents 144
89 Changing It Up Spatially 147

Chapter IX. Assessment and Variety   150
90 Formative and Summative Feedback 150
91 Assessment Dialogues 151
92 Study-Buddy Choreography 153
93 Assessment Improvisations Across The Floor 153
94 The Spice of Life 155

Chapter X. Teaching Dance through The Multiple
        Intelligences, by guest author Don Halquist   157
   1 Bodily-Kinesthetic Intelligence 158
   2 Visual-Spatial Intelligence 159
   3 Musical-Rhythmic Intelligence 160
   4 Interpersonal Intelligence 161
   5 Intrapersonal Intelligence 162
   6 Verbal-Linguistic Intelligence 163
   7 Logical-Mathematical Intelligence 164
   8 Naturalist Intelligence 165

Appendix A	*Resource Texts*	169
Appendix B	*Embracing Non-Eurocentric and Multicultural Perspectives*	172
Appendix C	*Applying Concepts from The Laban/ Bartenieff Movement System and The Franklin Method of Dynamic Alignment through Imagery*	179
Appendix D	*My Take on Bartenieff Fundamentals*	185
Appendix E	*How The Body Changes Its Form*	192
Appendix F	*Movement Qualities*	198
Appendix G	*The Geometry of Movement*	203
Index		209

Contributors

Selene B. Carter (foreword) is an associate professor and associate chair in the Department of Drama, Theatre and Contemporary Dance at Indiana University Bloomington. She previously taught at the Dance Center of Columbia College Chicago and received the Ruth Page Award, Chicago's highest honor in dance. She is a Certified Evans Teacher.

Ashley A. Friend (anatomical simulation drawings) is an independent choreographer, performer and teacher who was based in New York City for 15 years before relocating to Port Townsend, Washington in 2021. She earned a BFA at Cornish College of the Arts in Seattle and an MFA at The Ohio State University in Columbus.

Don Halquist (guest author of the book's final chapter) danced in the Evans Dance Company for 36 years and co-founded the Bill Evans Dance Teachers Institute in 1999. He has been a college dean, department chair and professor but recently returned to his first calling, teaching second graders, in the Salish Coast School in Port Townsend, Washington. He earned a PhD at the University of New Mexico in Albuquerque.

Jude Clark Warnisher (movement drawings, symbols and graphs) is a lecturer in the Department of Theatre and Dance at California Polytechnic State University, San Luis Obispo, California. She earned an MFA at the University of California Irvine and is a Certified Evans Teacher.

Foreword

Selene B. Carter

> The war of an artist with his society is a lover's war, and he does at his best, what lover's do, which is to reveal the beloved to himself and with that revelation, to make freedom real.
>
> James Baldwin

In this book, Bill Evans reveals his beloved profession. It is the living, moving body, dancing in this world as a practice of the human spirit in the fullest manifestation possible. The moving, dancing body as it is, not as a limited ideal or as others want it to be. This book is a love letter to a meaningful life in dance, to teaching dance, to Bill's teachers, and to his thousands of students, who in many ways are also his teachers. This book is a map to our own revelations of real freedom in teaching dance, and learning about ourselves, learning about our living bodies, and learning in a healthy, loving community as we study and grow together.

My mother, also a dancer, first encountered Bill Evans at the American Dance Festival in 1979 and found a revelatory experience in Bill as a master teacher, and dancer at the height of his powers, who was teaching from an anatomical/kinesiological and Laban/Bartenieff framework. For her, a student primarily of Graham's, to study modern dance beyond the stylistic preferences of a singular, idiomatic choreographic artist was a radical discovery. She brought Bill and his company to our community for a residency. My mother recently reminded me that it was at age 12, after a master class with Bill Evans, that I returned home and proclaimed to her that I would be a dancer for my life. What a gift that she enrolled me in the Bill Evans Summer Dance Intensive.

Between age 13 and 15, (1982–84) my foundational dance studies were with Bill and his company members. Those summers were a whirl of intense, exhilarating and deep discovery for me. I was seeded with a way of learning to dance from creative and conceptual explorations, of discovering the truth of what my body could do, holistically, synergistically, safely, and without strain beyond my own growth and physical limitations. Witnessing Bill and his dancers perform his works was the model for what I aspired to as a young dancer. From my early study with Bill and his dancers, I was seeded with a philosophic approach that flourished within me, always burgeoning me towards moving and learning to move that was rooted in somatic inquiry, self-reflection and holism.

Decades later, teaching in a college dance program I was required to teach dance techniques. Having been steeped in a post-modern praxis, I struggled with what mode or style I would teach. At age 40, the same age Bill was when I studied with him in my early adolescence, I began the certification program in Evans Somatic Dance. Once again, spending my summers dancing in the diverse, multigenerational community of dancers learning from Bill and his company. What I continue to find in those spaces and what is here in Bill's book is a template for living a meaningful life through dance.

Bill's journey in dance is profound, and he offers us nothing less. This book is a potent template for any dancer, or dance teacher who seeks to know more than a cursory indication of learning to dance. Bill offers myriad inroads, hard-won through his own lifelong explorations. As with any great teacher, he gives you the tools, and when he offers them, they become much more than a simple directive. The depth of what he offers brings us to the leading edge of our own growth. This edge of growth is what Bill has practiced as a teacher for over half a century. He invites you into his own questions of what it is to learn from the living body, and to encounter the world in all its glorious complexity, always a relationship, a dance between self and other. Be it space, nature, poetry, science, the realm of the spirit, the body is the conduit to these aspects. This book is a map to find who we are and what we value as teachers, he offers explorative, not replicative approaches.

Within Bill's own dancing body and life, he has embodied many styles, cultures and identities. I recall watching him perform a solo tap concert, where he narrated his autobiography as he danced. He remarked, "In the late nineteen-sixties when I was a ballet and modern dancer, I was in a closet of tap." It struck me at that moment, here is a white, culturally Mormon, man, whose first love of dance, tap, an African American dance form, who at the time he refers to being a closeted tap dancer, was a closeted gay man, yet now is out of both closets. He continues to relish these embodiments and deeply honor all the progenitors of the many dances he has learned, and in turn offers us, always cited, always contextualized in history, and Bill's lived experience.

Bill Evans danced his way to his own freedom, the freedom of the healthy, aging, wise, freely expressive body. He danced his way to the revelation of full acceptance of who he is in all the facets of himself. I want this for my students. I want every class I teach to be an inclusive space where each student finds one of Bill's central aims, their personal uniqueness. When Bill gathers us together after exploring a concept, image, or idea, after our full, spacious, specific, intentioned, and luscious dancing, he beckons us to the circle and asks, "What is most alive for you?" This book will guide you to find what is most alive for you, and in turn to ask this of your students. In essence, what is most alive is learning from the living body, and moving, lovingly towards real freedom. Bill has wrapped words around this.

Introduction

1 The Backstory

I started writing this book because the COVID-19 pandemic presented me with unexpected free time, just before the horrifying murder of George Floyd in Minneapolis ignited global protests against systemic oppression of Black Americans. Those events motivated me to reflect deeply on who I am and on how I might contribute to the changes I profoundly hope to see in our world before my life has ended.

I thank Cheryl Ossola, former editor-in-chief of *Dance Studio Life* magazine, for inviting me to write a monthly column called "Tips for Modern Teachers" from January 2012 to December 2014. Even though those original suggestions were extremely short, I was able to capture in them essential values I had come to embrace over decades of teaching that I hoped would be relevant to the diverse and vital community of private dance studio teachers for whom that magazine was published. I had expected to be teaching and performing in several European and Middle Eastern cities in the months surrounding my 80th birthday in April 2020. Instead, since the pandemic left me quarantined in Port Townsend, Washington,[1] I decided to expand on those original *tips* and crystallize a more complete account of my thoughts and feelings about teaching. I have again written for private studio teachers, but for a larger audience as well, especially college dance teachers wishing to reflect on their practice, college students expecting to become dance teachers and professional dancers who teach as part of their residency activities and to make ends meet between gigs.

From ages 5 to 18, I lived in a small, all-white, racist community. People of African descent (of whom there were none in our little town) were said to have been "cursed by god" by the prevailing church, which influenced all aspects of our lives.[2] The oppression of Indigenous Americans, which I witnessed first-hand, and the fear and hatred of Black Americans, which were revealed by the inflammatory language used by some school teachers and family members, caused me despair and anguish as a child. I felt in my heart that if there were a heavenly being overseeing our lives, such a beneficent force would love all people equally. The unconcealed racism with which I was surrounded wounded my soul and violated the predominant commandment I heard and embraced in Sunday school: "Love one another as I have loved you." I ultimately chose to leave the world of organized religion at age 19 because of the sanctioned racism, misogyny and homophobia of the organization into which I was born.

As a decidedly effeminate boy in a macho, cowboy culture, I was marginalized, harassed and bullied almost daily, sometimes brutally. My consequent self-loathing and feelings of hopelessness were often overwhelming and, like many gay teens, I contemplated suicide. I developed empathy for those who are different or disenfranchised at a very young age, and I escaped to the world of my imagination to find comfort and to the dance studio to find acceptance. I became an artist to flee a narrow and judgmental world in which I felt trapped.

My lifetime journey as a dancer, choreographer and educator has brought me into countless cherished interactions with students and artists who are Black, Indigenous and other people of color, in many parts of the world. For more than six decades I have endeavored to celebrate the dignity and sacred value of all human beings in my choreography, performance and teaching. Nonetheless, I know that I was imprinted with attitudes and habits of which I am unaware by my racist upbringing and my subsequent decades as a privileged, politically liberal white person.

There is no question that the color of my skin has made my life safer, more secure and less difficult than it would otherwise have been. I acknowledge my white privilege, and I vow that this remarkable time will impel me to excavate and address my own biases and to strongly support the elimination of both overt and camouflaged institutionalized racism wherever I encounter it. I cannot fully grasp the terror Black parents must experience whenever their children leave the house. I fervently hope that the rising awareness of systemic injustice will finally ignite a turning point in the oppressive practices of the dominant European-American culture. I will do all I can within my spheres of influence.

This is NOT a book about the scope of my dance technique,[3] even though it does reveal the evolving values that guided me as I developed it. As a teacher of pedagogy in three different colleges over 30 years, I found the ideas shared in these essays to be meaningful to students who have not studied Evans Technique, as well as to those who have.

I humbly offer these 94 essays to any established or emerging modern, contemporary, ballet, jazz, tap, hip-hop or other teachers who would like to consider the heartfelt suggestions of a dancing man whose life has been devoted to sharing what he loves. I had planned to stop at 80 essays, one for each year of my life as I began writing, but I uncovered 14 additional topics that felt fundamental to my teaching. The final chapter was written by Don Halquist. In it, he discusses how he and participants in the Evans Somatic Dance Certification Program have applied the Theory of Multiple Intelligences to their teaching of dance.

I consider the information in the appendices to be crucial to a meaningful understanding of the suggestions included in the body of this book. I encourage the reader to look over the appendices before reading further and—depending on one's knowledge of the content of each appendix—consider reading them in preparation for studying Chapters I–IX.

In Appendix A, **Resource Texts**, I enumerate excellent books on pedagogical approaches, the Laban/Bartenieff Movement System (L/BMS) and other somatic practices that have impacted my work. I suggest that you look at any of these books that might be new to you. In Appendix B, **Embracing Non-Eurocentric and Multicultural Perspectives**, I articulate the importance of embracing non-Western thoughts and practices to my evolution as a teacher and artist.

In Appendix C, **Applying Concepts from the Laban/Bartenieff Movement System and the Franklin Method of Dynamic Alignment through Imagery**, I discuss the decades-long significance of L/BMS and more recent influence of the Franklin Method on my thinking and teaching, and how those systems have helped me make my work relevant and accessible to students. In Appendices E through G, I reveal what the L/BMS framework of **Body, Shape,**

4 *Introduction*

Figure 0.1 Photograph of Bill Evans Performing His Work "Soliloquy," 2006 (Photographer Jim Dusen).

Effort and **Space** means to me and how I personally define concepts that have been most illuminating and transformative for me as a mover and teacher. For the reader with limited exposure to the work of Laban and/or Bartenieff, I strongly suggest that you study these four appendices before reading Chapters VI–VIII.

Figure 0.2 Photograph of Bill Evans and Don Halquist Performing Claire Porter's "In Gloves," 2010 (Photographer Jim Dusen).

Figure 0.3 Photograph of Bill Evans Teaching in the Bill Evans Teachers Institute, Hobart and William Smith Colleges, 2016 (Photographer Kevin Colton).

2 Why This Title?

I discovered early on that the best way for me to fully learn something is to teach it. When I attempt to explain a concept or practice to someone else, I gain an understanding of what I do not yet clearly understand. When I was named Scholar/Artist of the year by the (U.S.) National Dance Association in 1997, I titled my keynote address *Teaching What I Want to Learn*. It was later published as an article in *Contact Quarterly*.

I believe that the *how*, *why* and *where* are often as important as the *what*. Each of us is shaped by the lives we lead, and the kinds of dance to which we dedicate ourselves. Therefore, in many of the 94 essays, I share the autobiographical backstory of the thoughts, notions or practices I discovered, borrowed and evolved to arrive at my pedagogical values and strategies. I celebrate the process through which teachers are formed by their unique lived experiences, and I encourage each reader to reflect on and enjoy the journey through which your personal pedagogy is being created.

I offer these ideas not as a rulebook to be adhered to but as a model to be considered as you respond to your own time and place in your teaching of ballet, modern/contemporary, jazz, tap, hip-hop and other styles. I encourage you to excavate your own embodied experiences to identify, crystallize and follow your unique pedagogical values and goals.

3 Citing My Sources

I have sought out many guides since I took my first dance class in 1948. The positive influences of some of those mentors have merged with my DNA to lead me toward satisfaction and success, and I offer my profound gratitude to those teachers whose legacies live within my body-mind.

I studied with June Purrington Park, an unsung but superb teacher in Salt Lake City, from ages 9 to 15. At age 16, I switched to the classes of Willam Christensen, founder of the San Francisco Ballet, the ballet program at the University of Utah and later Ballet West. As an undergraduate at the U. of Utah, I majored in both English and ballet, and I was also continuously active in the modern dance program headed by Betty Hayes, Shirley Ririe and Joan Woodbury. After college, I spent two years as a U.S. Army officer at Fort Knox Kentucky, while also dancing with the Louisville Civic Ballet, directed by Fernand Nault. After my honorable discharge from the armed services, I became a trainee at Harkness House for Ballet Arts, under the direction of Patricia Wilde. In 1966, I joined the Ruth Page International Ballet, which performed extensively in Chicago and toured through 60 other U.S. cities in 1967.

I became a modern dance MFA (Master of Fine Arts) student at the U. of Utah in the spring of 1967 and joined the newly-formed Repertory Dance Theatre (RDT) almost immediately. I worked 48 weeks a year with that company and became its leading resident choreographer as well as one of three artistic coordinators. In 1975, while serving as an assistant professor at the U. of U., I formed the Bill Evans Dance Company (BEDCO). We relocated our base to Seattle in 1976 and became the most-booked professional troupe in the country over the next eight years, touring through all but two of the 50 states. The Evans Company School attracted students from throughout North America and many other parts of the world.

In 1986, I became a part-time dance company director/performer/choreographer and a full-time university professor, first at Indiana University Bloomington, then at the University of New Mexico Albuquerque, then at the State University of New York College at Brockport and finally at Dean College in Franklin, Massachusetts. BEDCO has been through several permutations and had several homes, but we celebrated our 40th anniversary in 2014 and continue to work on a project basis. My freelance professional work has taken me to 27 countries on five continents.

I founded the ongoing Bill Evans Summer Institute of Dance in 1977. Since 1999, we have focused primarily on intensive workshops for dance educators and a Certification Program in Evans Somatic Dance Technique. I founded the international Evans/Williams Somatic Dance Conference and Performance Festival in 2013.

My work as an artist has been affirmed by numerous grants and fellowships from the National Endowment for the Arts, the Guggenheim Foundation, other private foundations, several state and provincial arts agencies, the University of Utah (which named me a Distinguished Alumnus) and the Cornish College of the Arts (which made me an honorary Doctor of Fine Arts). The American Dance Guild bestowed a Lifetime Achievement Award for my choreography and performance in 2014. My contributions to dance education have been recognized with Lifetime Achievement Awards from the National Dance Education Organization and Dance Teacher Magazine, as well as accolades from the International Association of Dance Medicine and Science, the National High School Dance Festival and several other entities.

A few of the renowned dance teachers who enlightened me immeasurably through my long career are: Jack Cole, Kitty Daniels, Betty Hayes, Margaret H'Doubler, Betty Jones, Debra Wright Knapp, Larry Long, Donald McKayle, June Purrington Park, Eva Encinias, Dianne Walker, Elizabeth Waters and Ethel Winter.

My approach to teaching dance technique was formed in collaboration with students and members of my professional modern dance company, whose exceptional kinesthetic intelligence and willingness to explore my ideas inspired me to embody a philosophy that I could not have uncovered entirely on my own. Foremost among them are Gregg Lizenbery and Debbie Poulsen, who started studying with me in the mid-1960s, and Debra Knapp and Don Halquist, who have worked with me since the mid-1980s.

Since turning 70, I have increasingly relied on younger dancers to act as "Bill's body," serving as demonstrators and collaborating in ongoing somatic investigation. Dancers who have functioned brilliantly in that capacity include: Heather Acomb, Jolene Bailie, Kathy Diehl, Don Halquist, Anna Hansen, Linda Johnson, Jenny Showalter, Kyla Wallace and Courtney World.

I am *not* a dance scientist, but I studied anatomy and kinesiology with several superb leaders in the field: Karen Clippinger, Kitty Daniels, Sally Fitt, Ginny Wilmerding, John M. Wilson and Eric Franklin. I became a certified Franklin Method Teacher in 2021.

I *am* a Certified Laban Bartenieff Movement Analyst. My primary mentors were inspired visionaries: Peggy Hackney, Janet Hamburg, Janice Meaden, Tara Stepenberg and Pam Schick. Other teachers of somatic practice who influenced my work are Sondra Fraleigh, Bette Lamont, Suzie Lundgren, Nancy Romita and Allegra Romita.

My teaching methodology was shaped by many dedicated and innovative teachers, including Percival Borde, Jim Coleman, Janet Collins, Anne Green Gilbert, Peggy Hackney, Don Halquist, Janyce Hyatt, Debra Wright Knapp, Janice Meaden, Dianne Walker and Elizabeth Waters. It has been insightfully defined by Melissa Hauschild-Mork and Daniela Wancier.

Margaret Gisolo, Janyce Hyatt and Cynthia J. Williams are extraordinary dance educators/administrators whom I wish to thank for generously and skillfully facilitating my teaching and performing in annual gatherings of dance educators—Margaret from 1969 to 1982, Jan from 1975 to 1986 and Cynthia since 2013. Other teachers, theorists and artists who have positively influenced my work are mentioned within the essays that comprise the body of this book.

Notes

1 I acknowledge that the land on which I live and write is unceded homeland of Chimakum and Klallam Native Peoples. I deplore the history of violence on these stolen lands and express respect and gratitude for those original caretakers.
2 I was relieved when official church doctrine was modified in 1978, and people of African heritage were no longer officially discriminated against. However, the tax-exempt organization still impedes social progress, particularly women's rights and LGBTQ rights.
3 As of January 1, 2022, I am in the process of creating DVDs and online videos of me teaching the Evans Somatic Dance Technique with members of the Bill Evans Dance Company acting as demonstrators. For further information on those videos, please consult evansomaticdance.org. If I live long enough, I will write specifically about that technique/style in a different book.

I Notes to Self

1 Remind Yourself That You Love to Teach

As you walk from the office or dressing room to the studio, take a moment to notice your breath, ground yourself and remember that you love to move and to teach. Sometimes, the difficulties of managing a challenging workload or interpersonal conflicts with parents, colleagues or students can deprive us of the joy that is waiting for us if we remember who we are and why we chose to become teachers.

It is possible to let external circumstances come between us and our ability to be fully present in each moment of our interactions with students and colleagues. Before entering the studio, initiating a Zoom session, beginning a conference with a student or attending a faculty meeting, it usually helps to take a few moments to return to the peaceful home we can find in the body and remind ourselves what a rare privilege it is to follow one's bliss and do for a living what we would want to be doing even without remuneration.

I had two highly-accomplished brothers. My older sibling, a university professor of physical education, retired at age 62, exhausted by academic politics. My younger brother, a family court judge, retired at age 60, because the work to which he had dedicated decades of his life generated more stress and anxiety than he could continue to endure.

I kept teaching full-time as a college dance professor through age 78, and I still teach as an online adjunct, in summer gatherings of dance educators and as a guest artist in academic and professional programs whenever someone offers me an interesting gig because *my work is my joy*. Nonetheless, there are moments when overwhelming demands of the moment make me forget that I have chosen the work I do because it brings me profound satisfaction.

DOI: 10.4324/9781003290209-2

If we reflect on how fortunate we are that our livelihood focuses on encouraging, guiding and witnessing positive transformation in the people we teach, we can affirm that our time is extraordinarily well spent. Yes, there are challenges in the studio, on the internet, in the classroom or in the conference room, but being positive, open-hearted, grateful and alive in the moment will help us face those challenges and continue a forward journey toward positive change for ourselves and those we teach.

> **FOR YOUR CONSIDERATION:**
>
> I encourage you to describe an "embodiment practice" that helps you prepare to enter the classroom or studio or to begin an in-person or online interaction with students, peers or parents.
> I invite you to write three things you love about being a dance teacher. What might occur that could cause you to temporarily lose sight of what you cherish about teaching? How could you cope with such an obstacle?

2 Embrace Evolving Values

Our beliefs don't matter to those we teach until we act on them, incorporating them into our professional practice and interactions. Sometimes, teachers will say words that were said to them that are not truly reflective of their current convictions. Sometimes they pass on exercises learned in the past without modifying them to incorporate or accommodate knowledge gained from their own lived experiences.

I find it important to "take inventory" of the things I say and do in my classes frequently. I want to make sure that I'm not repeating things out of habit that no longer represent the thinking/sensing/feeling educator I have become and that my most deeply held current beliefs about learning and moving are reflected in what I share in the studio or classroom.

As we teach, we also learn. Our beliefs evolve as we immerse ourselves in new experiences. However, we don't always take time to recognize that we have changed, and it is often easier or more convenient to continue passing on practices we no longer fully value than to incorporate new knowledge into our teaching. We may not want to "rock the boat." We may not want to say something to students that contradicts what they are hearing from our colleagues. We might want to avoid confusing students by changing what we said and did in the past or fear that our new words and practices could make them frustrated or uncomfortable.

When you discover new information, even if it contradicts previous beliefs, don't be afraid to let students and colleagues know that you are exploring new ideas and practices. Students need to know that each of us can be a life-long learner and that new information sometimes forces us to re-evaluate or reconsider what we have previously thought to be true or essential. Without judging ourselves or others, and without apologizing for changing our words and movement phrases, let's explain to our students and colleagues that our research has led us to new information, and invite them to support us as we meet the challenges of refining our language and modifying our methods and materials as we move forward.

I like to remind students that we have "commencement" ceremonies because finishing a degree or a course of study is the beginning, not the end, of the life-long process of figuring out who we are and what we most want to contribute to our chosen field. Growth is change. Embrace your evolving beliefs. I encourage teachers to continually ask themselves, "Is this still what I want to be saying or doing?" As Maya Angelou famously said, "Do the best you can until you know better. Then when you know better, do better."

> **FOR YOUR CONSIDERATION:**
>
> Have you changed a teaching practice based on new knowledge or convictions? If so, was it worth it? Why?
>
> Have you developed a significant belief that has not yet influenced your teaching? If so, I invite you to relate it to yourself now. What might account for the delay in applying it to your practice? How could you modify language or movement experiences to make room for that belief in your exchanges with students?

3 Teaching's Not Easy, But If It's Your Calling, Nothing Else Will Be as Satisfying

We will encounter reluctant learners, students who are afraid of change or don't yet realize that change is an ongoing, life-long process. It can be challenging to engage such students in new ways of thinking and moving. Jack Cole[1] an iconic and dynamic teacher who had an enormous impact on me as a young professional dancer in New York City, often asked, "Did it say in the brochure that it was going to be easy?" I often hear those words in my head when I am endeavoring to guide resistant students toward positive change and growth. Every now and then, to reduce undue tension in a teaching/learning situation, I ask students almost the same question. "Did it say on the website that it was going to be easy?"

The arts are usually at the bottom of the pecking order in our schools and colleges, and dance instructors are often given heavier workloads and less pay than teachers of the other arts and, especially, professors of business and science. Teachers of most subjects are not generally respected or appreciated as I believe they deserve to be in the U.S. culture. When I taught in other parts of the world, particularly India, Japan, Guatemala and Brazil, I was more demonstrably valued than in this country. Nonetheless, the internal satisfaction I experience as a dance teacher anywhere, even in difficult circumstances, makes me grateful to have chosen this path. When I encounter reluctance, I take a deep breath, remember the big picture and long-term goals, and do the best I can under the circumstances of the moment.

Our world has never needed what dance educators have to offer as much as at this time. The wisdom of the body moving with integrated harmony is sorely lacking in most of the political and corporate leaders who are determining the fate of our planet, and in those who emulate them.

I say, "I didn't choose dance; dance chose me," and I feel that I was born to be a teacher. After a lifetime of guiding, nudging and encouraging people toward positive change, I can attest that the intrinsic rewards you will receive as a teacher of dance will make it well worth confronting all the obstacles that will come your way. If teaching dance is your calling, nothing else will satisfy you as deeply.

FOR YOUR CONSIDERATION:

Have you recently confronted a difficult challenge as a teacher, or have you observed another teacher confront a daunting situation? If so, please describe how you or the observed teacher reacted to that challenge. Could it have played out more effectively? If so, How?

4 You Always Have Something to Offer

About 20 years ago, I received a letter from a former MFA student at the University of Utah, where I was an assistant professor of modern dance in the mid-'70s. She told me that I was the "best teacher she ever had." I was astonished by her proclamation because she had studied with me *before* I had generated meaningful knowledge about anatomy, kinesiology, Laban/Bartenieff Movement Studies and pedagogy. "How," I thought, "could I possibly have been her best teacher?"

It took me a while to figure out that what I *did* have to offer at that time were: a passionate curiosity about both functional and expressive human movement, a love for interacting with dedicated young people and abundant, almost explosive, physical energy. I came to understand that those were qualities this particular student needed and valued at that point in her journey. Even though I was only one step ahead of her in my knowledge base, I was able to motivate her to do her best work and to feel good about herself.

So, don't be afraid to teach because there are things you just don't yet know. We know different things in different ways at different times. Go deep inside, trust yourself, draw on what drives you to be a teacher and share who you are and what you know at this unique point of your journey, enthusiastically and generously. When you don't have the answer to a student's question, you might say, "I'm not sure. Let's figure it out together."

FOR YOUR CONSIDERATION:

I invite you to reflect on your current strengths as a teacher and then describe at least three traits, dispositions or strategies you rely on to be effective.

What specific teaching strengths do you admire in others that you might like to develop in yourself?

---

5 It's OK to Be Unpopular

I have long felt that it is my ethical responsibility to tell students what I think will most benefit them. Since those I teach are most often enrolled in a required course in a degree or certification program, I don't need to tell them what they want to hear to keep them coming back.

I occasionally perceive that teachers who are the most popular and receive the highest praise from their students are among the least effective in fostering student growth or achievement. One of the dilemmas I struggled with as the dance executive in college dance programs was knowing how to determine the significance of questionnaires in which students evaluate their instructors. It is sometimes true that we will not appreciate (until later) mentors who nudge us out of our comfort zones, even though they help us achieve positive change and growth. Teachers must try to find a balance between making students feel good about themselves and endeavoring to initiate a process of transformation.

I imagine what my teaching will mean to current students in 10 years, in 20, in 50. One major goal is to help people develop healthful habits that will serve them for a lifetime of vigorous, joyful and full-bodied movement, whether they stay in dance or not. When I perceive that several students share a way of thinking or a movement habit I know to be destructive to their efficient functioning and/or long-term health, I take the whole group "back to the beginning" in my unpacking of fundamental movement concepts and processes, even in the most "advanced" courses. This usually makes some students unhappy and me unpopular, at least for a while, especially if they expect a fast-paced workout and an endorphin buzz.

I have found that even the most advanced student can generate valuable new levels of knowledge by returning to the basics, slowing down and going deep inside. Over time, many students look back on such experiences under my guidance, understand in retrospect my reasons for doing what I did, and acknowledge the value of such a process they had been unable to perceive "back in the day."

FOR YOUR CONSIDERATION:

How do you balance giving students what they say they want and what you believe they need?

Are you able to value the knowledge you gained under a former teacher's guidance even though you didn't "like" them at the time? If so, please describe how you separated what you learned from your feelings about the teacher.

6 It's OK to Say You're Sorry

Like most dancers of my generation, I had a few teachers who were rude or even cruel, and many of my early ideas about effective teaching were based on their words and actions. Occasionally, when I am particularly stressed, fatigued or overworked, I hear some of my former frustrated teachers' words coming out of my mouth, or sense that I am embodying their frustrated body attitudes. This happens rarely, and when it does, I am surprised and dismayed. I try to say "I'm sorry" to those I feel I have harmed as soon as I have regained my composure, and I am striving to learn to remain my best self in stressful situations.

Debbi Knapp,[2] a former Bill Evans Dance Company[3] member once told me, "A person who never makes a mistake never makes anything." I believe this to be true, and I have noticed that most students and colleagues are willing to forgive our unfortunate words and actions if we sincerely apologize.

I have noticed that some students want to be yelled at or even belittled as an indication that the teacher is being tough enough to prepare them for the "dog-eat-dog" world of professional dance. Indeed, some students seem to mistake a teacher's kindness for a lack of seriousness. However, I believe that we can set appropriately challenging standards for our students while also treating them with respect, and that we can engender joy in the demandingly rigorous process of helping students become highly skilled dancers.

> **FOR YOUR CONSIDERATION:**
>
> Can you remember and describe a time when a teacher apologized to you or a classmate? If so, what were your thoughts and/or feelings?
>
> If you can recall a time when you apologized to a student or colleague for a behavior you regretted, could you express what you learned from that process?

7 Follow Your Personal Aliveness

Jan Hyatt[4] believed in me at the early stages of my career, served as host to me and my company in numerous professional engagements and helped me understand what I have to offer as an educator and artist. As I prepared to deliver a lecture/demonstration or teach a class in one of the many residencies she produced for me or my troupe in Ashtabula, Ohio or Meadville, Pennsylvania, she would encourage me to "follow my intuition." She perceived that when I opened myself to the vibes coming my way from a gathering of audience members or students and then responded to what came alive within me, I found a message that better captured their attention or constructed a class that more successfully suited their needs than if I relied entirely on a prepared script or plan.

Jan helped me understand that the best teacher is also a student, and that I need to remain curious and engaged in my own process of life-long learning, and to leave my own comfort zone regularly, if I am to avoid taking myself too seriously and falling into stagnant ruts.

If we take time to reflect and truly notice what resonates inside us as we continue our journeys through life, we can honor and respond to that inner vibrancy each time we teach a class or address a gathering. In this way, our work helps us satisfy our curiosity, opens us to new possibilities and allows us to stay fresh, engaged and excited.

If we have the courage to follow intuition and *teach what we want to learn* (but don't yet quite fully know), we will experience continual newness. Many students will recognize our passion and genuine interest in investigation and exploration, and they might decide to explore with us and collaborate in the generation of new knowledge, as we all open ourselves to the possibility of positive change.

> **FOR YOUR CONSIDERATION:**
>
> When are you at your best as a teacher?
> Please relate how a teacher, mentor or colleague who believed in you at a crucial juncture in your life and/or career helped you understand yourself better and/or achieve success.
> How have you served in a similar role for someone else?

Notes

1 Jack Cole's career trajectory was unique for an American dance artist. He started at the very roots of modern dance with Ted Shawn, Ruth St. Denis, Doris Humphrey and Charles Weidman, and he studied what was then called "ethnic" dance extensively with La Meri. His career later spanned three major arenas: nightclub, Broadway stage and Hollywood

film. He selected me to study intensively with him for several months in 1966, when I was an apprentice to the Harkness Ballet in New York City.
2 Debra Wright Knapp, EdD, is professor emerita at New Mexico State University in Las Cruces. She earned her master's degree under my guidance at Indiana University, where I served as an associate professor and director of contemporary dance. Debbi performed in the Bill Evans Dance Company for many years before launching an international career as a rehearsal director and specialist in dance pedagogy and andragogy. She is a Certified Evans Teacher (CET) and has taught in our summer gatherings of dance educators over two decades.
3 The Bill Evans Dance Company was founded in 1975. From 1976 through 1983, it was based in Seattle, where it became the fifth-largest performing arts organization in Washington State and the most-booked professional dance ensemble in the United States for several consecutive years. BEDCO performed in the American Dance Festival, the Jacob's Pillow Dance Festival, the Kennedy Center for the Performing Arts and many other significant venues. It performed in many parts of Canada and Mexico and in 48 U.S. states. (I performed in the other two—Delaware and New Hampshire—as a member of Repertory Dance Theatre.) From 1988 to 2004, BEDCO was based in Albuquerque, and from 2004 to 2014, our home theatres were in Rochester, New York. Since celebrating its 40th anniversary in April 2014, the company has worked on only a project basis and is now based in Port Townsend, Washington, where it performs occasionally under the auspices of the Evans Somatic Dance Institute.
4 Janyce Hyatt, EdD, is an exceptional arts administrator and dance educator whose purpose has been to bloom where she was planted and strive to make her "little corner of the world a better place." She was the director of dance at the Ashtabula (Ohio) Arts Center for many years and then established the Program of Dance and Movement Studies at Allegheny College in Meadville, Pennsylvania. She received numerous grants from the Ohio Arts Council, the Pennsylvania Council on the Arts and the National Endowment for the Arts to bring just me or my company to her communities for extended residencies.

II Underpinnings

8 Planting Seeds

We never know when something we say or do in a dance class will have an impact that could last for the rest of a person's life. Each student has crystallizing moments—those occasions when she/he/they is ready to fully perceive something in an integrated way, those moments when a "light bulb goes off" and new clarity is gained. Sometimes, we are able to witness those empowering realizations in those we teach, but often they are delayed and happen even years later when a person is finally ready to absorb and make meaning of what we said or did.

Over the decades, I have received several messages from former students telling me that something I helped them experience back in the day when they were in my classes is of significant value to them in their current lives. Such communications encourage me to always give current students the best I have to offer, including those who appear not to be appreciating what we are investigating at the moment.

I encourage you to dig down deep inside yourself, figure out what is most important, and then *plant the seeds*—the ideas, concepts, possibilities and movement challenges you believe in. Do so now, as clearly, enthusiastically, patiently and compassionately as possible. You just never know when those seeds might come to fruition.

> FOR YOUR CONSIDERATION:
>
> I invite you to search your memory for an idea or practice that you may have dismissed as a student but later came to embrace.
> If a student were to "roll their eyes" or otherwise appear not to value something you were sharing, how would it make you feel? If you have found yourself in such a situation, how did you react? How else might you have dealt with that situation?

9 Crystallizing or Paralyzing Activities or Experiences

I developed an appreciation for the difference between an *activity* and an *experience* by reading *Unleashing the Power of Perceptual Change: The Potential of Brain-Based Teaching*, by Renate Nummela Caine and Geoffrey Caine. When we "give class," focusing primarily on the overtly physical aspects of dancing, I would say that we are leading people in an *activity*. Such classes can be satisfying and valuable, helping students develop stamina and cardiovascular endurance, and giving them practice in picking up the external aspects of dancing. However, when our teaching addresses the cognitive (intellectual) and affective (emotional) domains as well as the psychomotor (physical domain referred to above), we are inviting students to join us in a whole-person *experience*. Because such experiential classes can engage multiple functions of each student's psyche—thinking, sensing, feeling and/or intuition—they often have more profound and long-lasting results than classes primarily focused on physical activities.

Whole-person experiences are not necessarily always positive, however, because they can be *paralyzing* as well as *crystallizing*. Paralyzing experiences, in which a student feels humiliated or attacked and "shuts down," can also have a lifelong impact. In such situations, fear and uncertainty create emotional barriers to learning, and little useful knowledge can be generated.

When we create an atmosphere of trust, open-heartedness, kindness, fairness, empathy and compassion, students can safely feel free to confront learning challenges with the whole of themselves. Such situations can provide "aha" moments in which people experience transformation, leaving the class more empowered than when they entered it. By avoiding negative, paralyzing experiences and organizing positive, crystallizing experiences in our classrooms, we can help to create better places in our corners of the world.

FOR YOUR CONSIDERATION:

Could you describe at least one crystallizing and one paralyzing experience you had as a student in a dance class or rehearsal? How have such experiences of either kind influenced your teaching practice?

When might teaching class as an activity rather than a whole-person experience be appropriate in your practice?

10 All Students Are Smart

Individual students possess unique aptitudes, interests, goals and lived experiences. After more than six decades of teaching, I am still amazed, delighted and challenged by the fact that each incoming class of students has its own personality and chemistry, making it fascinatingly different from all those who came before.

Howard Gardner, a professor of education at Harvard University, formulated the Theory of Multiple Intelligences (MI), which helps us recognize and understand the richness of such personal differences. Gardner enumerated the following intelligences: Naturalist (nature smart), Musical (sound smart), Logical-mathematical (number/reasoning smart), Existential (life smart), Interpersonal (people smart), Bodily-kinesthetic (body smart), Linguistic (word smart), Intrapersonal (self smart) and Spatial (picture smart).

The MI Theory was first shared with me by Don Halquist, CET (Certified Evans Teacher), a dancer in my professional company and educator in my summer programs, when he was also teaching second grade in Enchanted Hills Elementary School in Rio Rancho, New Mexico. As a master's student in education, Don had learned of Gardner's conviction that there are many different ways to be smart, and he taught from that perspective from his first day in his classroom and in our summer programs for dance educators.

When we established the branch of the Bill Evans Summer Institute of Dance known as BETI (Bill Evans Teachers Intensive) in 1999, the initial schedule and curriculum were: Morning—Bartenieff Fundamentals followed by Evans Technique (Bill Evans); Afternoon—Applied Kinesiology followed by Anatomy-Based Ballet (Kitty Daniels); Evening—Multiple Intelligences for the Dance Teacher (Don Halquist). Over the years, we have played with many variations of that curriculum and have invited many other artists/educators to join the faculty. By now, because each of the BETI faculty has incorporated aspects of the MI theory into their teaching methodologies, we no longer offer a separate MI course.

My first encounter with Gardner's work was life-altering. I had long recognized that people are bright and capable in different ways, but the MI framework enabled me to see individual attributes more clearly and speak about them more concretely. I am more effective as a teacher when I look for what each student brings rather than what is missing, when I notice just how each student is smart and then try to figure out how to help her/him/them build on those innate and cultivated intelligences to experience success.

Note: Don Halquist has contributed Chapter X, Teaching Dance through the Multiple Intelligences, to this book.

> **FOR YOUR CONSIDERATION:**
>
> Has Gardner's MI Theory already influenced your teaching? If so, please describe three adaptations you have made to former practices.
>
> If Gardner's theory is new to you, what thoughts are coming up for you? What new practices could you consider based on the idea that each student is smart in a unique way?

11 Preparing Students for Their Future, Not Our Past

Even with such empowering tools as MI Theory, we continually face new challenges. One of the most daunting is the fact that each incoming class of students is even more different from the one before because of rapid developments in technology. Each half-generation of students accesses information and perceives the world in new ways. To serve their needs, we must strive to understand the reality they inhabit. We must also discern which of the materials we have taught in the past are still relevant in our rapidly-changing world.

Lesson plans and teaching strategies that we previously found successful may not be right for the particular students we are teaching now. Skills, knowledge and coping strategies that served us and former students as young professionals in the world of dance may no longer be adequate. We need to deeply look, listen and respond to the unique needs, interests, capabilities and future prospects of current students if we are to help them generate the knowledge and cultivate the skills that will enable them to cope with the evermore-changing world they will encounter when they leave us.

John Dewey (1859–1952). An American philosopher, psychologist and educational reformer whose ideas have been influential in education and social reform, said in the '40s: "The world is moving at a tremendous rate. No one knows where. We must prepare our children not for the world of the past, not for our world, but for their world—the world of the future." These words are immeasurably truer today than they were in my boyhood, when Dewey uttered them. If we fail to stay abreast of the changes in how information becomes available, and what is important to each new group and individual, we might be *preparing students for our past rather than their future.*

> **FOR YOUR CONSIDERATION:**
>
> How has your teaching evolved in response to changes you have perceived in your incoming students?
>   I invite you to ask yourself, "What do I have to offer that could help the unique individuals I am currently teaching, or expect to teach in the near future, prepare for the ever-changing world they will enter when their time with me has ended?" Of the many things you have to offer, which do those students most need?

12 Honoring Personal Uniqueness

KLee Cooper[1] said to me and the others in her Evans Teacher Certification cohort some years ago: "*I don't teach technique, I teach people.*" To me, she meant that even though she earned her living teaching dance technique classes, her primary mission was to recognize and honor the unique humanity of each of the people in her studio, and I embraced and borrowed that thought and that language on the spot.

A few years earlier, while serving as a guest artist/adjudicator at a Regional Dance America Festival, a gathering of pre-professional regional ballet companies, I surprised myself by saying, "Your personal uniqueness should be your most prized asset." I was teaching a modern technique class to a group of young teen girls, all wearing identical black leotards and pink tights with their hair in tight buns. I realized at that moment that I was troubled by many of the standardized protocols of that well-established and laudable corner of our dance world. It seemed that each student was trying her best to surrender her individuality and become an "idealized ballerina." It seemed that the "perfect" dancer on whom these girls were modeling themselves was bone thin, hypermobile, silent and obedient. She was an "instrument" (or object) to be molded by her teachers, choreographers and directors.

The great ballerinas of the world, I believe, are those who endured such generic learning environments but figured out how to reveal their special qualities anyway. For example, I had several opportunities to choreograph for and perform with the stunningly brilliant American Ballet Theatre star Cynthia Gregory in the '70s (at the Jacob's Pillow Dance Festival) and '80s (in concerts I directed at the Seattle Center

Playhouse and Opera House). When I marveled at the naturalness and ease with which she embodied the classical ballet lexicon and asked her how she developed those qualities, she said, "I stopped listening to my teachers when I was 12 years old. I just listen to the music."

It struck me as profoundly sad that the best dancers might need to ignore what their teachers are telling them in order to cultivate and reveal their individual qualities. How heartbreaking it would be for me as a teacher to know that my most successful students had "tuned me out."

Of course, other styles value individual differences more than ballet, but I often meet young modern, contemporary, jazz and tap dancers who wish they were like someone else, rather than being grateful for the minds and bodies they have inherited and developed.

Dance belongs to everybody and every *body*! I believe that dance is primarily an experience of the human spirit, not dependent on being born with or cultivating a particular body shape or size. One of my goals as a teacher is to help each student honor her/his/their singular features, dispositions and qualities. I encourage dancers to figure out just who they uniquely are, and I try to help each of them develop tools to become a more complete and fulfilled version of the person and artist they are meant to be.

> ### FOR YOUR CONSIDERATION:
>
> What are the qualities or attributes that contribute to your personal uniqueness?
>
> I invite you to strategize three ways in which you could encourage each of the students you teach to recognize and value their unique blend of characteristics, traits, dispositions and capacities.

13 Knowing Themselves to Adapt to Different Styles

There are rare people whose body structure comes close to the "perfection" of idealized beings around which some dance styles evolved, but most dancers will need to distort themselves to emulate or copy "perfect" lines and positions. Students who force themselves to appear different from who they actually are will make stress-producing physical compensations that will likely result in traumatic (sudden) or chronic (gradual) injuries. People seldom feel good about themselves when they pretend to be different from, or mask, who they really are; as a result, their self-esteem, perhaps the most significant factor in finding success in any pursuit, will be diminished.

I think it is crucial that students generate knowledge about both themselves and a dance style they wish to study. To empower our students, we can unpack the aesthetic ideas or "rules" underlying both the style we are teaching and older styles that formed the historical bases for its aesthetic values. If students also understand themselves—their unique anatomical, intellectual and emotional capacities—we can help them accommodate who they are to the demands of the style or styles they wish to explore in ways that are healthful and sustainable. Instead of fitting their bodies into a style of dance, they can allow and guide that style of dance to fit itself into their bodies.

Not everyone is best-suited to any particular dance style, but there are kinds of dance that are right for each person. Students deserve to understand that, with knowledge, self-confidence, patience and thoughtful guidance, they can learn to embody the essence of a chosen dance form without betraying their physical or psychological well-being.

FOR YOUR CONSIDERATION:

How did you determine which style(s) or form(s) of dance you would pursue?

How can you be useful to students as they decide which styles or forms interest them?

Did you ever need to learn more about anatomy or movement theory to adapt yourself to a dance style you wanted to embody? If so, what did you discover that you can share with students?

---

14 Students Don't Need to Be Fixed

When I first started teaching, I assumed that it was my job to "fix" what was "wrong" with students. So, I looked for what wasn't working and focused primarily on that much of the time. I felt irresponsible if a student moved on to the next step of her/his/their journey through the curriculum with what I perceived as a technical deficiency or inappropriate movement habit that I hadn't helped them correct. As the years went by, however, I discovered that I was of more use to the people in my classes, and that my job was more rewarding, if I *looked for the good* instead.

If we notice the ways in which each student is smart—what she/he/they already understands and/or embodies—and use that foundation for building additional knowledge and skills, we witness more success, experience more satisfaction and have a whole lot more fun than if we're always looking for what is wrong.

I now believe that our primary responsibilities as teachers include:

a   affirming that students are OK just as they are, that they are not broken and don't need fixing;
b   honoring the person each student is born to be;
c   helping each student understand what her/his/their strengths are or could be;
d   guiding those who want to perform and/or teach toward the kinds of dance in which they might experience satisfaction and success;
e   encouraging them to establish personal and professional goals; and
f   facilitating the generation of knowledge and the development of the skills they will need to accomplish those goals.

FOR YOUR CONSIDERATION:

How can we help ourselves and students learn to understand rather than to judge?

How can you guide students in the development of self-confidence and personal agency, so that they can take ownership of their journeys toward personal goals?

---

15 We Are All in This Together, but Each of Us Is Having a Different Class

I make it clear from the early moments of our first gathering that I consider each participant to be a fully-franchised member of our learning community. I might say,

> We are all in this together. I am here to support your growth, and I invite you to support the growth of each of your peers, and mine as well. You will all be taking the same class, and yet each of us will be having a different class.

Each student is different physically, cognitively and emotionally and has different needs, interests, dispositions and goals. Each is at a different stage of a different journey. As a guide to a group of unique individuals, I structure learning opportunities that I hope will have some relevance for everybody. However, I also encourage each student to serve as her/his/their own guide, and take responsibility for having their own class. That means remaining curious, establishing short- and long-term personal goals, maintaining an inner dialogue while moving, bringing their whole self to each investigation and collaborating with peers to help one another succeed.

Particularly when teaching adults, I invite dancers to modify what I ask of the whole group if they feel that something is not right for them. I encourage each student to share the responsibility for personal injury prevention by deciding when their level of cardiovascular conditioning, strength and/or flexibility, their lack of mental clarity or an emotional condition might make a particular movement experience I request inappropriate.

There are always a number of creative modifications that could make any movement phrase more appropriate for an individual dancer. I encourage students to figure alternate ways of investigating the underlying concepts we are examining, either on their own or by collaborating with a peer. They can "stay in the dance" while also honoring their personal truths.

I am fortunate that dancers in their 60s and 70s join my classes frequently. Because they know that their creative adaptations of the movement material I design are encouraged and welcomed, they dance alongside 20- and 30-year-olds without hesitation or apologies. Multigenerational groups of dancers are able to enjoy the stimulating experience of sharing movement through space and time with participants from many of life's developmental stages, each student experiencing the same class differently.

FOR YOUR CONSIDERATION:

When you feel like an equally-valued member of a learning community, how does it impact the quality of your participation in a class or a course?

If you ever felt compelled to do something in a technique class that seemed inappropriate, how could you have dealt with that situation differently?

16 Learning Is Active

Some people imagine the dance teacher to be a "fount of wisdom" who pours information into the minds of obedient students and tells them what to do with their bodies. I believe that the teacher should be a guide who organizes learning opportunities in collaboration with students, and that the best teacher is also engaged in learning. I often say to dancers, *"Bringing your body into the classroom is only the beginning. I encourage you to also be fully present in each function of your mind-body: thinking, sensing, feeling and intuiting."*

Learning is deeper and more efficient when we invite students into our process by letting them know why we are doing what we're doing, and when we encourage them to explore the investigations we orchestrate with the whole of themselves. We might sometimes ask them to structure part of those explorations themselves.

To use the framework of Bloom's Taxonomy,[2] we can address each student through the psychomotor (physical), cognitive (intellectual) and affective (emotional) domains in which knowledge is generated. Students who are fully engaged in *body, mind and spirit* can become *active learners* and *co-creators* of our classes, able to take full ownership of the process of exploring possibilities as they seek the kinds of positive change and growth that are individually important.

It important to recognize that active learning looks different in each student. Some may need to constantly move in order to generate knowledge. Others may need to construct knowledge socially by discussing questions with others. Still others prefer to go deep inside, becoming still and quiet, detaching from external tasks and perhaps appearing to daydream. Let's not be quick to judge; rather let's take the time to watch, listen and honor the ways in which each student engages in active learning.

> **FOR YOUR CONSIDERATION:**
>
> How do you most effectively learn with the whole of yourself?
>
> I invite you to select or devise two strategies for encouraging the students you are currently teaching (or expect to teach soon) to be more active generators of knowledge within your classes.
>
> Which of Bloom's three domains do you address most often in your teaching? How could you engage the other domains more frequently?

17 Thought Creates Action

I once noticed Suzie Lundgren, MA, CFP, CET, write "Thought creates action" in her journal during one of my movement classes. Suzie has been my summer teaching colleague over four decades. Since retiring from a career as a professional ballet and modern dancer, she has developed exceptional expertise as a Certified Feldenkrais Practitioner who especially enjoys sharing her insights with dancers. I treasure her rare ability to love unconditionally while also telling friends what they need, but may not want, to hear. Because she has witnessed my evolution as a teaching artist over such a long time, I often turn to her for guidance.

Suzie's statement is a shortened version of the famous Mahatma Gandhi quotation: "Your beliefs become your thoughts; your thoughts become your words; your words become your actions; your actions become your habits; your habits become your values; your values become your destiny." I recognized the significance and usefulness of her streamlined phrase immediately, and I've passed it on many times.

To change how we act, we must change what we think. To help students improve the way they dance, we need to help them notice, evaluate and perhaps change what they tell themselves as they move. We are all creatures of habit, so most often we need to help students unpack the origins of their unconscious responses and perhaps figure out what desires, needs, intentions or circumstances led them to create such habitual patterns. In movement re-education, we search for new or refined thoughts or ideas through which we might discover new actions that are more in tune with the body-mind's needs. Over time, new actions become new habitual movement responses.

We can help students become aware of their deeply-ingrained movement tendencies, which usually seem to them like the "natural" way they function. We can explain that most of our patterned-in habits were initially choices or instincts that helped us to survive and become who we are, but that not all of those ingrained patterns are still serving us. We can help them recognize "fallback" movement responses, without judgment, and ask, "Is this habit serving me well, or could I perhaps form a new one that would serve me better?" New or refined thoughts can create new or refined action patterns that might add years to a dancer's healthy functioning and increase their kinesthetic enjoyment of daily life.

> **FOR YOUR CONSIDERATION:**
>
> What are three thoughts that have helped you create new actions to form more efficient movement habits. What previous thoughts did they replace? What did you learn from that process?

18 Inefficient Movement Patterns Are Not Moral Weaknesses

It is crucial to recognize that inefficient movement patterns are not permanent physical conditions. Neither are they moral weaknesses! They are simply modes of behavior that evolved consciously or unconsciously as we became who we are. Each of our movement habits took root because we needed them, or perceived that we needed them, to function at a former stage of our development. Our movement habits have made it possible for us to arrive where we are today, and they have served us, even if we now recognize that modified or different habits could serve us better.

Students cannot reach their full potential without our guidance, but it is crucial that we learn to give feedback constructively. When we offer "corrections" or suggestions for different ways of approaching the investigations we organize for them, we can do so in verbal and body language that will allow students to understand that we are discerning, not judging, and that they are being supported, not "criticized," diminished or disrespected.

I sometimes jokingly say, "I still like you," or "You are still a good person," when helping a student notice a movement pattern that is not serving them, to make sure they know in a lighthearted way that they are not defined by inefficient habits and neither should they feel guilty about them.

In fact, students should not feel compelled to eliminate inefficient movement habits. A person might be a powerfully expressive dancer and yet also rely on some movement habits that diminish efficiency or might even be slowly creating chronic injuries. By noticing without judgment, a person can decide whether and/or when the time is right to engage in the challenging process of replacing inefficient behaviors.

> **FOR YOUR CONSIDERATION:**
>
> How can you offer "corrections," or guidance, in a manner that students feel supported by it?
> How do you know if/when you are ready to engage in the process of following new thoughts into new action patterns?

19 Replace. You Can't Just Erase

Like many of my own teachers, I used to tell students to "let go" of an inefficient movement habit. One of my teaching mottos was "Erase the brace!" "Brace" is my word for immobilizing tension in our bodies. Braced parts of us are not allowed to participate in the continuous reorganization that needs to occur in all parts of a well-functioning body.

Peggy Hackney,[3] a beautifully expressive dancer and renowned movement analyst, joined my professional dance company in 1976. During rehearsals and cross-country tours, she shared with me and other company members her profound knowledge of fundamental human movement. One of the many things Peggy helped me understand when I reconnected with her in 1996 is that we can't just let go of habitual movement patterns. That is, one can't just *erase*. We have used those sometimes-inefficient habits to develop the skills and artistry that now define us. Just "letting them go" could leave us with a sense of emptiness, frustration and perhaps an inability to accomplish even simple movements. What we can do, instead, is *replace* the habits that are not working well for us with new patterns that might serve us better.

So, I changed my motto to "*Replace* the brace!" Replacing a deeply-ingrained pattern takes time and patience, and students should know they may not be immediately successful. Grasping a new movement idea intellectually is relatively easy; noticing when a no-longer-desirable pattern wants to re-assert itself, and then intervening and replacing it with a new response, is considerably more challenging.

Therefore, instead of merely telling students what is "wrong" or what not to do, let's invite them to focus on "what could be right" and then help them develop the tools they need to engage in the change process. Let's encourage them to notice inefficient habits, to establish personal goals for positive change and to enjoy the gradual and challenging process of replacing no-longer-useful habits with the positive patterns they would like to establish.

For several years, we played with mottos in the Bill Evans Teachers Intensives.[4] In addition to "Replace the brace," we said "Research the lurch" and "Rehab the grab." "Lurch" was my name for a sudden jolt or jerk within an otherwise smooth phrase of movement, a momentary loss of flow that occurs when we interrupt the continuous reorganization process in the body and try to fast-forward to the end of the phrase. "Rehab the grab" was contributed by Debbi Knapp, to help us notice involuntary isometric or "grabbing" muscle contractions.

Levity can help to relieve the frustration we sometimes encounter when pursuing movement re-education. So, we often giggled while encouraging each other to, "Research the lurch, replace the brace and rehab the grab."

> **FOR YOUR CONSIDERATION:**
>
> If you ever tried to "just let go" of a movement habit, what was your experience?
> I invite you to "coin a phrase" you might use to help students seek improved function through lightheartedness or humor.

Notes

1 KLee (or Kathleen) Cooper, Certified Evans Teacher and founder/director of Pioneer Dance Arts in Sequim, Washington, joined the first cohort of educators studying to become CETs in 2003. She has been my professional associate for more than 40 years and has produced performances by me, Don Halquist and my professional company in her neighboring community of Port Angeles, Washington.
2 In 1956, Benjamin Bloom, with collaborators Max Englehart, Edward Furst, Walter Hill and David Krathwohl, published a framework for categorizing educational goals: *Taxonomy of Educational Objectives*. Familiarly known as *Bloom's Taxonomy*, this framework has been applied by generations of K-12 teachers and college instructors in their teaching. It recognizes that people learn through three domains: Cognitive—which includes remembering, understanding, applying, analyzing, evaluating and creating; Affective—which includes the manner in which we deal with things emotionally, such as feelings, values, appreciation, enthusiasms, motivations and attitudes, and Psychomotor—which includes physical movement, coordination and use of the motor-skill areas.

Development of these skills requires practice and is measured in terms of speed, precision, distance, procedures or techniques of execution.
3 Peggy Hackney is one of the world's foremost Laban/Bartenieff specialists. She studied and collaborated extensively with Irmgard Bartenieff and has spent the decades since Bartenieff's passing evolving and disseminating her ideas and practices. She joined the Bill Evans Dance Company and the faculty of our company school in 1976, and for several years she shared her knowledge of Laban/Bartenieff theories with me, company members and students in our school and summer programs. In 1996–97, I became certified through the Integrated Movement Studies Program that Peggy founded with colleagues Janice Meaden, Pam Schick and Ed Groff. *In the late 90s,* Peggy completed a book that has become a beloved text for dance and movement courses throughout the world, *Making Connections: Total Body Integration Through Bartenieff Fundamentals.*
4 The first session of the Bill Evans Teachers Intensive (BETI) was held in 1999 at the University of New Mexico in Albuquerque, where I was a professor of dance for 16 years and am now distinguished professor emeritus. There have now been 58 sessions of BETI in 17 locations in five countries, and thousands of dance educators have participated in our intensive workshops. In 2003, we added a certification program to our summer gatherings and many current BETI participants are Certified Evans Teachers or CET candidates.

References

Bloom, Benjamin, Max D. Engelhart, Edward J. Furst, Walker H. Hill and David R. Krathwohl *Taxonomy of Educational Objectives: The Classification of Educational Goals.* David McKay Co., 1968.

Caine, Renate Nummela, and Geoffrey Caine. *Unleashing the Power of Perceptual Change: The Potential of Brain-Based Teaching.* Assn. for Supervision & Curriculum Development, 1997.

Gardner, Howard E. *Frames of Mind: The Theory of Multiple Intelligences.* 3rd ed., Basic Books, 2011.

Hackney, Peggy. *Making Connections: Total Body Integration through Bartenieff Fundamentals.* Routledge, 2001.

III Cornerstones

Note: Words with specialized meanings in the Laban/Bartenieff Movement System, are capitalized in this chapter and in the remainder of this book (e.g., Yield and Push to Reach and Pull).

20 Positive Self-talk

In her essay, *Whole Person Education*, pedagogical theorist Linda MacRae-Campbell says that "…the willingness to confront emotional issues not only benefits learning, it also influences self-image, the single most important factor in determining an individual's success in any endeavor in life." I have certainly found it to be true, in my relationship with students as well as myself, that how we feel about ourselves as we move makes a huge difference in the amount of success and satisfaction we experience.

In the dance school I attended from ages 9 to 15, I experienced joy in every class. I loved dancing to my teacher's expertly-played live piano accompaniment and embracing the challenges she offered us, which were usually just a little beyond our grasp, and therefore conquerable. In a thoughtful and soft-spoken manner, she gave positive reinforcement to each student. I smiled almost constantly, believed that my teacher was pleased by the results of my hard work and felt that the dance studio was a haven in which I could be myself.

When I switched at age 16 to ballet classes in the continuing education division of a large university, I found a more competitive and less encouraging atmosphere. My teacher there preferred to teach by challenging his students, calling us such things as "clumsy elephants" to motivate us to become more graceful. He constantly pounded a long black stick on the floor to accentuate the beat of the piano accompaniment, and he yelled loudly to make himself heard over the cane and the music. More than once, that cane was hurled toward my feet when I didn't respond to a correction as he had hoped. In those classes I developed a habit, that amplified over years, of staring at myself in the mirror, focusing on what was not "perfect," grimacing at the end of each combination and then beating myself up a little for not being better.

If we judge ourselves and feel that we are not good enough, or if we focus on how difficult a movement might be, we will interfere with knowledge generation. If we think about what could go wrong, it probably will. When I look back on those years now, I wonder what aspect of my human nature kept me repeating that self-defeating syndrome, and I feel sad for the lack of joy experienced by the young person I was then.

The habit of negative self-talk persisted during my early years as a professional dancer, but I gradually learned to replace it. For the past 50 years, I have increasingly sent positive messages to myself as I dance. When my self-talk focuses on what could be right, when I feed myself encouraging images, my *body's wisdom* works for me to help me accomplish movement challenges with awareness, efficiency and joy.

Positive self-talk is powerful. When we affirm, we experience a sense of well-being and fulfillment, even while also recognizing that our work is not yet done. We can enjoy the trial-and-error process and support ourselves with inner validation while also accepting the challenge to improve.

FOR YOUR CONSIDERATION:

Do you consciously engage in self-talk while dancing? If so, what are some of the things you have recently said to yourself?

Could you recount three motivating phrases you might tell yourself as you seek to embody new movement material?

How could you encourage students to offer themselves supportive self-talk as they engage in the process of meeting new challenges?

---

21 Compete or Excel?

When dancers compete with others, their focus is *outside* their bodies, on how they look. But they learn more meaningfully and efficiently when they are deeply aware of *internal* processes, sensations and feelings. Therefore, I encourage students to *excel, not compete*. When pursuing their own excellence, they need to be just a little bit clearer, more efficient, more expressive, more connected to the music or more integrated this week than last to deserve kudos and experience success.

I often invite students to establish three primary personal technique goals for a semester and to track their progress toward them. I check in with each of them in a mid-session conference and receive a full report at the end of our time together. Often, they collaborate with a peer, helping one another clarify and refine those goals and develop strategies to reach them. Dancers' initial goals might change as new information becomes available or as they gain deeper understanding of what their movement habits and possibilities really are. I encourage such reassessment of goals, as well as the addition of supplementary goals if they arise and are personally meaningful.

Each of us can become a more fully-realized version of ourselves. Over time, I have witnessed students develop more growth in skill and artistry by seeking self-defined personal progress than by comparing themselves to others or some idealized external standard.

FOR YOUR CONSIDERATION:

Could you describe a time when you pursued and achieved your own internally-determined goal?

How could you help students formulate their own personal, relevant, suitably-challenging and achievable goals?

---

22 High Challenge but Low Threat

Renate and Geoffrey Caine tell us in *Unleashing the Power of Perceptual Change* that students learn best in a "high challenge, low threat" environment. Most people need to feel safe if they are to dive into learning with the whole of themselves. It is crucial to assure students that they can trust the environment of the learning community, that they are welcome just as they are, and that their individual differences and needs will be noticed and honored. We effectively generate new knowledge only when we leave our comfort zones, but if we never experience a sense of belonging and accomplishment, we might stop believing in ourselves and stop trying.

For me, low threat means without judgment. I have noticed that when I judge myself or feel judged by others, insecurity rears its head and learning stops. It is important to recognize the difference between judgment and discernment or understanding. I do not mislead students by failing to notice behaviors that might not be serving them, but neither do I make students feel guilty about the things they don't yet know. Discernment can be defined as insight, clear perception or awareness. It can be developed with a sense of objectivity. Judgment implies opinion, comparison and hierarchy. It elicits emotional reactions that can get in the way of positive change.

All students need challenges in order to grow, and some students are immediately comfortable with struggle and uncertainty. Others may need to feel assured of the low threat in our classrooms before they are willing or able to pursue new achievements. Such students may feel overwhelmed by struggle and need the chance to repeat a movement investigation several times, perhaps over multiple lessons, to feel good enough about themselves that they are ready to confront new challenges.

My colleague Debbi Knapp shared with me a formula for providing both challenge and success: "A class should provide both repetition of something familiar and two challenges, one that can be accomplished in the length of a given class and one that will require practice over time."

> **FOR YOUR CONSIDERATION:**
>
> How could you create a low-threat environment in your classes?
> How could you provide high challenges for students who want it without discouraging those who might fear it?

23 The Value of Refined Repetition

There is always more than one thing going on at a given time in any human movement experience. Repeating movement phrase-work or investigations for students needing more time with the material can still include growth opportunities for students not wanting more time, if a familiar pattern is taught from a new perspective or with an emphasis on a different layer that might be considered. If we unpack (or differentiate) additional aspects of the material as we offer repetition of phrase-work, dancers can engage with the degree of specificity and nuance that meets their needs.

Refined repetition can reduce the threat level for students who are uncomfortable with uncertainty, and it can also challenge students already acquainted with the external aspects of a sequence because they can be invited to seek more specific internal sensations, different expressive qualities, more clearly-defined spatial intent or more nuanced musical phrasing.

It is important to recognize the value of refined repetition for all our students. If the information contained within our dance phrases is to penetrate deeply, and be stored in the student's body-mind memory, we need to offer repeated opportunities to re-examine it. Colette Bennett[1] and other educational researchers have determined that in order for a new vocabulary word to make the journey into the brain's long-term memory, a student must be exposed to the word in 17 timed intervals. That means that we need to allow our students to experience the same movement concept investigations repeatedly, with intervals for reflection and meaning-making.

> **FOR YOUR CONSIDERATION:**
>
> I invite you to identify three different "layers" of a dance combination you could emphasize in each of three repeated investigations.
>
> How can you organize learning experiences to allow information you value to deeply penetrate the student's body-mind?

24 There Is No Meaning without Context

In 1972, English social scientist Gregory Bateson wrote, "Without context, words and actions give no meaning at all." One of my pleasures in studying with the iconic Black rhythm tap artist/teacher Dianne Walker[2] is the way she intersperses personal and professional anecdotes throughout her classes. She brilliantly uses seemingly casual verbal interludes to provide historical context and meaning, as well as recuperation from intense exertions of unpacking and coordinating complex rhythms.

I was also enriched by the teaching of Percival Borde,[3] who passed on traditional African dance studies researched by Pearl Primus to us Harkness Ballet trainees in New York City in the mid-'60s. His classes included fascinating anthropological information that gave me context from which to create meaning.

Most of my dance teachers, however, all the way through college and my early years of professional study in New York, Chicago and elsewhere, did not mention the sources of the movement materials they passed on. I usually had no idea of the origins of what we were dancing, and often assumed that my teachers had invented it themselves. As a teacher, I have learned that telling students where and how I first encountered an idea or movement phrase will allow them to grasp a bigger picture by locating what we are studying in a context of time, culture and world events.

I majored in both ballet and English as an undergraduate at the University of Utah. If my literature teachers had borrowed from essays, plays or poems without citing their authors, it would have been considered academically dishonest plagiarism. Why and how, I wonder, did it become common practice in the dance world for teachers to share material they learned elsewhere without revealing its sources? Is this not also a kind of plagiarism? This practice deprives students of information that could enable them to understand how smaller parts contribute to the larger scheme of things.

To empower our students, and prepare them to make integrative meaning, we need to cite our sources. This is not always possible in master classes or short workshops, but when we teach students over a period of weeks or longer, we have a responsibility to tell them about our first experience of the movement phrases, concepts and styles we are sharing with them. I enjoy contextualizing the ideas and practices I have come to value, explaining why they are meaningful to me and what students might derive from investigating them.

I was fortunate as a child to have a tap dance teacher in Salt Lake City who had studied extensively in Hollywood with Louis DaPron, Donald O'Connor's teacher and choreographer. June Park[4] mentioned DaPron as the source of rhythmic patterns she shared with us, and I am grateful that she made it possible for me to embody his sophisticated and challenging material. Those rhythms still live in my body-mind and offer profound kinesthetic and rhythmic pleasure.

However, I wish I had then known more about the historical/social milieu from which those rhythms and body attitudes evolved. As an adult, I discovered that DaPron and other famous white Hollywood tap dancers of his era were strongly influenced by seminal Black American tap artists who had settled in southern California when Vaudeville expired.

Knowing of the origins of rhythm tap in Black American and Irish American immigrant communities would have been empowering for me as a child. It would have broadened my vision and understanding of how dance connects to our larger lives. It would have empowered me to understand as a child that the art form I loved so much was primarily a creation of Black artists, and that rhythm tap and jazz music, which I also dearly loved, were inextricably connected in their developmental stages. I grew up in an all-white, systemically racist community, and such fundamental information about my most passionate interests would have elicited larger questions to which I would have sought answers at that formative stage of my life.

FOR YOUR CONSIDERATION:

How could you include contextual information in the limited time available in your technique classes without interrupting the flow or continuity?

I invite you to identify three movement phrases you have passed on without acknowledging how they became significant to you. What could you say about them that might help students understand the larger context in which you came to value them?

---

25 Learning Can Be Serious Fun

I believe that almost every technique class should include opportunities for students of all ages to make discoveries through light-hearted but serious fun. Play is the work of toddlers and young children, who follow their curiosity to generate knowledge about the fascinating world in which they find themselves at amazing speed. Playing opens them to discoveries of the physical world and the life of the imagination. The trial-and-error problem-solving of developmental movement progressions connects mind, body and spirit.

In his dance pedagogy courses, Don Halquist encourages teachers to always make learning fun. He suggests beginning each class by asking, "Who has a joke?" He recommends that we keep a supply of light-hearted, non-political, non-religious jokes on hand, in case a student can't think of one. I've taken his advice with many groups of students and found that after a while most will come prepared with their own jokes and share them eagerly.

Humorous moments often arise spontaneously in our classes, and it is important to stay alert for their appearance and to revel in them. By speaking in a joyful voice, moving with a carefree body attitude or interspersing a cheerful comment, a teacher can encourage spontaneity and reduce physical and emotional tension when students are struggling to learn complex and demanding material. A whimsical moment can bring students back into heightened engagement when they become distracted or fatigued.

The brain and body respond positively to laughter, which promotes learning by increasing dopamine (a brain chemical that helps us move and learn), endorphin (a brain chemical that reduces the perception of physical and emotional pain) and breathing volume (more oxygen). When a lesson starts with or includes humor, the creation of new knowledge and/or sharing of information with peers is enhanced by the positive sensations and emotions elicited by laughter.

> **FOR YOUR CONSIDERATION:**
>
> I invite you to find a new joke to share with your students in each of your next three classes and then notice if it affects the mood of the class. If you perceive a positive impact, how might you encourage students to bring their own jokes to subsequent classes?
>
> Could you describe three strategies you have used or witnessed that lightened the atmosphere in, or added some levity to "uptight" or "stressed-out" teaching/learning situations?

26 Uncover to Discover

Teachers sometimes talk about what they "covered" in their classes, or check off items on a list of topics they have included in their lesson plans. I have even noticed teachers making sure they are "covering" anatomical information by yelling it out to students as they are dancing complex movement phrases.

I don't want to "cover" a topic; instead, I try to "uncover" it, so that students can "discover" aspects of that topic that are personally meaningful. I have found that students want to learn what has personal relevance. I can mention a topic in the syllabus, include it a lesson plan and then speak enthusiastically about it repeatedly, but none of those attempts will guarantee that students have embodied it. Before expecting students to engage, I must first *get their attention* and cooperation. They must "buy into" or become curious about the topics I feel are important.

Sitting and listening, or even watching and copying, are not immersive enough for most students to retain, reflect and make meaning of new ideas or experiences. I try to organize opportunities through which I can help students discern the relevance of ideas we investigate to their personal journeys toward significant goals and then embody those ideas or concepts in a variety of ways.

When students are fully invested in the exploration of movement phrases or ideas, they are more likely to "dive in" with the whole of themselves as we actively uncover, unpack or differentiate the many layers of an experience. Students can then add what they learned to the arsenal of tools they are assembling to become more fully-realized versions of themselves.

> **FOR YOUR CONSIDERATION:**
>
> In what other words could you delineate the contrast between what I call "covering" and "uncovering" information you wish to share with students?
>
> Could you describe two ways you could help students find personal relevancy that may not be immediately apparent in something you want to teach?

27 Never Work Harder Than Your Students

More than a decade ago, I required a book entitled *Never Work Harder Than Your Students and Other Principles of Great Teaching*, by Robyn R. Jackson, in a graduate-level dance pedagogy course I designed and taught at the State University of New York College at Brockport. I have integrated ideas that came alive for me while engaging with that text into my teaching ever since.

Effective teaching is often more about asking relevant and timely questions than about giving wise answers. The Laban/Bartenieff Movement System (L/BMS) has given me tools for observing without judging. I can help students learn to look, differentiate, discern and understand, without telling them what to see. My questions sometimes invite students to paraphrase information I've shared verbally or asked them to read. More often, my questions will offer opportunities for them to figure things out. Each kind of question is valuable, and they accomplish different purposes. Sometimes I pose a couple of contrasting hypothetical possibilities and then ask, "What if?" I've found those words to be a powerful invitation to active learning.

When we ask problem-solving questions, we can't expect immediate answers, but need to give students time to reflect and come up with personally-meaningful responses. We might ask them to discuss a question with a peer before sharing their answers with the class.

The technique class can be a laboratory. We might say, "What are you curious about?" When we guide students as they investigate and seek answers, we are motivating them to develop personal agency. After inviting students to delve into questions about movement theory and materials we should get out of their way and let them do the exciting and potentially transformative work of discovering and making meaning. When they draw on their own lived experience and wrap their own words around their findings, they know things in a profoundly different way than if we had simply told them, no matter how passionately we may have spoken.

If we do most of the work, we derive most of the benefit. By unpacking and uncovering ideas we consider essential, and then structuring inquiries through which students can construct their own problems and solutions, we are making room for them to experience the challenges, joy, satisfaction and empowerment of investigation and discovery.

FOR YOUR CONSIDERATION:

I invite you to think of a lesson plan you love to teach and to identify three ways within that lesson that you could do less so that your students could do more.

Could you describe two strategies for making sure that every student has an opportunity to answer when you ask a question to the whole class?

---

28 Teaching the People in the Room

As we enter the studio, it is wise to look and see, to listen and hear, to open ourselves to the vibes coming from the individuals or the group in the room. We can never know in advance what may have happened to students before they arrive. No matter what we have prepared in advance, it's a good idea to notice what is happening at the moment and be willing to modify our plans. If we make it a priority to tune in to who they are today and then meet them where they are, we are more likely to facilitate a collaborative experience in which knowledge is co-created by as many participants as possible.

Sometimes, we must completely shelve a prepared lesson plan and spontaneously create, or co-create with student participation, a new one. After all, we are not just teaching technique; we are teaching these people on this occasion, and we need to figure out which of the things they need today we are prepared to offer. At other times, we may be able to deliver most of the class we had planned if we first attend to a situation at hand. We might spend more time than usual checking in and discussing or just hearing about factors that are causing them concern. Through honest and compassionate communication, the mood of the group might be altered and they might be ready for a streamlined version of the class we had planned.

Some teachers will tell students to "leave your emotions at the door." I know that our emotions are interwoven with all the other things we are and that we cannot leave them anywhere. They come with us, and if we try to press them down and ignore them, they will reveal themselves inadvertently or inappropriately and cause frustration, distraction or other interference with learning. Sometimes, giving people a few moments to share strong feelings with a peer, whose only job is to listen, can help them become calm, focused and able to embrace emotional truth while also participating in class. I believe that we should encourage students to acknowledge feelings and engage with them. They might make the decision to defer dealing with an emotional situation until after class, or to take some time out of class to compose themselves, without fear of being judged. Either of those are healthier alternatives than pretending that feelings don't exist.

FOR YOUR CONSIDERATION:

Could you describe a process you would like to explore for checking in with students at the beginning of class?

How could you encourage students to acknowledge emotional realities in your classes?

I invite you to scan your memory for a time when you taught or observed a class that wasn't appropriate for the people in the room on that occasion. If you recall such a class, what might have been done differently?

29 Learning from the Living Body

I earned an MFA degree in modern dance at the University of Utah, while also dancing full-time with Repertory Dance Theatre,[5] the Salt Lake City-based professional modern dance company that is still going strong. During that exciting and challenging time, I had multiple opportunities to study with Margaret H'Doubler,[6] whom I consider the "grandmother of somatic dance." In mesmerizing classes, H'Doubler explained that kinesthesia is the perception of motion in our muscles and proprioception the sense of body positions. She guided us with anatomically-based imagery into internal explorations, rather than expecting us to visually follow her demonstrations and/or look at our reflections in a mirror.

Dr. Elizabeth R. (Betty) Hayes,[7] the director of the modern dance program and an early graduate of H'Doubler's groundbreaking modern dance major program at the University of Wisconsin-Madison, made sure we didn't rely on mirrors. In fact, only one studio in the building had a mirror—old, small, warped and usually hidden behind a curtain—that could be consulted if a choreographing student felt it was absolutely necessary.

As an assistant instructor in Hayes' beginning modern dance course, I explored teaching with minimal demonstration. This required me to develop analytical and verbal skills that would enable student learning in other ways. I had to tune kinesthetically into the initiation, sequencing and sensations of the movement phrases I wanted those undergraduates to learn, and then wrap words sufficiently around my internal experiences that I could share them.

Eventually, I found myself combining physical demonstration and verbal imagery, articulating internal sensations as I experienced them. In addition to being a visual model, I was learning to teach basic anatomy through words and touch, musicality through rhythmic sounding and movement qualities through vocal inflection. I felt vibrantly alive as I encouraged younger dancers to see, hear, sense and feel, to become fully present within kinesthesia and proprioception. Ever since those days as a graduate teaching assistant, I have found that students engage more deeply and activate more parts of themselves when they are encouraged to listen, sense, feel and embody rather than primarily look, follow and copy.

I have one caveat: Our *kinesthetic perceptions can sometimes be erroneous*. If we tell ourselves we are doing one thing while actually doing something else, we learn to associate the kinesthetic sensations of the imprecise movement with the thoughts and words describing what we had intended to do. For example, we might be telling ourselves to flex the spine laterally and reach the head toward Side Middle while actually reaching the head toward Right (or Left) Forward High.[8] (I have observed this mind-body disconnect in hundreds of dancers over the decades.) In instances of erroneous kinesthetic feedback, it is important to rectify a misperception from both the outside and the inside. Through guiding touch or verbal cues, a learning partner or teacher could help a student achieve the desired action and confirm that their kinesthetic feedback matches their intent.

FOR YOUR CONSIDERATION:

Could you describe a time when you learned from your own living body?

If you have had one or more somatic-based teachers, what are some ideas you learned to value under their guidance?

I invite you to describe three ways in which you could guide students toward embodied knowledge.

---

30 The Mind-Body Organizing Power of Intent

Rudolf Laban (1879–1958) was the founder of systems of movement analysis and documentation that are studied throughout the world. Irmgard Bartenieff (1900–81), who studied with Laban in Germany before coming to the U.S. in 1936, was a dancer, choreographer, physical therapist and pioneering dance movement therapist. Laban/Bartenieff (L/B) and the Laban/Bartenieff Movement System (L/BMS) refer to the work of the former as brought to North America and interpreted, developed and refined by the latter and her numerous collaborators and successors.

Note: Please see Appendix C for more information about both these somatic pioneers.

Bartenieff Fundamentals (BF), is a system of somatic investigation and repatterning that was founded in New York City in the 1950s. It was first shared with me by Peggy Hackney in the middle and late '70s, and has given me and countless others multiple inroads through which we recognize and understand our most basic movement habits and engage in a process of movement re-education toward more efficient and expressive body to mind and mind to body functioning.

A guiding BF principle is that "intent organizes the neuromuscular system." From the beginning of life, we have moved to satisfy intents—instincts, needs or desires. Intent is a purpose (while intention is a course of action). Many movements that were once conscious decisions have become habitual responses that no longer rise to the conscious level. Since our ancestors moved to satisfy conscious or subconscious purposes, we are "wired" to move in response to an intent, and doing so can give us access to inherited bodily wisdom.

I invite students to experiment with a variety of specific purposeful intents and courses of action (concerning body functions, expressive movement qualities, musical phrasing, spatial forms, directions, pathways or other factors they care about) and to notice which of those guiding images or ideas and strategies allow them to function most efficiently and expressively.

Moving without clear cognitive or affective intent, perhaps by simply copying the outer form of a movement sequence being demonstrated by a teacher, or learning a series of body forms on the basis of how they look and on what counts they are made, engages only a portion of a student's body-mind-spirit. When we are not fully present or embodied, we might struggle with the coordination of even basic actions. Moving with appropriate intent, in harmony with the body-mind's organic functions, will help students integrate the whole of themselves efficiently in the accomplishment of movements tasks or challenges.

FOR YOUR CONSIDERATION:

I invite you to wrap words around the primary intent behind three of your favorite dance movements. Could you play with different purposes for the same movements?

Since our intent doesn't always reach the conscious level, I invite you to improvise a dance, record it, and then study the video until the dance becomes accurately repeatable. Once you have learned to repeat your improvised dance, could you bring what might be the unconscious intent behind some of the movement to the surface, where it can be identified, clarified, refined and used to guide you?

31 Movement Occurs in Phrases

In Bartenieff Fundamentals, it is emphasized that *movement happens in phrases,* not in isolated segments. A movement phrase is similar to a group of words that comprise a grammatical phrase, clause or sentence, as contrasted with individual words. In her classes, Peggy Hackney, author of *Making Connections: Total Body Connectivity through Bartenieff Fundamentals,* says that phrases are "perceivable units of movement which are in some sense meaningful. They begin and end while containing a through line."

In my experience, most dance teachers focus on counts, steps or positions rather than on phrases when teaching. Since we have moved in variable phrases rather than an arbitrary number of counts throughout our lives, teaching through single counts, separate positions or long chains of undifferentiated movement can make it difficult for many students to learn.

Here's how I describe the different BF-defined parts of a movement phrase:

a   *Preparation*—when the mover experiences a conscious or subconscious intent to move;
b   *Initiation*—when in time and where in the body the movement begins;
c   *Main Action*—when a viewer might see the motion; and
d   *Follow-Through*—when the phrase is completed or when a transition into the next phrase begins.

Revealing a whole phrase before breaking it down makes it easier for almost everyone to embody it. Movement sequences can be phrased in more than one way, so it is helpful if a teacher clearly communicates desired dynamics during that initial sharing. Students might later be encouraged to play with different ways of phrasing and enlivening the same sequence.

Accents can be an important aspect of phrasing. They can be *Impulsive* (at the beginning), *Impactive* (at the end) and *Swing* (in the middle), or a phrase can be *Even*, with no accent. Each stride and weight transfer in walking can be perceived as a separate phrase, with an emphasis at the beginning, in the middle, at the end or with no emphasis. My customary walking/stride accent is Impulsive, but it can change depending on the intent motivating my traveling in space or on my mood any given day.

Most of us rely repeatedly on phrase lengths and patterns in which we feel at home. Individual phrasing preference is a significant component of what is known in L/BMS as a person's *Movement Signature*. (The Impulsive accent in my stride coheres with much of what I know about myself. I love beginnings, new ventures and new ideas.)

FOR YOUR CONSIDERATION:

Did you emphasize the counts/moments or the phrases the last time you taught an extended dance combination? Could you try "teaching" it to yourself now and allow your vocal inflections as well as your physical embodiment to indicate phrase lengths and accents?

Could you go for a stroll and notice if you experience an accent in each short walking phrase—each stride and weight transfer? If so, is it at the beginning, in the middle or at the end?

---

32 Neutral Alignment/A Change in the Part Creates a Change in the Whole

Many teachers believe that "neutral" alignment is important. I agree, but we must understand that neutral does not mean placed, held or unchanging. It means *in a functional relationship, available and ready to respond*. In fact, every part of a neutrally-aligned body will change continuously as a person breathes, moves and dances. Neutral alignment is dynamic!

Bartenieff Fundamentals practitioners say, "A change in the part creates a change in the whole." When I first heard that concise description of something I had experienced in my own body for years, I breathed a deep sigh of recognition. That principle gave me permission to own and proclaim what I was already doing but feeling guilty about, which was letting my whole body reorganize subtly to support gestures and weight shifts. Much of my earlier dance training had focused on "isolations," in which only one part of the body was supposed to move. I was told to "stabilize" (which I interpreted as *hold or immobilize*) other parts of myself in order to focus on the isolated motion.

Even small immobilizations or energy blockages in one body part will interfere with total body freedom. Such holding patterns block force absorption and cause strain and unnecessary wear and tear that will eventually create chronic musculoskeletal injuries. The body is a complex organism composed of many interactive systems, and it serves us to allow the whole body to reorganize continuously and harmoniously as we dance.

Functional, efficient, resilient, adaptive and, therefore, "neutral" total body organization is crucial to both a dancer's short-term skill development and long-term health and well-being. Life is movement and movement is change. Alignment is not a position; it is a dynamic balancing act.

FOR YOUR CONSIDERATION:

What does the term "neutral alignment" mean to you?

I invite you to notice two or three parts of your own body that tend not to respond to the changes taking place in the rest of you in a technique class. What images might help you invite those reluctant body parts into a process of total body reorganization?

---

33 Brace, Collapse or Give and Take/Yield and Push to Reach and Pull

I like to differentiate three attitudes we can embody toward our flow of energy:

a   We can *Brace* or close the body's outer surface, keeping the inside in and the outside out.
b   We can *Collapse* or become passive rather than actively engaging with our energy.
c   We can *Yield* or invite our energy into an active give-and-take relationship with the environment. This means opening the body's outer surface, which can be compared to the selectively permeable membrane that controls the movement of substances in and out of the cell. An *open body wall* will allow the outside energy to pour in and the inside energy to pour out. Bracing creates too much tension, and *collapsing* results in too little control. *Yielding to and bonding with* the environment establishes an active dialogue with gravity and the world around us. Because there are many degrees of *yield*, we can modulate our flow toward either the bracing or collapsing ends of the spectrum without going so far that we shut it down or give up altogether.

Through the study of Bonnie Bainbridge Cohen's Body-Mind Centering[9] and Bartenieff's Fundamentals, we know that we rely on developmental movement patterns formed in utero and during the early months after birth for the rest of our lives. In utero, we:

d   *Yield* before we *Push*.
e   *Push* before we *Reach*.
f   *Reach* before we *Pull*.

In the study of dance, we can consciously apply this phrase, "Yield and Push to Reach and Pull," to find increased efficiency and connectivity in just about any movement we explore.

I think of Yield as bi-directional Flow—exuding outpouring and absorbing inpouring energy simultaneously—that establishes an active partnership with gravity and a readiness to move. I am then able to Push from each point of contact to the earth, initiating the motion by sending energy from the earth through open pathways of Flow to my body's core. It is then the Reach that sends energy to or through my body's edges to permit an integrated gesture and/or shift of weight. I can then Pull myself to a new body form and/or a new point in space.

We can coordinate our breathing with this phrase: Yield/Push has an affinity for exhalation, and the breath cycle completes itself with inhalation in the Reach/Pull. There are times when the Reach and Pull might begin first, but they can be supported by an almost simultaneous Yield and Push. We can call upon this four-part phrase whenever we move, in small or large ways, to ride our breath, utilize momentum and find continuity of movement.

FOR YOUR CONSIDERATION:

I invite you to perform one of your favorite dance combinations three times: first, as you normally do; second, consciously *disallowing* any Yield and Push and relying entirely on Reach and Pull; third, consciously preceding each Reach and Pull with a generous Yield and Push. Could you wrap words around the differences you experience in these three experiments? Could you repeat the combination one more time, while either bracing or collapsing in each place where you had previously Yielded, and describe your experience?

Notes

1. Colette Marie Bennett is the Curriculum Coordinator for English Language Arts, Social Studies, Library Media, and Testing for the West Haven Public School System in West Haven, Connecticut. She blogs about education at *Used Books in Class*: http://usedbookclassroom.wordpress.com/ She tweets at Teachcmb56@twitter.com.
2. Dianne "Lady Di" Walker (born in 1951) was a pioneer in the resurgence of the art of rhythm tap and has created a four-decades-long career spanning Broadway, television, film, international jazz concerts and tap festivals. As a mentor and teacher, she has enormously influenced generations of tap artists. I studied with her on many occasions, including a residency that I coordinated at SUNY Brockport and in tap festivals and master classes across the country.
3. Percival Borde (1922–79) was an African and Caribbean dancer and choreographer who was connected professionally and personally to Pearl Primus, the great modern and African dancer, choreographer and anthropologist. He was one of several iconic teachers hired by director Patricia Wilde to work with apprentices at Harkness House for Ballet Arts in New York City. For me, he connected dance, ritual and everyday life. He followed my career and reached out supportively during the years in which he taught and choreographed at SUNY Binghamton.
4. June Purrington Park (1914–2008) was born into a dancing family. Her parents were vaudeville performers and her father established the Purrington School of Dance Art in Salt Lake City, where I took my first tap/ballet lessons at age eight and first studied with Willam Christensen at age 16. June studied ballet with Ernest Belcher and tap with Louis DaPron in Los Angeles before returning home to teach first in her father's studio and then to establish her own June Park School of Dance. I studied with June from ages 9 through 15, and she influenced who I am as a teacher more than any other role model. She was an accomplished pianist and accompanied all her classes and performances on a grand piano. She taught me about music as well as dance and modeled for me what it means to be a skilled, honest, dedicated, articulate, compassionate, dignified and responsible professional person in dance. She facilitated my participation in summer dance conventions in Los Angeles in my tweens and early teens, where I saw exciting Black vernacular jazz dancers who inspired my early choreography. She attended my Salt Lake City performances over more than four decades and was often the first person to come backstage at the end of a show.
5. The Repertory Dance Theatre (RDT) is a professional, touring modern dance company based in Salt Lake City, Utah. It was founded in 1966 and has operated continuously and successfully since that time. I was a dancer, choreographer and administrator (first chairman and later one of three artistic coordinators) with the company from 1967 to 1974. I have created 19 works for RDT and have returned many times over the decades to teach, perform and reconstruct or create choreographic works.
6. Margaret H'Doubler (1889–1982) is the author of *Dance: A Creative Art Experience* and four other books on her pedagogy and the importance of dance in education. She was an assistant professor of basketball,

baseball and swimming when she discovered dance, and she drew on her knowledge of movement and the body to define dance as both an art and a science. She founded the world's first higher education dance major and a dance group called Orchesis, at the University of Wisconsin at Madison, and women graduating from her program with BS degrees in women's physical education, emphasis in dance, founded seminal dance programs and Orchesis performing groups in colleges and universities throughout the country. H'Doubler was retired and living in Tucson, Arizona in the late '60s, when I was a graduate student in dance at the University of Utah, where she served as a frequent guest/master teacher.

7 Elizabeth R. Hayes (1911–2007) was an early graduate of H'Doubler's Wisconsin dance major program. Betty provided leadership for modern dance at the University of Utah for 48 years and was also a leader in dance education nationally. She wrote several books, including *The Evolution of Visual, Literary and Performing Arts*, which was published when she was 93. She and I became colleagues after I earned an MFA, and she accepted my invitation to serve on the RDT advisory committee for several years. In 1970, I choreographed *For Betty* to honor her. It has been performed thousands of times by several different companies over the decades. In 1974, she selected me for the position of assistant professor of modern dance at the U of U. When she was honored with the National Dance Association Heritage Award in 1977, the Bill Evans Dance Company performed *For Betty* at the NDA award ceremony in Seattle. She remained my friend and mentor for almost 40 years.

8 Words with specialized meanings in the Laban/Bartenieff Movement System (such as "Side Middle") are capitalized in this book.

9 Bonnie Bainbridge Cohen, creator of Body-Mind Centering and author of *Sensing, Feeling and Action: The Experiential Anatomy of Body-Mind Centering*, conducts workshops and courses and has created numerous DVDs and other instructional materials through which she disseminates her ground-breaking theories and discoveries. She was once a student of Irmgard Bartenieff's and has become a unique leader in the world of somatic investigation. In 2017, she delivered a powerful keynote presentation at the Somatic Dance Conference and Performance Festival that I founded and which I co-direct with Cynthia Williams at Hobart and William Smith Colleges in Geneva, New York.

References

Bateson, Gregory. *Mind and Nature: A Necessary Unity (Advances in Systems Theory, Complexity, and the Human Sciences)*. Hampton Press, 2002.

Caine, Renate Nummela, and Geoffrey Caine. *Unleashing the Power of Perceptual Change: The Potential of Brain-Based Teaching*. Assn. for Supervision & Curriculum Development, 1997.

Hackney, Peggy. *Making Connections: Total Body Integration through Bartenieff Fundamentals*. Routledge, 2001

Jackson, Robyn R. *Never Work Harder Than Your Students and Other Principles of Great Teaching.* 2nd ed., ASCD, 2018.

MacRae-Campbell, Linda. "Whole Person Education: Nurturing the Compassionate Genius in Each of Us." *IN CONTEXT: A Quarterly of Humane Sustainable Culture #18*, edited by Robert Gilman, Context Institute, 1988.

IV Language

34 Words Matter

I choose the words with which I guide movement explorations carefully, differentiating more *objective language* (usually taken from anatomy or the Laban/Bartenieff Movement System) from intentionally *subjective language* (figures of speech, metaphors or similes). When using scientific and theoretical terms, I use some words that have variable meanings in everyday speech but specialized, specific meanings in the work I share. To facilitate students' understanding, I define the meanings of such words within the contexts of our explorations, so that we can communicate with clarity and efficiency.

My long-term teaching colleague Kitty Daniels,[1] a masterful teacher of ballet technique and anatomy, combines clear anatomical instruction with generous metaphorical imagery. She encourages teachers to collect numerous images that are congruent with their understanding of body science or somatic movement theory and to include several such visualizations in each class. When using subjective language, I offer a variety of choices because such words can have both denotative (dictionary definition) and connotative (personal connection) values for each of us. Subjective images that work well for one student may trigger unpleasant feelings or confusion in another and get in the way of her/his/their learning. I notice the response elicited by a specific mental picture, and if an image is not deepening student access to our investigations, I'll drop it and try something else.

The same is true of more objective language. L/BMS gives us numerous possible inroads—through the areas of Body, Effort, Shape and Space—to understanding any movement experience. If what I am saying through the concepts of one area of L/BMS is not helpful to a student, I'll try another area. For example, some students will respond well to a combination of Space Effort and Time Effort suggestions (e.g., "Scan the Horizontal Plane gradually") but not to Space and Flow Efforts (e.g., "...with Indirect² containment"); they might be confused by Space and Weight Effort images (e.g., "Spiral forcefully") but find clarity in Shape and Body invitations (e.g., "Enclose the body-half").

Even precisely-defined L/BMS terminology might trigger unpleasant feelings in some people. Certified Evans Teacher Mariah-Jane Thies was made uneasy by the word "Slash," a basic work action that is strong, quick and indirect. To her, applying that word felt violent and traumatizing. I encouraged her to find a replacement word, and she came up with "splash." She can now move with sudden, strong indirectness without those unpleasant feelings, and she also feels empowered to translate other L/BMS terms that don't quite work for her into language that both serves her needs and honors the system. Like Mariah-Jane, students can often find their own images that lead them to enhanced success and enjoyment in moving. I often invite them to do just that, and then share them with a study-buddy, me or the whole class.

FOR YOUR CONSIDERATION:

I invite you to select two of your favorite dance combinations. What words do you ordinarily use to describe them? Please teach one of these combinations to yourself or another using only scientific or theoretical language that feels objective to you. Please describe the other using only subjective or poetic language. Could you switch which pattern you describe objectively and subjectively? Can you compare and contrast these experiences?

---

35 Invite

I want the people I teach to willingly and eagerly engage with themselves, with me and with their peers in a process of investigating possibilities. Therefore, I "invite" students to participate in an experience rather than "tell" them to do so. Invitational teaching summons them to recognize their personal agency over their thoughts, feelings and actions. It motivates them to see themselves as able, valuable and responsible, and to behave accordingly. If I say, "I invite you to form a circle," for instance, it has a very different impact from saying, "Form a circle." By using words such as "invite," "encourage," "consider," "could you?" or "what if?," I am indicating to people that when they choose to participate, they are actively accepting a sincerely-offered request, not a command.

Deep learning requires students to think, question and synthesize—to take ownership of their progress toward individual goals. I avoid strongly-worded directives that might indicate that I am the authority, rather than a leader of exploratory experiences. I am a guide or a facilitator, not an autocrat with all the answers, and I want my word choices, the tone of my voice and my body language to convey an open heart and a desire to support each student's individual learning process. I want them to know that my primary goal is to assist them in the generation of useful and relevant knowledge, and that I always hope to learn something new myself.

> **FOR YOUR CONSIDERATION:**
>
> I invite you to describe three ways in which you could let students know that they have personal agency in your classes.
> How would you describe your role as a dance teacher in one sentence?

36 Allow

Each of us has inherited bodily wisdom, but many of us have been learned to ignore or override it through limited or erroneous ideas about human functioning that have been passed on by generations of well-meaning but sometimes misinformed parents, dance teachers and movement specialists.

Instead of telling students to *do* something with their bodies, I try to encourage them to honor their bodily wisdom and to *allow* the body-mind to guide them as they participate in the experiences I am organizing. For example, I might ask "Could you allow your sitz bones to widen and your feet to melt as you sink into a plié?" This has a different impact from saying "Widen your sitz bones and soften your feet." The goal of most somatic-based dance instruction is to help students get out of their own way and let their bodily wisdom—both their inherited kinesthetic intelligence and their cultivated mind-body patterning—work for them.

By offering appropriate mental pictures and encouraging students to embrace those images with body-mind and spirit, we can galvanize the unfolding of organic processes from the inside out. Students can learn to dance in harmony with innate needs, rather than imposing externally-motivated ideas upon themselves. By *allowing*, with appropriate objective and/or subjective intent, we can stimulate the mind-body to seek efficient solutions to the movement problems we encounter. Rather than trying to force body-level change, let's permit, encourage and guide positive organic change to occur.

> **FOR YOUR CONSIDERATION:**
>
> I invite you to recall a time when you tried to force a body-level change. How else might you have approached that situation?
> What are other words or phrases in which you could convey the essence of "allowing?"

37 Reach and Other Integrative Verbs

Instead of saying, "Point your toes," I might ask, "Could you *Yield, Push and then Reach* simultaneously through each toe?" Or I might say, "Could you allow energy to pour out through each toe tip?" The image of "pointing the toes" creates bracing contractions that limit the independent actions of the many joints in the foot and ankle. Instead of saying, "Flex your foot," I might ask, "Could you Yield, Push and then each through the heel?" As in the previous example, the act of "reaching" integrates the foot with the rest of the body, creating a resilient kinetic chain from the core through the hip, knee, ankle and calcaneus into the space beyond the distal ends.

Thinking of the foot or any body part as a separate entity can cause disintegration. By inviting students to "reach through the toe tips" or to "allow energy to pour out through the distal ends," however, we can help them create synergistic energy balance through the whole leg and foot with support from the rest of the body.

This is equally true in the arms/hands and spine. We can "Reach through the arm and hand, letting energy pour out through the open door in each fingertip and thumb tip," and we can "Yield, Push and then Reach and Pull through the spine, releasing energy through the open door at the top of the head and/or at the tip of the tail." Guided by such language, limbs become resilient and pliable, and they appear longer because the flow of energy and participation of the rest of the body are not blocked.

No part of the body functions separately. As we know, a change in one part of the body creates a change in the whole, and our word choices can help students connect rather than segment their bodies. A continuous goal in guiding students could be *integration*, recognizing that each toe, finger, vertebra or other body part is a continuously-adapting component of the whole organism, that all body parts are interconnected and continuously reorganizing.

FOR YOUR CONSIDERATION:

What language in wide usage among dance teachers might cause a student to think of one body part as a separate entity? When can such an idea be useful? When might it be problematic?

What kind of integrative language can you think of to describe three basic dance movements that you regularly invite students to experience?

---

38 We Are Not Objects

The body is not a thing. It is a process. If we say "lift" rather than "reach," for example, we might be causing them to *objectify* themselves, treating their body parts as if they were inanimate things to be manipulated from the outside. In fact, the continuous reorganization of each and every part of the body is more efficient when awakened, sensed, felt and integrated from the inside.

When we treat the body as if it were an object, to be "lifted," "placed," "put," "stacked," "held," "lowered," "aligned," "pointed," "straightened," "sucked in," "pressed down" or "tucked under," we are likely to become less resilient and less adaptable. Such words can create a *Reach and Pull without a preparatory or simultaneous Yield and Push*, causing energy to travel along the body's outer surfaces rather than through its core and central pathways. Words that "dehumanize" the body encourage us to engage superficial muscles without the integration of the smaller muscles closer to the bone and the organs and fluids within our internal pathways. Overloading superficial muscles creates overuse/underuse imbalances in our muscles and connective tissue, a common cause of chronic injuries. This overload of muscles and their fascial coverings creates excessive tension that masks sensation, and sensing is our most important tool in modulating efficient function.

Language

Using process-oriented verbs found in the L/BMS lexicon, such as "Shrink, Grow, Yield, Push, Reach, Pull, Lengthen, Shorten, Widen, Narrow, Bulge, Hollow, Rise, Sink, Spread, Enclose, Advance and Retreat," can awaken internal sensory aliveness and encourage the creation of resilient elasticity as well as the clarity of form sought in objectifying words.

Let's be fully embodied and tune into our own internal experiences as we teach, wrapping words around those sensations to accurately convey what is coming alive within us. Let's invite students to join us on kinesthetic journeys through internal processes and feelings that make us vibrant, resilient, fluid, pliable and, therefore, adaptable.

FOR YOUR CONSIDERATION:

What factors might have influenced the introduction of objectifying or potentially dehumanizing language into some traditional teaching practices?

Could you mention several verbs in addition to those mentioned above that might awaken internal aliveness?

Notes

1 Kathryn "Kitty" Daniels, MA, CET, is professor and chair emerita in the Dance Department at Cornish College of the Arts in Seattle. She is a former member of the Concert Dance Company of Boston and the Bill Evans Dance Company. She has developed an expertise in anatomically-based ballet instruction and has been a leader in the International Association of Dance Medicine and Science. I consider her a superb teacher and have invited her to be my summer intensive teaching colleague since 1977. Kitty, Don Halquist and I were the founding faculty member of the Bill Evans Teachers Intensive in 1999.
2 Words that have specialized meanings in L/BMS are capitalized in this book.

V Guidelines and Strategies

39 Noticing Each Student in the Learning Circle

For many years, I had an esteemed colleague who told me early in every semester, "I haven't figured out yet who my favorites are." I was always a little surprised by that declaration because it didn't jibe with the way I think about the people I teach. In fact, I often feel a special responsibility for students who don't seem to "get" me or appear disconnected from my approach. If I were to choose favorites from among the most gifted and focus more on them than others, I would lose some of the joy I receive from witnessing the often-unexpected changes that transpire in students when I notice and support each one of them as equally as possible.

It is easy to notice high-achieving students, and also those who are struggling, but all students deserve to know that they are seen and that their presence and engagement are valued. I believe that every group of students is a learning community in which each individual is important. To reinforce that belief, I begin and end class in a circle. *Learning circles* are significant in many indigenous cultures; circular formations are found in "folk" dances in all parts of the world, and improv circles are an integral part of my African-based rhythm tap heritage.

Circles are non-hierarchical and allow each of us to see and be seen. I look each person in the eye while in the circle and try to speak each student's name at least once in every class. As we disperse I invite dancers to take a little walk and make eye contact as they speak the name of every classmate before finding their place in the room to begin our movement explorations.

In one of my higher education positions, I received permission to observe one class in each course taught by every other faculty member in the department. I wanted to see and hear my colleagues in action, to figure out how I could mesh with the teaching team of which I had become a part. Just after mid-term I visited the last of those classes and was surprised to see a colleague still beginning a technique session by taking verbal roll, and then waiting for each student to respond before marking them present. I wondered how the students felt knowing that their teacher had not yet learned their names. I also wondered how the instructor was able to efficiently offer personal feedback without calling students by their names.

I encourage you to make it a priority to learn the name or preferred nickname and preferred pronouns of every student by the second session of your time together. It's not always easy, but it's worth putting in the time and concentration to memorize every name as soon as possible. I find that it matters to students that I learn their names quickly. I never need to "take roll" because I notice who is in the room and mark them present or absent in my office when class is over.

FOR YOUR CONSIDERATION:

When and why do you ask students to gather in a circle in your classes?

How could you help yourself learn each student's name early in each series of classes?

I invite you to describe three strategies you could use to let students know you see them as individuals and that they matter.

---

40 There Is No Front in Our Classroom

There is no designated "front" in my classroom; we change the direction toward which we orient ourselves several times during each session. I make sure that we all face each of the four walls of the studio at some point in each class, and that we face the corners of the room a few times each week. Sometimes I'll stand in the middle of the studio as each student faces a slightly different direction to see and hear me.

Some students love to be in "front" while others are more comfortable in a "back" corner. By having an ever-changing spatial format, every student is likely to be in each location from time to time. Those who always stand in the back discover how much more challenged by and aware of what we are exploring they can become when not following or "hiding" behind others.

We notice different aspects of one another when our spatial relationships are dynamic. I am in close proximity to every student regularly, and I get more chances to focus on each of them. They observe me and each of their peers from different perspectives and must often tune in to kinesthesia rather than mirrors for feedback. It also helps them sense the difference between their personal space and the space of the room in which we happen to be moving.

> **FOR YOUR CONSIDERATION:**
>
> If you have employed a changing-front approach to spatial organization in your technique classes, what were the results? If not, I suggest that you try it and notice any changes in student engagement.
>
> When are mirrors useful to your students? Are they ever problematic?

41 Wrapping Words around Perceptions/Pair and Share

"Reading without reflecting is like eating without digesting," said 18th century Irish Philosopher Edmund Burke. Furthermore, as Don Halquist has helped me understand, *there is no true learning in a dance class without reflection and personal meaning-making.* Therefore, I ask students to notice and speak about what they sense in their own bodies, what they see in the dancing of a peer and what meanings they derive from those experiences in almost every class.

To encourage students to be physically, cognitively and emotionally engaged, I structure frequent opportunities for them to find their own voices and to make them heard. I invite them to "wrap words around their thoughts and feelings" regarding the movement concepts we are embodying and then to share their responses verbally with "study-buddies." I borrowed this term for learning partners, and renewed my investment in this practice,[1] during my participation in the Integrated Movement Studies (IMS) Certification Program facilitated by Peggy Hackney, Janice Meaden and Pam Schick in Salt Lake City and Seattle in 1996–97. I was paired with a remarkable thinker and mover, Kathie Debenham, throughout our course of study. We generated knowledge and insights through our collaborative work that I would not have been able to access on my own.

Sometimes, after each student has spoken with one peer, I invite some or all of the dancers to share their thoughts with the whole class. I find that when they know their personal perceptions of our shared experiences are important to me and their peers, and that they will be invited to speak about their thoughts and feelings, they watch, listen and recognize personal relevance more intently.

This process also ensures that each student receives feedback. As Peggy Hackney told me, "It is a gift to be perceived." Receiving honest evaluative information from a mentor or peer is crucial to anyone's progress. I suggest that each student thank their buddy for "the gift of their perception," and I point out that by being appreciated, the buddy is likely to share non-judgmental perceptions in the future, even without being asked.

Some teaching colleagues have asked me, regarding this pair and share process, "Are they ready to give feedback? They're just students." Or, "How can you give up time from exercises for these conversations?" Honestly, I have found that students often have remarkable insights and can be of genuine help to one another when given the opportunity. I also believe that people learn more efficiently and deeply when they engage with the whole of themselves. In fact, since I've been inviting dancers to wrap words around and give voice to perceptions, the time it has taken most students to understand and embody concepts we investigate has actually shortened considerably.

> **FOR YOUR CONSIDERATION:**
>
> If you can you recall a time when a peer gave you a meaningful gift of perception, I invite you to enumerate some of the ways in which it was useful.
>
> I invite you to formulate three questions you might ask a student to keep in mind while observing a study-buddy explore.
>
> How do you encourage reflection and personal meaning-making in your classes?

42 Teaching through Touch

Touch has played a vital role in learning throughout my life. It will be fascinating to see how we continue and modify the implementation of this age-old modality after the COVID-19 pandemic. I expect it will become altered in ways we can't yet anticipate.

I have a vivid memory of struggling to tie my shoe laces. It was a sweltering summer day in 1944 in a rustic cabin my parents had rented at a trout fishing camp on the upper Provo River near the village of Francis, Utah. My aunt Dorothy took my fingers in hers and guided me through the bow-tying process a few times, and then—magically, it seemed—I could do it! I had a similar experience a few years later when my father snuggled behind me, took my hands in his and taught me the "tie-tying dance" as I dressed myself for Sunday school. It lives in my kinesthetic memory to this day.

Touch brings heightened awareness. Guiding touch conveys information and has been used throughout human history as a highly efficient way of passing on information. I have relied on it to assist students for the past 55 years, and have often asked them to *palpate* bony landmarks (examine them by touch) on themselves and peers as they explored functional anatomy.

It has become increasingly important to discuss my reasons for using touch *before* doing so. Some teachers have used touch inappropriately, and students have experienced or heard about invasive, sexually-loaded or otherwise abusive touch. I now ask for each student's permission in advance, and I honor any request not to be touched. I make it clear that people can talk to me in private or send a private message because some might feel uncomfortable speaking about this subject in public.

One of the many benefits of exploring movement through Bartenieff Fundamentals is that it allows us to learn from the "touch of mother earth" on our bodily surfaces as we move through supine and prone positions. As the body Yields to its Weight and fluidly exchanges energy with the floor, the brain receives a steady stream of sensed and felt messages to guide investigation.

> **FOR YOUR CONSIDERATION:**
>
> I invite you to wrap words around what you experienced when touch enhanced your generation of body knowledge. If you have passed that exploration on to students, how have you modified or amplified it?

43 Balancing Portions of the Class

It is immensely important to create proportional balance in technique classes among time spent on the floor, time spent standing/moving mostly in place and time spent moving through space. All three portions are valuable, and I usually try to follow a formula of 20/40/30 in a standard 90-minute class (20 minutes on the floor, 40 minutes standing/moving mostly within the kinesphere and 30 minutes moving the kinesphere through the general space).

Time spent sitting/lying on the floor, as in Bartenieff Fundamentals (BF), "release" techniques derived from or related to BF, Graham- or Hawkins-based Techniques and some styles of jazz, provides crucial opportunities for students to tune deeply into breath, grounding, kinesthetic sensation and basic patterns of total body organization. I view this as the time to "go in" to prepare to "go out" later.

The portion of class devoted to exploring various joint articulations, gestures and Posture-Gesture Mergers while standing and moving primarily within the kinesphere (in modern techniques such as Limón and Cunningham and jazz techniques such as Mattox, Luigi and Simonson, for example) is also essential. It allows students to focus on clarity of initiation, sequencing, phrasing, form and line while also developing muscular strength and control. Because students are not moving vigorously "across the floor," they can still attend internally to these processes.

The moving through general space portion of class develops much more total body integration, muscular activity and coordination than the earlier-mentioned parts of a class. To prepare students for actual performing, we must create opportunities for full-out, physically-challenging dancing that travels through the studio in almost every class.

It makes sense to proceed from simple to complex as the class progresses, but I also like to go from the floor to standing and back to the floor and to create structures that allow students to move through space before the final part of class, rather than leaving all of the 30 minutes devoted to moving across the floor until the end. That is, the three portions of class don't necessarily have to take place in a sequence of 1, 2, 3. They might be more like 1a, 1b, 2a, 1c, 2b, 3a, 1d, 2c, 2d, 3b, etc.)

FOR YOUR CONSIDERATION:

I invite you to create a guideline or formula you could follow to craft a well-balanced class.

If you tend to give more time and attention to one of these portions of class than to the others, can you say why?

When might facilitating a well-balanced class not be a priority?

44 Investigations, Not Exercises

I consider dancing to be primarily an expression of the *human spirit*, rather than essentially a display of physical skill. By "spirit," I mean the parts of us that come alive when the *ordinary becomes extraordinary*, when the details and nuances of even small and simple movements are so resonant and crystal clear that they feel compellingly rich and full. At such times, I feel connected to energies and processes of the larger world of which I am an infinitesimal but vital piece. There is no life without movement, and the vivacity we experience through motion can be venerated in each class. We can study dance to liberate, investigate and celebrate the essence of life itself.

We rely on physical skill to express our thoughts and feelings, but some of the most powerful moments I have experienced as an audience member have been the simplest—depending on the inner vibrancy of the performer, their focused attention to spatial and qualitative details or their refined and nuanced musical phrasing, rather than sheer physical virtuosity. I remember getting goose bumps watching Pearl Primus[2] move in simple ways on stage at the American Dance Festival at Duke University in the late '80s; I felt so aware of my own sensory and emotional experiences that the wondrous miracle of the human body moving resonated within me. At such rarefied times, either watching movement or dancing myself, I feel part of something universal, timeless and uplifting.

Students tend to approach "exercises" primarily or even only through the psychomotor domain (i.e., exercise means physical activity), but "investigations" or "dances" can enliven students' cognitive and affective domains as well (i.e., investigation means whole body-mind experience). To me, our explorations in the dance studio are more about the quality than the quantity of an experience. I stopped calling what we do "exercises" many years ago. Since words create thoughts and thought creates action, students become more cognitively and affectively engaged when I offer "investigations," "dances" or "celebrations" instead.

We are simultaneously seeking physical accomplishment and expressive power in the study of technique. Even beginning dancers can engage in class as an artistic practice rather than an athletic event. By creating and describing the movement materials we share with students as celebrations of sensing Weight, thinking about Space, intuiting Time and feeling Flow, we can simultaneously stimulate the development of physicality and expressivity. We can motivate students to become fully alive in the whole of themselves and in the moment.

> **FOR YOUR CONSIDERATION:**
>
> If you haven't yet done so, instead of asking students to do "exercises," I invite you to use the terms "investigations," "dances" and "celebrations" for a while and see if those words change the quality of student participation. What other terms might you use to encourage students to approach dance as both an athletic and an artistic pursuit?

45 Planning Backward

Students experience increased satisfaction when I design classes in which the parts contribute to the whole. That is, when there are unifying themes, concepts and movement inquiries interspersed throughout a class, students are able to participate in threading their separate experiences into a larger, more comprehensive dance and learning event.

For most technique classes, I create a culminating celebration or "big dance." Usually, it is the penultimate event, taking place just before the cool down/closing ritual. I design this climactic feature of class first and try to make sure it has been prepared for in some or all of the earlier explorations. Often, I will ask students to play with smaller portions of the final big dance as the class unfolds. This strategy is sometimes referred to as backward planning.

The term "backward design" was introduced to educators in 1998-99 by Jay McTighe and Grant Wiggins in their book *Understanding by Design*. In backward design, we begin by clarifying the objectives of a class or the whole course—what students are expected to learn and be able to do—and then proceed "backward" to create a lesson or lessons that achieve those desired goals.

This method offers students both repetition and newness because already-confronted challenges are revisited in a larger context in the climactic chance to "really dance." I have found that this strategy can enable students to experience heightened success because they can accumulate discoveries and accomplishments made in earlier, shorter portions of the class for its culminating event. This practice can help teachers design coherent classes that have a seemingly organic flow; because the details of its smaller components have already been unpacked or explained, there can be less explication and more moving as everyone enjoys the lesson's climax.

> **FOR YOUR CONSIDERATION:**
>
> I invite you to choose one of your favorite culminating "big dances," or to choreograph a new one, and then figure out how you could unpack and examine five or six of its shorter components in the earlier portions of class to support student success in that culminating event.

46 Managing Time

As we evolve as artists, teachers and people, we generate more and more knowledge that we want to pass on to students, and we are frequently forced to engage in self-negotiation concerning what to include or leave out. I have usually worked in private venues or institutions of higher education where technique classes are assigned 90-minute time slots. Even though this is the standard length approved by the National Association of Schools of Dance, I often find there is not enough time to include all that I would like in one session.

In some studios, colleges and secondary schools, where dance has to conform to an institution's overall schedule, technique classes may be as short as 50 minutes. I advise teachers in such situations to think of one class happening in two consecutive meetings, rather than to skip over essential class elements, and to seek support in lobbying for longer sessions.

For more than three decades, I have taught pedagogy courses (at Indiana University, then the University of New Mexico, then the College at Brockport, then Dean College and still in my Certified Evans Teacher program) in which students are required to design and teach 90-minute technique classes. Time management is almost always a major challenge. Many students over-prepare for and spend so much time on the early portions of class that they have to rush through or skip over the climactic big combination near the end of class, which most of the dancers have been looking forward to.

So what do I suggest after 68 years of teaching? Plan for fewer movement investigations than you really want to give, and organize them in a sequential outline. Then give yourself some optional variations on or supplements to those major explorations that you might be able to include if time permits, but that you are not so attached to that you will be disappointed if you can't include them. I often say to myself, "No matter what, we'll start moving expansively and 'really dancing' around the 50-minute mark." Even if I haven't guided the investigations I had hoped to by that point, I'll move on to the more full-bodied and physically-challenging experiences, perhaps modifying aspects of them for which I have not prepared the dancers.

In recent years, I have usually planned for five or six primary investigations/dances/celebrations in a 90-minute class, and I include guided improvisation in most of them. This formula usually affirms that "less is more" and provides enough time for students to engage productively in moving and generating knowledge without feeling rushed or oversaturated.

FOR YOUR CONSIDERATION:

How do you decide what to include and what to leave out of a given class?

I invite you to make a lesson plan for a class you would like to teach that includes a clear timeline from beginning to end. I suggest that you find an opportunity to deliver that class and then reflect on the impact on your time-management skills of keeping clock time continually in your consciousness.

---

47 Previewing the Whole, Differentiating the Parts and Integrating the Entire Investigation

In the past decade particularly, I have witnessed contemporary dance teachers present extremely long "phrase-work" and give kudos to dancers who "pick up" the material most quickly. That kind of teaching can be fun for the instructor and pleasing to students who like that kind of challenge, but I perceive limited value in what I consider prizing *quantity over quality*, and I question the benefit to students of learning copious amounts of movement superficially. People rely on their most ingrained patterns to rapidly copy phrase-work's external or visually-observed outward aspects, and if those ingrained patterns are inefficient, this kind of teaching might embed movement habits that are not serving a student's best interests more deeply into her/his/their neuromuscular system.

Peggy Hackney discusses the *whole-part-whole* teaching method in *Making Connections*. I have found that most students learn longer combinations more fully and efficiently if I follow that model. Below are the steps in which I might put this strategy to use:

a   First, I (or perhaps an assistant) will demonstrate the whole investigation as accurately, musically and qualitatively as possible, so that students can see the "big picture" or context. This establishes *oneness*.
b   Then, I will teach portions of the investigation consecutively, verbally revealing and examining concepts and ideas that I find important within it, and giving students opportunities to understand, sense, feel and embody them. I might repeat each portion a time or two. This offers *differentiation*.
c   When each part has been investigated, I will put the whole pattern together again. When returning to the whole with a differentiated understanding of the component parts, the pattern can be experienced in its many layers and can be more deeply sensed and felt. This provides *integration*.

Deep learning, with clear understanding of the big picture *and* the differentiated parts, is empowering. It makes artistic subtlety and nuance possible. It can also create a profound sense of ensemble in unison movement because dancers are revealing not just the outer form or sequence of their dance but also to its underlying intent or purpose.

> FOR YOUR CONSIDERATION:
>
> When and how have you had to cope with the issue of quantity vs. quality in your teaching or learning?
>   How do you usually teach longer movement phrases?
>   I suggest that you share the whole "dance" before breaking it down the next few times you teach a long combination and then notice any impact on student learning.

48 Addressing the Cause, Not the Result

Note: You may wish to look at Essays 71, 72 and 73, Arm Circles/ Scapulohumeral Rhythm, More Arm Circles/Gradated Humeral Rotation and Arm Circles With Shape Qualities, to better understand this essay.

72 Guidelines and Strategies

Teachers often "correct" the *result* of a phrase of movement, rather than noticing and addressing the *cause* of a pattern they would like to see modified, and they find themselves giving the same correction repeatedly because they are focused on the *main action* of a phrase rather than its *preparation and initiation*. To change the result, a dancer needs to modify the underlying conscious or subconscious intent, preparation and initiation that caused it.

For example, instead of saying "Press your shoulders down," or "Drop your shoulders," which went up when a student lifted her/his/their arms, we might perceive that the student has a habit of resisting the movement of the scapulae and clavicles as the arms rise. In this instance, it could be more helpful to say,

> I invite you to notice the gradated rotation of the humeral heads in the shoulder sockets as your arms move upward. Could you allow your scapulae (whose lowest points will slide along the back and around the sides of your rib cage) and your clavicles (whose distal ends will swing upward) to move with your humeri as you reach your arms into the high level?

By knowing that gradated humeral rotation and accommodating changes in the scapula and clavicle are natural components of rising arm gestures, the dancer is more likely to allow organic neuromusculoskeletal processes to fulfill themselves. In this example, when the humerus, scapula and clavicle are allowed to rotate freely, natural bone rhythms will occur and the scapula will have no anatomical reason to elevate as the arm moves upward.

Asking a student to press the shoulder down is trying to fix the result (or main action) after it has occurred. This does not address the cause of scapular elevation, which is bypassing or disallowing the preparation for and initiation of the arm gesture. Inviting the student to invest in the *whole phrase* of the arm gesture, including the preparatory thought of allowing the gradated rotation of the humerus to activate scapuloclavicular rhythms as the arms reach upward, will enable her/him/them to execute a more efficient main action and experience a different and more anatomically functional result.

This is true of all parts of the body. When we move one body part, other parts need to move in accommodation and support. Focusing on functionally-appropriate preparation and initiation, and then getting out of the way as the body fulfills it organic processes, will empower students to perceive and improve the causes of inefficient movement habits rather than feeling frustrated by the results of improperly-cued or unfulfilled movement phrases.

> **FOR YOUR CONSIDERATION:**
>
> If you can you think of a time when you felt unable to apply a correction you had been given repeatedly, what information or teaching strategy might have made it possible for you to feel successful?
> I invite you to describe an example of body-level feedback addressing the result in a gestural phrase you have found challenging to students, and another example addressing the cause.

49 Opening Rituals

I want students to feel supported by me, by their classmates and by themselves, and to feel that they can trust the environment and safely leave their comfort zones to delve deeply into movement exploration. Appropriately-chosen and guided "rituals" help to strengthen social bonds, develop a sense of community and prepare students for active learning.

One of my favorite *opening rituals* is to invite students to gather in a standing circle and tune in to Breath and Weight. After seeking permission, we place the palms of our hands gently on the lower backs of the people on either side. I take a few moments to make *eye contact* with each student, welcome everyone to today's session and invite them to make an internal body-mind scan to notice what is alive for them today. I might ask, "Is something from what we explored in our last class still resonating within you? Or, what question about your body moving would you like to investigate today?" I invite them to share their response with a student standing next to them, after which I encourage everyone to allow their personal curiosity to guide them as we explore today's movement investigations. We then enlarge our circle and spread out in the general space as each dancer makes eye contact with every other class participant.

Through such an opening ritual, students can transition from the complexity of their lives as they prepared for class and rushed to the studio to the clearly-focused centeredness of the learning community we have established, where they can be fully present in the moment and open to the possibility of positive change.

FOR YOUR CONSIDERATION:

What satisfying opening class rituals have you established, experienced or witnessed?

How else could you create an atmosphere of trust at the beginning of a class?

50 Closing Rituals

Closing rituals are equally important. I often witness teachers end classes abruptly; at one moment, students are "flying" across the studio, breathing heavily and perspiring, and then "poof," it's all over. Observing such inconclusive class endings unsettles me. The traditional ballet class concludes with the *reverence* for good reasons. A return to the familiar, with a summing up, resolution or affirmation fosters feelings of completion and satisfaction.

I like to wrap things up with a reaffirmation of community. Returning to our standing circle, we explore simple gestural or total body growing and shrinking patterns as the heart rate slows and we cool down. Sometimes, we stretch major muscle groups, as I guide us again into sensing our inner selves. I invite everyone to join me in a "circle hug," manifesting our support for one another other. While in the hug, I often ask students to notice what today's explorations brought them, intellectually, physically and/or emotionally. If time permits, I might share a general observation I made during the session or pose a question to be considered before we meet again.

I sometimes ask students to describe their personal before- and after-class rituals, and then invite the whole class to try them and notice what they offer. Rituals can support us teachers, too. Many of my educator friends enact their own personal rituals before and after a class, to prepare for and then savor the opportunity to serve as a guide to learning.

Our class rituals offer the comfort, security and sense of trust of the familiar, as a balance to the often new and challenging explorations introduced in the "body" of the class, and as a transition back to the less-ordered world students encounter outside the studio.

> **FOR YOUR CONSIDERATION:**
>
> What satisfying closing class rituals have you established, experienced or witnessed?
>
> I encourage you to notice and reflect upon your personal pre- and post-class rituals as well as those you organize for students.

Notes

1 I first asked students to "pair and share" in the early '70s, when I was an assistant professor of modern dance at the University of Utah, teaching 80-minute technique classes to as many as 60 students at a time. Because it was impossible to give individual feedback to so many, I frequently asked them each to watch a peer and share their observations. I recognized the benefit of doing so almost immediately, when students in those large classes began to approach their learning with heightened presence and joy because they no longer felt invisible. Since re-experiencing the power of this process as a student in the IMS program in 1996–97, I almost always include in it in my teaching practice, no matter how large or small, long or short, the class.
2 *Pearl Primus (1919–94)* was a Black American dancer, choreographer and anthropologist. Early in her career she saw the need to promote African dance as an art form worthy of study and performance, and she played an important role in the presentation of African dance to American audiences. In 1966, I studied her work with Percival Borde, her husband and professional collaborator.

References

Hackney, Peggy. *Making Connections: Total Body Integration through Bartenieff Fundamentals.* Routledge, 2001.

McTighe, Jay, and Grant Wiggins. *Understanding by Design.* 2nd ed., Assn. for Supervision & Curriculum Development, 2005.

VI Body Specificity

51 Lung Respiration

Our modern dance ancestors started with *breath*. Martha Graham called it "contraction and release;" for Doris Humphrey, it was "suspension, fall and recovery;" for Rudolf Laban, "Growing and Shrinking." Breath is our initial and most significant movement pattern; it underlies everything we do for the whole of our lives.

Many students have been encouraged to "suck in your stomach" when dancing. Teachers who use that word in this context are actually referring to the abdominal muscles. (Since the stomach is a hollow organ located in the upper-left area of the belly, below the liver and next to the spleen, the use of that word can cause confusion and a misunderstanding of human anatomy.) If we hold an isometric contraction (a shortening of muscles that does not produce movement) of the transversus abdominis/deep abdominal wall, we will partially immobilize the respiratory diaphragm, the breathing muscle. That is, if we suck in the abdomen and hold it there, we can no longer take a deep breath and experience full lung respiration.

Many teachers tell students to "press your navel to the spine," "pull your ribs down and draw them in," "press your shoulders down" and/or "straighten your spine" and then to try to hold those conditions as they move. As a result of such inappropriate cues from instructors, we often see dancers holding their breath or breathing shallowly in only the upper thorax and immobilizing most of their torsos. Such patterns limit force absorption throughout the whole body and set dancers up for injuries.

We cannot restrict movement in just one part of ourselves. In *full belly breathing*, the transversus abdominis is *engaged but not held*; the observer will see its motion; the mover will sense muscle filaments sliding closer together and then farther apart.

Movement is change, and breath is our most fundamental movement. The respiratory diaphragm must move to bring oxygen efficiently into the body in inhalation and let carbon dioxide escape in exhalation. As it does so, the belly will bulge and hollow; the spaces between the ribs will open and close like the pleats of an accordion; the curves of their spine will deepen and lengthen.

FOR YOUR CONSIDERATION:

Can you describe a time in your dance training when lung respiration became an important focus?

How would you describe the impact on your dancing of unrestricted diaphragmatic breathing?

What might you say to a student you observe breathing shallowly?

---

52 Cellular Respiration/We Are Mostly Water

For me, breathing is not just about the lungs and respiratory diaphragm; I like to notice that my cells are also involved. Cellular respiration begins in utero. Entering and exiting through the umbilical cord, blood carries nutrients to each fetal cell and carries away what is no longer needed. Cells swim in a sea of interstitial fluid; they fill and empty; they "breathe."

The lively interplay between outer and inner is a principle of Bartenieff Fundamentals (BF).

When we are born, cellular respiration is fed by lung respiration. Oxygen comes into the system as a gas but is converted in the lungs to fluid that travels through the arteries, capillaries and veins of the cardiovascular system to nurture and clean each cell. The heart's contractions work to move oxygen from the lungs into the blood, and to gather liquid carbon dioxide from the blood so it can be expelled as a gas through the lungs.

Humans are mostly water. In addition to interstitial fluid, we are composed of intracellular fluid, cerebrospinal fluid, synovial fluid, lymph, arterial blood, venous blood and fat. I like to imagine "liquid breath" traveling through us as we sense the filling-emptying and inpouring-outpouring that support us with vibrant aliveness on a cellular level.

College students are about 60–65% water. As an octogenarian, I am closer to 50%, but I still become more vibrant on a cellular level, more grounded and more pliable when I say these words: "I give all the fluids in my body permission to seek gravity." At this stage of my life, it is one of the first things I think as I prepare to move, but I have found that people of all ages can feel almost immediately more alive when they visualize their cellular respiration and imagine their fluids pouring freely and bonding them with the earth.

FOR YOUR CONSIDERATION:

I invite you to borrow or compose three thoughts that help you embody images of cellular respiration, and then to improvise a dance fed by those images.

Could you also improvise a dance about the lively interplay between outer and inner as oxygen pours into your body as a gas, is converted to fluid in your lungs, travels throughout your body in the blood and is then converted one again to gas as you exhale carbon dioxide?

---

53 Breathdancing

"Movement rides on breath" is an image frequently invoked by BF practitioners. Those words help us draw attention to our cellular and diaphragmatic respiration to become more integrated and efficient at anything we do. By affirming our breath support, we can become more fluid, resilient and adaptable throughout the entire organism.

For more than half a century, I have enjoyed doing "breath dances." I often think of breath as the dance of my internal organs, especially the filling and emptying of my lungs responding to the motion of the respiratory diaphragm. I enjoy exploring how that inner dance initiates and supports the sliding and gliding of my muscles and fascia, the gestures of my limbs, the postural changes of my spine and torso and the traveling of my body through space. I sometimes allow my breath to create rhythms that spark small movement impulses, and then permit those impulses to fulfill themselves into larger motions that take me where they will in the space without my conscious direction.

In the late '60s and early '70s, when I was first following my curiosity about my inner world to evolve my own dance style and teaching methods, Nana Shineflug, Lois Royne and other members of the Chicago Moving Company studied with me in Salt Lake City. When they returned home, they started sharing what they had learned in my classes, describing my style as "breath dancing." By 1976, Rebecca Rice, who became a prominent Boston-based choreographer and company director, Judith Nelson, who became a successful New York City-based performer of the Limón style of modern dance, and other distinguished former students were calling my work the "Evans Technique." It is not a term I initiated. It came from former students wanting to signify that what they had experienced in my classes, which had a whole lot to do with breath support, was different from what they found elsewhere.

I ride my breath to dance my life.

FOR YOUR CONSIDERATION:

I invite you to notice the continuous fluid changes occurring throughout your body (your cellular respiration) to become grounded as you enter the studio.

I invite you to draw students' attention to their diaphragmatic breathing to help them become present in body, mind and spirit as they begin class.

If you ever notice yourself holding or restricting your breath while dancing, what words or images could you invoke to help yourself find full breath support?

---

54 Dynamic Alignment/The Pathways Through

I have observed dance teachers physically manipulate a standing-still student's body to create a desired "look," only to have it disappear as soon as the dancer started to move again. That is *static alignment*. We need to help our students find *dynamic alignment*, pliable and adaptable relationships of body parts, and discover the corridors or pathways through the organism from one distal end to another. In BF this important concept is called *Throughness*.

I like to think that we move "from, through and to." That is, we can't just go *to* someplace new. We need to start *from* where we are, and move *through* specific pathways (within the body and/or within space) to travel *to* a new location. We don't just dematerialize and then rematerialize somewhere else; there's always a process, a journey. So, where we begin, and the route we travel, are as important as the destination.

Irmgard Bartenieff said that "the feet support the head and the tail supports the arms," meaning that we can sense internal channels of

80 Body Specificity

flow and connectivity (which we might compare to open tubes full of energy) from the soles of the feet through many *kinetic chains* to the top of the head, and from the tip of the coccyx through many kinetic chains to the tips of the fingers. These functional relationships are created through inner awareness and total body coordination, not through externally-motivated stacking of body parts. As Eric Franklin says often while teaching, "Alignment is a balancing act, not a position." By feeding ourselves appropriate intent and imagery, we can sense that our inner pathways remain open, adaptable and resilient as they shorten, lengthen, bend and twist.

For example, I might say, "Let the earth energy pour in through the tripod of each foot; notice it traveling through the network of corridors inside you, and allow it to pour out through the open door at the top of your head." These "corridors" include organs as well as connective tissue. For some dancers who have experienced injuries or trauma, the pathways through may be circuitous, and they might be different on one body side than on the other. I encourage each dancer to spend time exploring deeply, freely and slowly to sense the pathways of connectivity that are most available and efficient.

> **FOR YOUR CONSIDERATION:**
>
> What images or ideas have you previously embodied that resulted in static alignment?
>
> How did or could you replace those ideas or images with others that encourage dynamic alignment and a sense of from-through-to?

55 Body-Part Phrasing

BF differentiates three kinds of body-part phrasing. I find these ideas both simple and profound, like much of the BF lexicon:

a   *Simultaneous*—all parts move together;
b   *Successive*—one body part moves and then an adjacent part, in a wave-like progression;
c   *Sequential*—one part moves and then one or more non-adjacent body parts.

Dancers often fall into subconscious patterns in various parts of their bodies, moving some areas Simultaneously and others Successively without noticing the difference. Noticing these different body-part phrasings can almost instantly help students sense and understand themselves with increased clarity, and gain expressive and technical skills as a result.

I enjoy asking students to create a new body form with Simultaneous Phrasing—all parts moving at the same time. They often feel that they must make such a change quickly, so I invite them to experience it in Sustained Time. This can pose a coordination challenge for many and help bring subconscious preferences into their awareness.

Asking students to move Successively, starting either proximally or distally, can be enlightening. In such investigations, dancers can begin to notice habits of moving multiple joints as if they were one, rather than articulating each separately in a wave-live sequence. Joints that are not allowed to move freely on a regular basis become unavailable to us. Moving them independently brings and distributes synovial fluid, stimulates and lubricates fascia, offers a sense of ease and fluidity and heightens kinesthetic awareness.

A phrase in which the dancer moves non-adjacent body parts can be challenging and also fun. The spine is so long and has so many joints that its different regions can be doing different things at the same time. Some interesting and surprising movement sequences can emerge from investigations of Sequential Body-part Phrasing. For example, I can flex my cervical spine while extending my lumbar spine and vice versa.

> **FOR YOUR CONSIDERATION:**
>
> I invite you to explore different Body-part Phrasings and consider if you have conscious or subconscious preferences in different parts of your body.
>
> I invite you to move in non-preferred Body-part Phrasing and notice what doing so helps you learn about yourself.

56 Asymmetrical Body Sides

At age 16, in my first class with the renowned ballet master with whom I would study for eight years, I was repeatedly told to press my right hip down to keep the belt on my black tights parallel to the floor. In my undergraduate ROTC (Reserve Officers' Training Corps) drills, I was frequently told to press my right shoulder down to appear more symmetrical. Being an obedient student and cadet, I tried hard to make my hips and shoulders level, inadvertently causing patterns of excess tension, distortion and imbalance into my body that caused chronic injuries I had to manage for many years.

It was not until I was in my mid-30s that a perceptive medical practitioner took the time to notice that I have a lateral curve in my lumbar spine, the reason why my right shoulder and hip are higher. Because the scoliosis is mild, it was hard for untrained eyes, and even a couple of orthopedic surgeons I had consulted, to see. When I stopped forcing my body to be symmetrical and learned to balance the workload throughout my asymmetrical body architecture, I found increased ease and mobility and less pain. Instead of feeling inadequate for having uneven body sides, I learned to feel grateful for the strong and healthy body I have inherited. Instead of trying to make my body "square," I learned to be grateful for how it functions in its "un-squareness," and to sense balance and harmony in the forces traveling through it.

Here's another story regarding assumptions about asymmetrical body sides: At age 23, as a tank platoon leader in the U.S. Army, I suffered multiple fractures in my left talus, the hindfoot tarsal bone that takes the weight of the tibia and fibula and spreads the body weight into the calcaneus, the midfoot and the forefoot. The bones in my foot decalcified, a condition known as "death without infection," and I wore non-weight-bearing casts for almost eight months.

Note: Please see Figure 7.5.

The bones gradually recalcified, but it was ten years before I regained full mobility in my ankle. Teachers told me to "point your foot" thousands of times and I became self-conscious and frustrated because I was not able to do so to their satisfaction. It was often the only correction I received, so I learned to shut out the endless insistence that I do what was impossible. In all those years, only one of my many teachers, Mattlyn Gavers, asked me why one ankle was so different from the other. Gavers was a professor of ballet at the University of Utah and a frequent guest teacher during my years with the Repertory Dance Theatre. She modeled for me the importance of getting to know each student's history. Happily, at age 33, in a Matt Mattox[1] jazz class, scar tissue broke up suddenly, making a horrendous-sounding but painless snapping sound, and my ankle instantly regained its full mobility.

When I was 45, Anne Marie Welsh, critic for the *San Diego Union*, wrote these words: "When you watch [Evans], your eyes go not to his handsome face or *lovely feet*, but to his breastbone, the vulnerable, merely human spot that seems to be guiding him." I was overjoyed by that description of my feet. I had felt that they were not good enough for ten years, but then someone was celebrating them. What made my feet "lovely," I think, was not the degree to which they "pointed," even though they were by then symmetrical, but the way I enlivened them and connected them to what was happening throughout my whole being.

I hold no grudges against those who insisted that I "square off" my hips and shoulders or "point my feet," because I know they were trying to be helpful. However, I encourage all teachers to be careful about judging and "correcting" asymmetry in body sides. I strongly suggest that you dig a little deeper and help the student and yourself understand what is really going on. If you see bilateral differences, you might have a conversation with the student and perhaps encourage her/him/them to consult an expert.

FOR YOUR CONSIDERATION:

Why do you think that "square hips" and "pointed feet" are requested so frequently by dance teachers?

How could you and a student work together to understand the cause of asymmetry in her/his/their body?

---

57 Plié Is So Much More Than Bending the Knees

When I ask young dancers what a *plié* is, they often answer, "Bending the knees." That oversimplified idea of our most basic dance movement has caused countless dancers to become brittle and eventually injured. Plié should actually be an experience of change throughout the body. We use it to find power for rising and force absorption for sinking. If a person "tucks the pelvis under," they can bend their knees without flexing their hip joints, but that would certainly not be a plié!

Plié involves simultaneous flexion in the hips, knees and ankles, as well as subtle accommodating spirals and counter-spirals in the pelvis, legs and feet. The spinal curves deepen; the sitz bones widen as the "hip bones" and pubis narrow and retreat; the sacrum slides back and down; the femurs rotate out; the tibias rotate in and the feet sink and spread. All those processes reverse, of course, when the legs are extended.

84 *Body Specificity*

These "automatic" neuromusculoskeletal changes are likely to happen unless we resist or brace against them. If we think of plié as merely bending the knees, we will unintentionally block some or many of the other changes that should organically take place in a well-functioning body. Because teachers have implied that the knees are separate from and—because they are emphasized so frequently—more important than other body parts, training patterns have evolved that create inelastic dancers and are inherently injury-producing.

If we were to travel around the globe observing people's rhythmic movement, we would notice that dancing in most cultures takes place primarily in *demi plié*. Moving with "soft" legs, and the resilience, adaptability and force absorption it provides, has made sense to people almost everywhere for a very long time. The desire to lift up away from the earth (and toward "heaven") is associated mostly with dances originating in northern Europe. Because our theatrical dances in North America have drawn heavily on such traditions, many teachers here have become fixated on straight knees as an ultimate good.

I strongly encourage all teachers to stop calling plié a bending and straightening of the knees and acknowledge the integrated changes throughout the body that should be encouraged.

FOR YOUR CONSIDERATION:

How would you succinctly describe a plié?

I invite you to try bending your knees without flexing your hips. If you tuck your tail under, it's possible, right? Why is it not a plié?

Why do you think that "straight knees" are emphasized so frequently by many dance teachers?

---

58 Turn-Out Is Not All About the Feet

Many young dancers experience chronic injuries as a result of erroneous ideas or careless practices concerning "turn-out." Some students develop serious misalignment patterns (including excessive anterior tilting of the pelvis and overpronation of the feet) as a result of trying

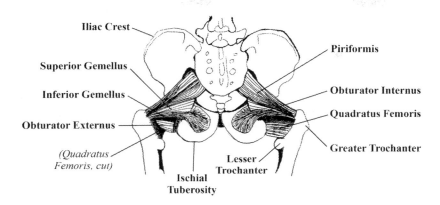

Figure 6.1 Simulation of the Deep Lateral Rotators as Seen from the Back.

for years to turn out primarily in the feet and/or knees. A change in one part of the body creates a change throughout the whole organism, and the entire body of a dancer with braced or immobilized feet (and therefore legs and pelvis) lacks Throughness, neutrality, connectivity and resilience.

The primary action in "turn-out" is outward rotation (also called lateral or external rotation) at the hip, a ball-and-socket synovial joint. The ball is the femoral head, and the socket is the acetabulum. The articulation of the pelvis and the femur connects the axial skeleton to the lower extremity. In efficient turn-out, the six deep lateral rotator muscles engage to move the femur around its own axis, away from the midline of the body; the greater trochanter (bony prominence on the outside of femur at the level of the pelvic floor, which one can easily palpate, or explore with the fingers) moves toward the ischial tuberosity (sitz bone). The lateral rotator group consists of six small muscles that outwardly rotate the femur in the hip joint: piriformis, gemellus superior, obturator internus, gemellus inferior, quadratus femoris and obturator externus. Other larger muscles in the leg assist in outward rotation, but thinking of initiating it in the deep lateral rotator muscles creates efficient initiation and sequencing.

I remember being required to turn my feet out to 180 degrees as a college ballet student, with no mention of the deep lateral rotators. Like many young people, I was able to force my feet into those positions (especially in plié), but the consequential misalignments in my pelvis, spine and feet caused me serious problems.

I did not learn of the six deep lateral rotators until age 27, when I had already worked for several years as a professional dancer. Betty Jones was a Humphrey/Limón dancer noted for her elegance, clarity and longevity as a performer and for her thoughtful generosity as a teacher. *She* was strongly influenced by the somatic approach known as ideokinesis,[2] and she incorporated genuinely helpful anatomically-based metaphors into her teaching. As a frequent guest teacher with RDT during the late '60s, she gave me my first clear, hands-on insights into appropriate initiation of outward femoral rotation.

Erroneous ideas about turn-out have persisted, however, and I remember modern technique teacher colleagues at the University of Utah in the mid-'70s telling students to "open the door," meaning to carry the knee from the front to the side as they moved a leg from parallel passé to turned-out passé. When I relocated to Seattle and asked dance kinesiologist Karen Clippinger[3] to join my new school's faculty, she told us that "First, you need to *turn the door knob*; then, you can open the door." That is, if you think first of taking your knee to the side, you will be overworking the superficial sartorius muscle, pulling your femoral head away from the socket and limiting the crucial rotation of the femoral head that would have prepared you for that action.

If you first "turn the door knob," the femoral head will remain comfortably at home in the acetabulum as you phrase into abduction to create a turned-out passé. This rotation of the ball in the socket feels very much like turning a door knob to most people I have taught, and I have passed on Karen's image to help countless dancers initiate outward femoral rotation efficiently. Classical ballet requires almost constant turn-out, of course, and master ballet teacher Kitty Daniels concurs that students should primarily focus on the engagement of the six deep lateral rotators, even though other muscles are involved.

I believe that dancers in all styles need to have access to efficient outward femoral rotation. I ask students to initiate outward rotation of the gesturing leg at the hip socket by reaching the greater trochanter freely toward the ischial tuberosity. Since both the greater trochanter and ischial tuberosity are easily palpated, noticing their changing relationships is an easy way to confirm that rotation is happening in the hip joint.

> **FOR YOUR CONSIDERATION:**
>
> What was the language your teacher used when you were first asked to turn out?
> Have those words been useful to you over the years or have you had to modify or replace them?
> How do you guide yourself and/or students into an experience of outward femoral rotation?
> Could you describe one of the ways a dance anatomy or kinesiology teacher has affected your own dancing and/or teaching?

59 Turn-In/Balancing Muscular Exertions

Balance is key to healthy functioning in all aspects of our lives, and activating proportional amounts of inward (internal or medial) and outward rotation in the hip joint is crucial to our well-being. In inward rotation of the femoral head, the greater trochanter moves away from the ischial tuberosity, so a dancer can confirm that there is inward rotation taking place in the hip socket by palpating the changing relationship of those two bony landmarks.

Turning out more than turning in creates imbalances in the neuromusculoskeletal system. Because muscles that are not regularly engaged become weak, and muscles that are overworked will retain too much tension when resting, it's important to give ourselves opportunities to balance outward femoral rotation, neutral rotation (parallel) and inward femoral rotation in every class. I enjoy creating and sharing phrases that move through turn-out, parallel and turn-in, and linger for crystallizing moments in positions that allow students to experience each, in both the supporting and gesturing legs. Sometimes ballet students will refer to neutral rotation (parallel) as "turned-in," and they can benefit from truly exploring inward femoral rotation. If I am teaching a group who mostly study ballet, I will offer many opportunities for them to kinesthetically savor the difference between turn-in and parallel, as well as to appreciate the functional necessity and aesthetic beauty of each.

The goal of providing balanced exertions should apply to all our joints. Moving the body regularly in all the ways it has evolved to function is of utmost importance to our ability to fully inhabit and enjoy our bodies. One of my favorite warm-ups is guiding students in a "liquid motion" journey: Starting in the atlanto-occipital joint (where the skull articulates with the top of the spine), we travel successively all the way through the body, ending in the toes. I encourage playfully and gently moving each joint in as many fluid ways as possible, in both small and large breath-supported motions. Most people complete this warm-up exploration feeling more alive and at ease than when they began.

> **FOR YOUR CONSIDERATION:**
>
> I invite you to choreograph a "big dance" for a technique class that explores a variety of ways of moving through turned-out, parallel and turned-in positions of the legs. Next, I invite you to come up with at least three shorter explorations of turn-out, parallel and turn-in you could give earlier in class to prepare for that big dance.
>
> How could you make certain that each joint in students' bodies has frequent opportunities to move fully and freely?

Notes

1 Matt Mattox (1921–2013) was a protégé of Jack Cole before becoming a dance star on Broadway and in Hollywood. In the early '70s he left the U.S. for Europe, where he became an enormously successful teacher, specializing in his "freestyle jazz" technique. He played a pivotal role in my career as one of my mentors at Harkness House for Ballet Arts in New York City and later as my colleague at L'Académie-Festival des Arcs in the French Alps. In that renowned international summer gathering he taught jazz and, on his recommendation, I taught my modern dance technique many summers between 1980 and 1998. When I formed my own professional company, Matt gave us his work *Opus Jazz Loves Bach*, which we performed all across the U.S.

2 Ideokinesis is an approach to improving alignment and fluency of movement through guided imagery. It uses metaphors, such as visualizing an object moving in a specific direction along various muscle groups throughout the body, while lying completely still. Many dancers have found that appropriate mental imagery can improve functional alignment and posture through the re-patterning of neuromuscular pathways in the absence of overt movement. Mabel Ellsworth Todd, author of *The Thinking Body*, conceived the ideokinesis approach and Lulu Sweigard and others contributed to its early evolution. Peggy Hackney was profoundly interested in this work and was often seen carrying a copy of Sweigard's book, *Human Movement Potential: Its Ideokinetic Facilitation*, under her arm while on tour with the Bill Evans Dance Company.

3 In my first Seattle Summer Institute of Dance, July and early August, 1977, I engaged New York City-based Gretchen Langstaff to teach a

course called Applied Kinesiology. (She was a colleague of Irene Dowd's, whom I came to admire when we interacted daily at the American Dance Festival in 1976. Irene has maintained and developed the groundbreaking somatic work of Mabel Todd and Lulu Sweigard.) At the end of that Seattle Institute, I invited Gretchen—an articulate and compassionate teacher—to return in '78. "I think you should hire Karen Clippinger," she said. "She knows more than I do." Karen was a dancer and largely self-taught dance kinesiologist who traveled from California that summer to study with members of my professional company. She accepted my invitation to join our summer faculty and soon relocated permanently to Seattle, where she taught in my school and in the Pacific Northwest Ballet School and pioneered an injury prevention and therapy practice for dancers. We co-taught many workshops over several years, and her influence impacted me profoundly. She later became a professor of dance kinesiology at California State University at Long Beach and the author of *Dance Anatomy and Kinesiology*. We last worked together in 2017, when she gave a stimulating keynote presentation at The Art and Science of Teaching Dance conference I directed at New Mexico State University.

References

Clippinger, Karen. *Dance Anatomy and Kinesiology*. 2nd ed., Human Kinetics, 2015.

Franklin, Eric. *Dynamic Alignment through Imagery*. 2nd ed., Human Kinetics, 2012.

Hackney, Peggy. *Making Connections: Total Body Integration through Bartenieff Fundamentals*. Routledge, 2001.

VII Anatomical Imagery

Note: Words with specialized meanings in the Laban/Bartenieff Movement System, are capitalized in this chapter and elsewhere in the book (e.g., Diagonal Knee Reach, Shape Qualities, Successive Sequencing).

60 Allowing the Pelvic Outlet to Open

Some teachers refer to the lowest part of the pelvis, the area surrounded by the ischial tuberosities on the sides, the coccyx in back and the pubic symphysis in front, as the "pelvic diamond." Eric Franklin[1] often calls it the "pelvic outlet." Its opening facilitates childbirth and excretion; its closing provides support for abdominal contents. Bartenieff referred to these changes as pelvic-femoral rhythm.

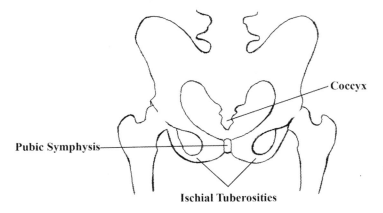

Figure 7.1 Simulation of the Pelvic Outlet as Seen from the Front.

DOI: 10.4324/9781003290209-8

Anatomical Imagery 91

When allowing the center of weight to move closer to the earth while standing on both feet (*as in plié or closed chain flexion of both hip joints and both knees*), there is a three-dimensional reconfiguration of the femurs and pelvis, resulting in an opening of the pelvic outlet/expansion of the pelvic diamond. Some people refer to the action at the hip as femoral flexion, but since there are two "femoral joints," the hip and the knee, others believe it can enhance clarity to call it "iliofemoral" flexion.

The ischial tuberosities (sitz bones) widen and advance a little; the anterior superior iliac spines (hip bones) and the pubic symphysis narrow and retreat a little; the sacrum nutates (slides down and then back); and there is a chain of spirals and counter-spirals/rotation and counter-rotation in the pelvis (turns in), femurs (turn out), tibias (turns in) and feet (turn out). The patellas slide down and the feet sink and spread toward the fifth metatarsals, like windshield wipers swiping horizontally.

When we rise from plié by extending the hips and knees, these processes reverse themselves and the pelvic outlet closes. The sitz bones narrow and retreat a little; the hip bones and pubic symphysis widen and advance a little, the sacrum counternutates (slides forward and then up) and the feet rise and enclose, as their spring-like arches re-express themselves. Once again there is a chain of rotation and counterrotation in the hips, legs and feet, with the femoral heads rotating in a little, the patellas sliding up, the tibias rotating out a little and the "windshield wipers" of the feet swiping toward the midline.

There are so many subtle changes occurring in our bone rhythms when we plié, that focusing on all of them at once could create sensory overload. I suggest that you guide students toward noticing a few of these experiences at a time and embodying all of them within a few classes.

Here are some sample cues you might offer:

a "As you flex your hips, could you notice the pelvic outlet opening and your feet melting like butter? As you extend your hips, is the pelvic outlet closing? Are the feet reclaiming their dome-like arches?"
b "I invite you to ride your exhalation, drop your heavy pelvic diamond and let the sacrum slide down and then back, as you allow your sitz bones to widen and your feet to sink into and spread upon the earth."

c "To rise, could you ride your inhalation as you push the earth away with the tripod of each foot? Is the space between the points of the tripod shrinking? Are your sitz bones narrowing? Is your sacrum sliding forward and then up?"
d "I invite you to enjoy the outward rotation of the femoral heads as you sink into plié and their inward rotation as you return."

> **FOR YOUR CONSIDERATION:**
>
> I invite you to engage in some vigorous movement that involves full flexion of your hip joints, with both feet on the floor most of the time. After playing around with this "dance" for a while could you tune in to the changes occurring in your pelvic diamond, legs and feet? Are you noticing the opening and closing of the pelvic outlet? If so, is this a sensation you regularly associate with plié in a dance class? If your body resists the opening and closing of the pelvic outlet or any of the other changes mentioned in this essay, what self-talk could you use to sneak under that reluctance and experience enhanced mobility?

61 The Pelvis Is Not Square

If you examine a disarticulated (not wired or bolted together) pelvis with your hands, you'll notice that it is composed of two spiral-shaped pelvic halves and a sacrum, each of which is built to move independently, and that there is nothing "square" about it. However, for decades, or perhaps centuries, dance teachers have told students to "keep the pelvis square." This directive causes dancers to resist accommodating changes the pelvis needs to make each time a femoral head moves within its acetabulum/hip socket. When we resist or disallow organic reorganization of the musculoskeletal system, what Eric Franklin calls "bone rhythms," we wear away at our tissues from the inside, gradually harming them and diminishing efficiency. I believe that the idea of a "square" pelvis is one of the reasons why generations of dancers have needed hip replacement surgery.

In BF, we speak often of pelvic-femoral rhythm, pointing out that articulations of the hip joint—flexion, extension, abduction, adduction, circumduction, lateral rotation, medial rotation—are supported by accommodating changes in each pelvic half and the sacrum/coccyx.

When the femur moves in space, the hip socket must go with it. The pelvic half "wheels" or spirals with the femur in whatever direction it travels. This happens with every walking stride and with every open chain (non-weight-bearing) leg gesture in the dance lexicon. The two pelvic halves move independently, and the supporting pelvic half will often move in actual or relative counter-wheel or counter-spiral in the opposite direction from the gesturing pelvic half.

The idea that the pelvis should not respond to changes of the legs and spine is a pernicious one. Without judging themselves for having given that directive in the past, I encourage teachers to stop making that request, remember that a change in one part creates a change in the whole, and seek a more complete and updated understanding of healthy pelvic-femoral functioning.

FOR YOUR CONSIDERATION:

I invite you to notice your relationship to the idea of a "square" pelvis.

If you find your body resisting accommodating and spiraling changes in the pelvic halves when you move your legs, can you unpack the origins of that resistance and devise a plan to replace it with a more healthful and efficient response?

If your body does not resist these changes, can you recall instructions you were given or realizations you experienced that help you enjoy organic pelvic-femoral accommodations?

---

62 Open-Chain Pelvic-Femoral Rhythm/Thigh Lifts and Leg Swings

When we are born, the pelvis consists of three different bones on each side, the ilium, ischium and pubis. The sacrum and coccyx function as parts of both the pelvis and the spine. As we mature, the three bones on each side fuse, so that we have two pelvic halves that articulate with the femurs in the hip sockets (acetabula) and with the spine in the sacroiliac joints.

Bartenieff left us with her *Basic Six* fundamental explorations: (1) *Pre-Thigh Lift/Thigh Lift*; (2) *Pelvic Sagittal Shift*; (3) *Pelvic Lateral Shift*; (4) *Body-Half*; (5) *Diagonal Knee Reach*; (6) *Arm Circles*. I write more about them in Appendix D. They are discussed in depth in Peggy Hackey's *Making Connections* and in some detail in

94 *Anatomical Imagery*

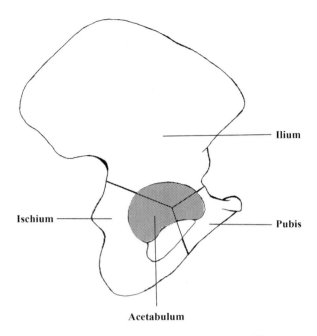

Figure 7.2 Simulation of the Right Pelvic Half.

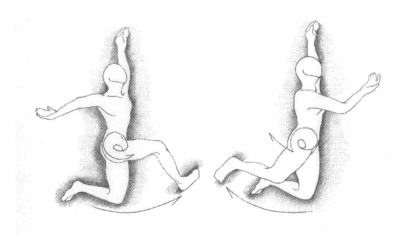

Figure 7.3 Illustration of Thigh Lift and Side-Lying Leg Swings.

Anatomical Imagery 95

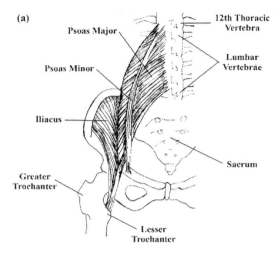

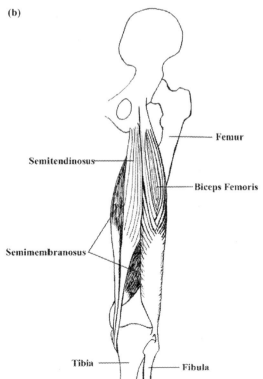

Figure 7.4 (a) Simulation of the Right Iliopsoas. (b) Simulation of the Right Hamstrings.

Bartenieff's *Human Movement: Coping with the Environment*. In the back-lying *Thigh Lift* and a variation I call "side-lying leg swings" we bring our attention to open-chain pelvic-femoral rhythm, the accommodations of each pelvic half to iliofemoral flexion and extension.

In *Thigh Lift* (which I prefer to call an arc-like heel reach), we are encouraged to notice the motion in the sacroiliac joints and pubic symphysis as each pelvic half moves with the corresponding femur when each thigh is flexed beyond 90 degrees and then returned to 45 degrees. These are wheel-like motions, in which the lowest part of each pelvic half spirals toward either the gesturing or (in relative motion) the supporting femur. That is, the sitz bone travels in the direction of the heel, while the highest part of each pelvic half, the iliac crest, wheels in the opposite direction.

In Bartenieff-based *side-lying leg swings*, we can tune in to the counter spirals happening more fully in the pelvic halves. We can notice the lowest part of one pelvic half spiraling freely forward with the gesturing leg and the other spiraling slightly backward with the supporting leg as we engage the *iliopsoas* to fully flex the gesturing limb. We can then notice the lowest part of the pelvic half of the gesturing leg spiraling backward and the other spiraling a little forward as we engage the *hamstrings* to find pure extension of the gesturing femur. We can imagine each pelvic half to be a wheel or clock; when the lower part (6 o'clock) rolls forward, the higher part (12 o'clock) rolls back.

We can also notice the rotation taking place in the sacroiliac joints and the limited but vital rotation occurring in the lumbar spine as they move in the direction of the gesturing femur, as well as other accommodating changes throughout the body.

FOR YOUR CONSIDERATION:

I invite you to select one of your favorite dance exercises that focuses on leg gestures (what in ballet terminology we might call *développé, enveloppé, grand rond de jambe* or *grand battement*). Could you "teach" it to yourself and notice the words you use? Does your language encourage the continuous reorganization of the pelvis and wheeling of the pelvic halves to facilitate efficient and integrated leg gestures? If not, how might you modify it?

63 Pelvic Shift Happens

I find that moving through space is more about the pelvis than the feet. Walking forward involves shifts of weight from one pelvic half to the other as well as a "wheeling" of the pelvic halves, as one spirals slightly toward the reaching leg and the other counter-spirals toward the pushing leg. When we allow the sagittal and lateral shifting of the lowest part of the pelvis, the weight transference through the pubic symphysis and the spiraling of the pelvic halves to propel us, our legs and feet know just how to respond.

Too many dancers have been taught to "place," "stabilize" or "hold" the pelvis, rather than to allow it to take the lead and reorganize continuously as they move in space. They have learned to resist the fluid momentum of the pelvis and the organic bone rhythms within it. They have been encouraged to brace against the integrated changes of the femoral heads, the pelvic halves and the sacrum that would allow them to move powerfully and freely across the floor.

To prepare students to travel with ease and efficiency, I often devote time early in technique classes to explorations of pelvic shifts and other concepts and practices bequeathed to us by Bartenieff, who considered sagittal (forward and back) and lateral (side to side) pelvic shifts and the thigh lift discussed in essay 62 to be among our most fundamental human movements. In such explorations, we learn to transfer weight efficiently, with the main action traveling through the pelvic diaphragm and pubic disc as the two halves of the pelvic diamond reorganize continuously. By bringing awareness to the shifting and spiraling of the pelvic halves that occur when weight is transferred from one foot to the other, or from the lower body to the upper, we can replace tension-holding patterns with fluid mobility.

FOR YOUR CONSIDERATION:

I invite you to "give your pelvic halves permission to propel you freely through space." As you do so, can you "allow your legs and feet to accommodate and support the traveling and counter-spiraling pelvis?

Next, I invite you to "ask your feet and legs to move you through the space, while 'stabilizing' or 'holding' the pelvis." Could you describe in detail the differences you experience as you follow these two sets of opposing instructions?

64 Let's Liberate Our Elbows and Knees

I see an "epidemic" of locked mid-limb joints among many of today's young ballet, jazz, modern and contemporary dancers. I believe that this problem comes from some teachers' and choreographers' obsession with "straight" knees, and a desire to make the arms match the legs. An overemphasis on "longer" legs and arms can cause students to lock their elbows and knees, disrupting the flow of energy from the body's core to its distal ends and blocking force absorption.

The instruction to "straighten the knees" can cause pressing back when rising from plié, creating anterior tilt in the pelvis and exaggeration of the lumbar curve. A misaligned pelvis will block the bone rhythms (described in essay 60) that need to take place in a healthy plié. Bracing in the knee can cause internal damage. With each plié and rise, there should be spirals and counter-spirals occurring at the knee. As the femur and tibia counter-rotate, the femoral condyles roll and slide on the menisci, which spread and narrow on the tibial plateau. The patella rotates as it slides down and then up. All these organic actions at the knee contribute to healthy and efficient functioning, but they will be diminished by pressing the knee back and bracing it against change.

Many teachers encourage students to hyperextend their elbows as well. Since we can't immobilize just one part of ourselves, that practice will limit the mobility of the shoulder girdle and torso. It will also diminish expressivity because energy will not be allowed to pour from the torso through the arms and out the distal ends. I find such locked arms to be energetically shorter, rather than longer. Students deserve to know the difference between *extension* of the knee and elbow, which can accommodate open, resilient pathways from the torso through the leg and arm, and *hyperextension* of the mid-limb joints (which is likely to separate limbs from the torso and create brittleness and misalignment).

I never say, "Straighten your knees or elbows." Instead, as dancers prepare to return from plié, I might say:

a   "I invite you to extend your hips by pushing the floor away and allowing the patellas to slide freely upward."
b   Can you notice the counter spirals of the tibias rotating out a little and the femurs rotating in a little as the sitz bones narrow?"
    To guide leg gestures, I might say:
c   "Could you yield and push on the supporting side and then reach and pull through the whole leg and foot on the gesturing side?"

Anatomical Imagery 99

d   "Do you sense a through-line in your open joints from the core through your distal ends?"
   To guide arm gestures, I might say:
e   "I invite you to sense the kinetic chains from your tail to your scapula and from your scapula to the distal ends of your fingers as you reach your arms into space. Are you enjoying the rotation of your humeral heads, scapulae and clavicles?"
f   "Could you notice the rotation of the radius around the ulna at the elbows and the resilient elasticity of the kinetic chains from your torso through your shoulder girdle to your hands?"
g   "Can you sense that energy pours in through your feet, travels through your legs, torso and arms and pours out through your fingertips?"

When I headed the dance program at Indiana University, I invited Dr. Jesus Dapena, a noted professor of biomechanics, to observe some contemporary dance classes and give me feedback. After watching a class in which the teacher repeatedly said "straighten your knees," he was astounded. "Why," he asked, "is he asking them to destroy their bodies like that?"

I know that many people find hyperextended joints beautiful. Over the years, as I have learned more about how human beings have evolved to function, I have become increasingly disturbed by locked joints. Could you prepare dinner or play the piano with locked elbows? How then, could they be desirable in dance, where adaptability is crucial? I find dancing that is harmonious with a well-functioning body to be truly beautiful, but I have a hard time perceiving beauty in dancing that violates the needs of a healthy body. We must acknowledge the importance of every joint in the body and the fact that they all need to coordinate in continuous processes of orchestrated change.

> **FOR YOUR CONSIDERATION:**
>
> Could you lock your elbows or knees and still experience energy pouring freely through your distal ends? Why or why not?
>   Could you borrow or create three total body images you might share with students to help them differentiate extended and hyper-extended mid-limb joints?

65 Walking Feet/Foundations and Levers

We talk about walking as "putting one foot in front of the other," and we often begin teaching children to dance by introducing the five positions of the feet. That is, we have inherited teaching language and practices that separate the foot in students' consciousness from the rest of the body. Walking is more about the pelvis than the foot, but restrictive footwear and erroneous ideas about what happens as we travel through space have caused some students to partially immobilize their feet, thereby distorting the functioning of their legs and pelvises. It is crucially important to understand how the foot has evolved to function.

We have 26 bones and 33 synovial joints in the ankle and foot, and all of them need to move freely on a regular basis if we are to be strong and adaptable. Our distant ancestors walked on uneven terrain in bare feet or skins. We move mostly on flat surfaces in often rigid flat-soled shoes. Since the evolution of our feet has not caught up with the changes in our lifestyles, it is important for us to move in bare feet or flexible footwear and on uneven surfaces as much as possible. If uneven surfaces are not available, we need to roll our feet on soft balls or move on sponge-like surfaces regularly.

In his teaching, Eric Franklin tells us that our feet serve us in five primary ways: foundations, propulsive levers, force absorbers, balancers and proprioceptors. He says passionately that human beings have "evolved to walk," and, as we walk, the feet change alternately from *lever mode* to *foundation mode*.

During each stride, our weight spirals longitudinally through the *pushing foot* from the heel to the ball. This is the *propulsive mode*, in which the hindfoot and forefoot are twisted, creating a rigid lever as the heel swings in and supinates and the forefoot pronates, with the weight on the first metatarsal. (We also activate this propulsive lever mode when we *relevé* or jump.)

During each walking stride, our weight spirals longitudinally through the *advancing foot* from the heel, forward along the outside of the foot, and then horizontally in a successive sequence through the metatarsals and toes from lateral to medial (5-4-3-2-1), ending in an untwisted *foundation mode*, with the weight on the whole foot. (We also use this foundation mode when we descend from a *relevé* or land from a jump.)

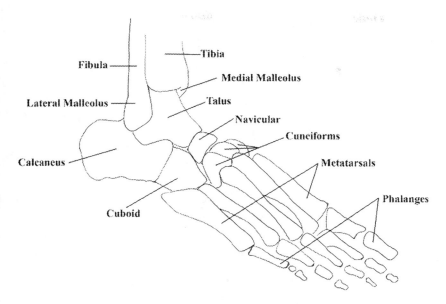

Figure 7.5 Simulation of the Bones of the Right Foot and Ankle.

The seven tarsal bones (hindfoot—calcaneus and talus and midfoot—navicular, cuneiforms and cuboid) and the forefoot (metatarsals and toes) reorganize with each step. At the ankle, the body's weight descends through the tibia (90%) and fibula (10%) to the talus, which distributes it from the calcaneus to the midfoot and forefoot. We can imagine synovial fluid "lubricating" the rolling of the talus, which can be thought of as a ball bearing, as it slides in the tunnel created by the distal ends of the tibia and fibula. We can image continuous and successive longitudinal spirals and counter-spirals flowing from the heel through the midfoot to the toes as we move in space. When each walking stride is complete, we arrive at least for a fleeting moment at an even distribution of weight on the tripod of balance (discussed in essay 67).

> **FOR YOUR CONSIDERATION:**
>
> I invite you to go for a walk. Once your flow is outpouring freely, could you notice the motion in each foot? Can you sense longitudinal spirals/counterspirals from heel to toes? Do you sense differences in the propulsive lever and foundation modes? Can you sense the weight rolling into the earth successively from the outer border of the advancing foot through each of the metatarsals and toes—5, 4, 3, 2, 1? Is one foot the same as the other? Could you diminish these actions? Could you allow them to happen more fully?

66 The Feet Reorganize Continuously in Each Plié

In BF, we are encouraged to notice our feet responding to the changes in the pelvis, hips and knees in both the flexion and extension phases of each plié. We notice the feet Sinking and Spreading (or "pouring into the earth") as we descend and then Rising and Enclosing (or "reclaiming their dome-like arches") as we ascend.

As the hip and knee flex, the tibia and fibula slide over the talus, which moves back-in-down as the heel swings out and the toes and metatarsals spread and swipe to the outside. The whole foot becomes lower and wider. As the hip and knee extend, the tunnel created by the tibiofibular mortise (tunnel) slides back over the talus, which moves forward-up-out, ending in vertical; the heel swings in, and the toes and metatarsals enclose and swipe in. The whole foot becomes higher and narrower.

Many students have developed bracing patterns in their feet. Some have been told to "lift and hold their arches or insteps" in a misguided attempt to correct over-pronation caused by forcing turn-out in the feet. All 26 bones in each ankle/foot need to articulate continuously as we move through the world. Bracing tension in any part of the foot will diminish the mobility of the whole foot and, therefore, lessen resilience and balance throughout the entire body. Since we execute plié more than any other dance movement, it is crucial to our efficiency and expressivity that we permit ankle and foot bone rhythms to occur each time we Sink or Rise.

Mobilizing my feet brings vibrancy to my whole body. I like to go barefoot as often as possible and wear sandals or flexible shoes that allow my feet to be mobile. I keep small, soft rubber balls under my desk so that I can roll my feet on them as I read or work at my computer. I find that doing so reduces fatigue and allows me to stay focused on projects like writing this book.

> **FOR YOUR CONSIDERATION:**
>
> Do you allow your feet to reorganize as you Sink into and Rise from each plié? If not, in what ways are your feet resisting the changes described above?
>
> I invite you to roll one foot on a small, soft rubber ball for about three minutes, playing with as many different actions and qualities of movement as possible. Make sure to ground the heel and spiral the forefoot in and out over the ball and then ground the metatarsals and spiral the hindfoot, noticing the twisting and untwisting of the foot. Next, I invite you to notice the differences between your two feet, and between your whole body-halves. Then, I invite you to repeat the rolling explorations on the second foot, before once again noticing the results of enlivening the many joints in the feet and ankles.

67 Tripods in the Feet and Near the Hip

When Bella Lewitzky[2] accepted my invitation to teach a master class in 1989, she told our University of New Mexico dance majors that "the big toe, little toe and heel in each foot form a tripod." I took her class and found the idea of the foot as a tripod immediately useful in distributing weight in a balanced way throughout my body. I passed it on to other students for decades.

In 2017, Nancy and Allegra Romita[3] shared with me and other participants in my summer teachers' intensive what they call the *Tripod of Balance*, a more refined idea about the foot that I find even more useful. I now sense the points of the tripod in each foot to be located:

a   between the distal ends of the first and second metatarsals,
b   between the distal ends of the fourth and fifth metatarsals, and
c   in the portion of the calcaneus that lies under the malleoli, the bony prominences at the lower end of the tibia and fibula. The calcaneus or hindfoot is the largest of the tarsals. It is located

104   *Anatomical Imagery*

under the talus, articulates anteriorly with the cuboid, and includes the "heel" at its posterior end. It is important to sense the difference between the back of the calcaneus/heel and the point under the malleoli that is the posterior point of the Tripod of Balance.

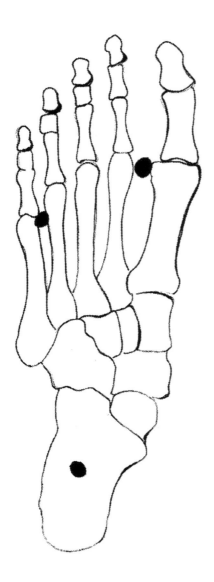

Anatomical Imagery 105

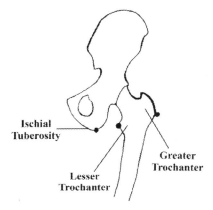

Figure 7.6 (a) Simulation of the Tripod of Balance, Right Foot as Seen from Below. (b) Simulation of the Tripod Near the Right Hip as Seen from Behind.

I find enhanced balance and mobility in my whole body by distributing my standing weight so that it is shared equally among these more specific three points. It provides resilient feet-to-head connectivity, and I can easily sense the pull of gravity through the vertical joint centers of my hips, knees, ankles and my spinal curves.

It is important to notice that the tripod exists only when weight shift has taken place and we are standing "still" on one or both feet. Even then, the tripod is not static, because the spaces between the points of the tripod enlarge when we plié and condense when we extend. That is, as discussed in essays 65 and 66 because the foot is constantly reorganizing, the *tripod is dynamic*. Its size changes each time we Sink or Rise when standing in place and with each shift of weight as we travel in space.

Even though the image of the tripod crystallizes only when the weight spreads onto the whole foot, it is powerful and useful. I discussed the problems caused by hyperextension of the knees in essay 64. Happily, most students find it impossible to lock their knees when distributing their weight evenly on their dynamic *Tripods of Balance*.

I also enjoy playing with the idea that there is a *tripod at the hip* with kinetic chains to the tripod in the foot. I sense a neuromuscular connection from the portion of the calcaneus under the malleoli to the sitz bone, a connection from the distal ends of the fourth and fifth metatarsals to the greater trochanter and a connection from the distal ends of the first and second metatarsals to the lesser trochanter. To make this visualization simpler and easier, I can simply think "heel to sitz bone, little toe to greater trochanter and big toe to lesser trochanter."

I can "steer" circumduction, rotation, flexion and extension at the hip by enlivening and reaching through each metatarsal and toe, and I can send energy back and forth between the tripod of the foot and the tripod near the hip. Sensing the relationship of these proximal and distal tripods through the kinetic chains that join them helps me spread the workload throughout my whole leg and foot and enhances ease and clarity in both proximal and distal articulations.

FOR YOUR CONSIDERATION:

Do you arrive on your tripod of balance when a weight shift is complete?

If you play with the idea of the points of the "Lewitzky" tripod (located in the little toe, big toe and heel), and then the "Romita" tripod (centered between the distal ends of the fourth and fifth and the first and second metatarsals and in the calcaneus under the malleoli) what different sensations do you experience?

If you stand on your Tripods of Balance are you able to hyperextend your knees?

If you explore the idea of corresponding tripods in the foot and near the hip, what do you notice?

---

68 Honoring Spinal Curves

When I took her SUNY Brockport somatics course for dance majors in 2004, my colleague Sondra Fraleigh[4] said, "I invite you to allow the curves of the spine to express themselves." I borrowed Sondra's statement and speak it frequently. About 15 years before that, a well-respected BF teacher told me to correct my "cervical lordosis" when lying on the floor to explore the Basic Six. I responded to her well-intended comments by developing a habit of over-lengthening my neck. The first feedback Sondra gave me that semester concerned my cervical blockage, and I soon realized that the BF practitioner who had cautioned me about the lordosis had misunderstood what it means for me to have a healthy spine. I thank Sondra for noticing my habit and setting me on a pathway of honoring the integrity of all my spinal curves.

Parents often tell their children to "stand up straight." Many teachers will say that and also "lengthen your neck." "Tuck your tail," to flatten the lumbar curve, was requested often by many dance technique teachers in the early decades of my life. Exaggerated curves of the lumbar or cervical spine (*lordosis*) or thoracic spine (*kyphosis*) can be noteworthy problems, but *overcorrecting* such problems can lead to *flat back*, which can be equally or even more problematic. Diligent students told to "straighten" the spine might actually succeed in diminishing its curves, causing brittleness that will almost certainly result in injury. Several dancer friends with naturally loose ligaments approached their dance training so zealously and followed teachers' instructions to straighten the spine so vigorously that they actually removed their spinal curves. All suffered herniated intervertebral discs and many underwent spinal fusion surgery.

At birth, the spine has just one curve from head to tail, which reach toward each other in the front space. As we progress through our developmental stages in the early months of life, we create first the cervical curve by activating the head reach, as we lie on our bellies and respond to what we want to see, hear, smell and taste, and then the lumbar curve, as we start to kick, shove, belly-crawl and propel ourselves through space. As we learn to walk, we develop the double S cervical, thoracic, lumbar and sacral curves. Each curve functions differently within the spring-like obelisk of the spine to provide both stability and mobility.

Together with the intervertebral discs, the spinal curves provide force absorption, allowing us to spread the impact of movement throughout the whole body. By imaging the cerebrospinal fluid in the skull and spinal cord and the fluid-filled intervertebral discs, I experience the head-tail connection as a "liquid" relationship, in which a change in the head creates a change in the tail and a change in the tail creates a change in the head. I can enhance my sense of a liquid spine by imaging the synovial fluid bathing the bilateral facets—the small planar joints on the back-top and back-bottom of most vertebrae, which interlock like shingles on a roof and slide/glide over one another as we flex, extend, laterally flex and rotate the spine.

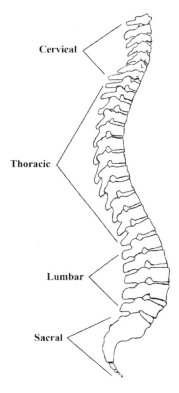

Figure 7.7 Simulation of the Curves of the Spine as Seen from the Right Side.

Some Body-Mind Centering practitioners speak of the "soft digestive spine," and at times, I like to imagine my spine as a double-S-curved and hollow tube opening at both the mouth and anus.

Alternately, I like to sense a Lengthening up the front of the curves of the spine and out the "open door at the top of the head," as my skull floats like a hot-air balloon toward the sky, my jaw bones hang toward the earth and I imagine my ears rotating forward. With the next breath, I can sense a Lengthening down the back of the curves of the spine, and out the "open door at the tip of the tail," as my sacrum and pelvic diamond ground themselves Heavily. With the next breath, I can sense the Shortening of the spine and remind myself to enjoy both Growing and Shrinking throughout my body.

The flow of energy in the spine can be bi-polar or uni-polar. In bi-polar organization, we might experience the combination of a Light head and a Heavy pelvic diamond. In uni-polar organization, the head and tail move in the same direction, and both may be Light or both may be Heavy, depending on our total body intent. In both these patterns, the changes in the depth of our liquid, resilient and open spinal curves make us elastic and adaptable.

FOR YOUR CONSIDERATION:

How do you usually refer to the spine in your self-talk or teaching? Can you trace the history of how that language became part of what you say?

What might you say to a dancer who has a habit of tucking their tail?

I invite you to visually embrace and embody the image of a "soft digestive spine" and notice what it brings you.

---

69 Celebrating Spinal Possibilities

In the Franklin Method, we are asked to explore 12 different ways in which the spine can move. In addition to (sagittal) flexion and extension, the possible movements in a disc/vertebra unit include lateral flexion to both the right and left sides, rotation to the right and left, translation right and left, translation front and back, compression and distraction (lengthening). I take a few minutes each morning to move my spine freely in all those ways as a preparation for the day ahead.

The cervical spine has considerable mobility in the sagittal, vertical and horizontal planes. The thoracic spine has more lateral flexion and rotation than flexion and not much extension. The lumbar spine can flex and extend much more than it can bend to the side or rotate. It is crucial that we articulate each joint in the spine fully within its particular range of motion regularly (and the "use it or lose it" principle applies to our joint mobility throughout the body). I find that individual dancers have widely-varying amounts of flexibility in the different regions of the spine, and it is important that each dancer understand and explore her/his/their own full range of spinal motion rather than replicate the degree of spinal mobility they perceive in a teacher or other dancers.

There are more than 100 joints in the spine, and giving each one of them an opportunity to mobilize freely will support fluid multi-dimensional movement in the whole body. As I plan explorations of spinal articulations for each technique class, I include arm circles with eye-tracking in the sagittal, vertical and horizontal planes as well as spirals that travel from plane to plane and three-dimensional cycles through the Diagonals of the Cube. In such circles and spirals, the spine reorganizes continuously.

Note: See Figures 7.11, Three Cardinal Planes, and 7.12, Diagonal Pathways.

When the spine rotates, it also shortens a little, because of "coupled motions" of rotation and lateral flexion. Eric Franklin refers to this as "screwing down." Lateral flexion of the spine will be accompanied by a little rotation toward the bending side in the cervical and thoracic vertebra and a little cross-lateral rotation in the lumbar spine. I encourage students to notice and enjoy these three-dimensional coupled or automatic motions rather than resisting them by imagining that the spine is moving in only two dimensions.

I enjoy noticing how the shoulder girdle and pelvic girdle respond to the movements of the spine. I like to think of *initiation and accommodation*. I can focus on initiating with head-tail articulations while also noticing how the rest of my body moves in accommodation to the changes in my spine. For example, as I flex my thoracic spine, my scapulae will upwardly rotate (the inferior angles sliding around the back to the sides of my rib cage) unless I interfere by bracing against that accommodating movement.

FOR YOUR CONSIDERATION:

How can you include opportunities for exploring all the ways in which the spine can move in the "warm-up" portion of a technique class?

How can you encourage each student to take responsibility for knowing and activating their individual range of spinal mobility?

70 Successive Spinal Sequencing, with a Partner

I share the process described in this essay as one example of how students can work together to co-create knowledge by investigating a fundamental movement experience through guiding touch (outer perspective) and kinesthetic sensation (inner perspective).

When investigating wave-like/Successive Sequencing through the spine, I often invite students to work in pairs and offer each other tactile support. In this investigation, students focus on the articulation of each set of *facet joints* from the bottom of the second cervical vertebra to the top of the sacrum. There are 92 facets (46 overlapping pairs) in these regions of the spine. The facets are bi-lateral planar joints located posteriorly on the top (superior) and bottom (inferior) of each of these vertebral bodies. They are synovial joints that move with curvilinear sliding and gliding. In the cervical and thoracic spines, they overlap like shingles on a roof; in flexion, the inferior facets of the superior vertebra slide up and forward over the superior facets of the inferior vertebra. Eric Franklin likens this action to laminated playing cards sliding up and then forward over one another. In extension, the inferior facets of the superior vertebra slide back and down.

The orientation of the facets in the cervical and thoracic spines can be thought of in relationship to the Door Plane (with cervical facets oriented 45 degrees forward from vertical and thoracic facets oriented at about 60 degrees). In the lumbar spine (L-1 through L-4), the facets are oriented at 90 degrees but in the Wheel Plane. Instead of playing cards, an image for the movement of lumbar facets is of a head sliding up and out of earmuffs on flexion and sliding back into those cozy earmuffs on extension. The action at L-5/S-1 (the last lumbar vertebra over the sacrum) is more like the playing cards.

After asking permission to use non-invasive touch, one student stands behind the other and places both index fingertips firmly but sensitively on either side of the C2 spinous process, the bony protuberance one can easily palpate at the back of the vertebra. They place their thumbs on either side of the C3 spinous process. The student doing the touching lingers at what they perceive as the inferior facets on the superior vertebra and encourages them to slide up and forward with their fingertips as that disc/vertebra unit flexes. Both students notice (one seeing and the other sensing/imaging) the opening of the back of the joint as the space between the fingers and thumbs enlarges. They then bring their fingers and thumbs closer together and slide down to the next two vertebrae. The journey travels from the inferior facets of the second through the seventh cervical vertebra (neck) and then the 12 thoracic

112   Anatomical Imagery

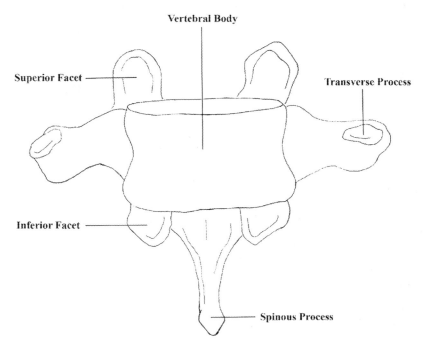

Figure 7.8 Simulation of a Thoracic Vertebra as Seen from the Front.

vertebrae (connected to the rib cage). In the first four lumbar vertebrae (lower spine), the guiding student encourages each set of lower facets to slide up and out of imagined earmuffs before flexing forward. At L5-S1, both can once again imagine a sliding up and forward.

The process can then be reversed, focusing on the sliding of lumbar facets down and in and then thoracic and cervical facets back and down in Successive extension of each disc/vertebra unit.

The student receiving the touch is invited to close her/his/their eyes and tune in fully to the tactile/kinesthetic experience of this excursion, focusing on the independent life of each vertebra while gaining internal awareness of the structure and relative mobility of each spinal curve.

I like to ask students to explore the difference between *Successive* spinal flexion and extension (moving one set of facets at a time, as in the exploration described above) and *Simultaneous* flexion and extension (moving all or a group of facets at once) in their very first class because I find that doing so heightens embodied spinal awareness almost immediately.

> **FOR YOUR CONSIDERATION:**
>
> Why is it important to assure that each set of facet joints can move independently in a Successive wave?
> I invite you to devise explorations of both Simultaneous and Successive spinal Phrasing for students.
> How could you also explore Sequential Phrasing (non-adjacent sequencing) of the spine?
> Could you design explorations of fundamental biomechanical processes involving other parts of the body in which students could work together to offer non-invasive touch?

71 Arm Circles/Scapulohumeral Rhythm

Many students have been told to "press the shoulders down," "place the arms" in static positions, "hold the hands" in various shapes or designs, "carry the chest forward and the shoulders back," and "stretch the elbows." These instructions reduce mobility and expressivity throughout the whole upper body, leading to inefficiency and mal-function.

As we explore BF *Arm Circles*, we are encouraged to tune in to *scapulohumeral rhythm* and notice that the arm and shoulder girdle are constructed to move harmoniously together, that when we gradate the rotation of the humeral head while moving the arm up, down, forward or back, there is also motion in the scapula and clavicle. If I engage in what Bartenieff called "eye-tracking," following my fingertips with my eyes (also called eye-hand coordination), I can sense the rest of my body moving in accommodation to my arms and enjoy a satisfying sense of total body integration.

The *shoulder/glenohumeral joint* consists of a ball and socket. The head of the humerus is the ball and the *glenoid cavity in the scapula* is the much smaller socket. The articulation of the scapula on the rib cage is known as the *scapulothoracic joint*. It is not a typical joint in which bone articulates with bone; instead, the scapula is sliding on the fascia surrounding the muscles on the back and sides of the rib cage that enables the rotation of the

114   *Anatomical Imagery*

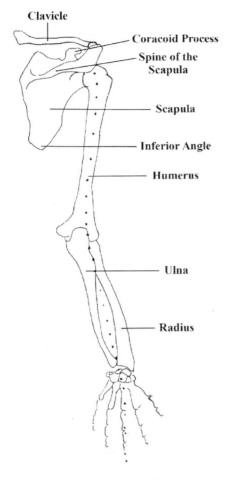

Figure 7.9 Simulation of the Right Scapula, Arm and Hand as Seen from the Back.

shoulder blade, in coordination with the movements of the arm and collar bone.

The *appendicular skeleton* is composed of the shoulder girdle, arms, pelvic girdle and legs. The *axial skeleton* is the head and trunk. The appendicular skeleton articulates with the axial skeleton *only* at the sternum, in the *sternoclavicular joint*, where a disc allows it to function like a ball and socket to provide considerable mobility at this crucial junction. I like to imagine that my arm starts at the sternoclavicular joint, that is, that my clavicle moves my arm, and to sense support for my arm gestures in my rib cage and spine.

In joints where there is smooth movement between bones, such as the shoulder joint, we have *synovial fluid*. Bonnie Bainbridge Cohen tells us that synovial fluid has the consistency of olive oil, and I love to imagine "soothing, warm olive oil lubricating the motion" as I lead with my distal ends to carve arm circles in my kinesphere. I sense fluid ease in the circumduction of the arm in the glenohumeral joint, the (non-synovial, but fascial) gliding and sliding of my scapula around the back and sides of my rib cage and the spiraling movements of the clavicle.

I enjoy the synovial articulations of the phalanges (fingers and thumbs), the metacarpals (bones of the hand), the carpals (bones of the wrist) and the radius and ulna (forearm), which twist and untwist at the elbow.

Kitty Daniels shared with me a visualization that I find extremely useful to students who have developed immobilization of the shoulder girdle:

> Circle your arm while imagining that light is pouring from the glenoid cavity/socket of your scapula through your arm and hand. Wherever the hand travels in your kinesphere, the socket travels with it, aiming its outpouring light through each finger and thumb into the space beyond.

FOR YOUR CONSIDERATION:

With what words do you usually describe gestures of the arms and hands?

I invite you to take a little walk while imagining your arms swinging from the sternoclavicular joints and then compare that with imagining your arms swinging from the glenohumeral joints. What differences do you experience?

I invite you to explore Kitty Daniel's "light pouring" image described above, leading with your fingertips to carve sagittal, vertical and diagonal arm circles, and then put into words what this image brings you.

Could you try it again with eye-tracking, and recount any bodily changes you notice?

72 More Arm Circles/Gradated Humeral Rotation

In Bartenieff's Arm Circles, the concept of "gradated" or gradual is key. A useful image for gradation is a dimmer light switch, which can be rotated continuously to provide more or less light, in contrast to a "flip" switch that provides all or nothing. Every two degrees of rotation in the humerus creates one degree of rotation in the scapula. The rotation of the scapula initiates rotation of the clavicle. When we consciously activate humeral rotation, the scapular and clavicular rotation are automatic coupled motions unless we brace against them. If we flip the rotation of the humerus (rotating it completely in one moment at the beginning of an arm reach), the scapula will not participate fully in the process.

In BF, we are encouraged to experience a kinetic chain from the tip of the little finger to the lowest point/inferior angle in the scapula

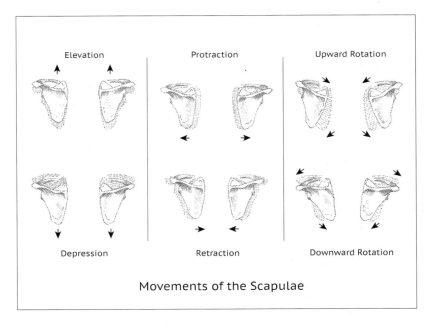

Figure 7.10 Movements of the Scapulae.

Anatomical Imagery 117

and another from the thumb to the most-forward point/coracoid process, the prominence on the scapula located toward the front of the body that can be palpated under the clavicle. We can "steer" our gradated humeroscapular rotation with our distal ends/fingers and thumbs.

While exploring Arm Circles, we can affirm that:

a   Rotation takes place around an axis, from the proximal end/head of the humerus to the distal end of the middle finger.
b   Gradated rotation of the humerus can activate gradual rotation of the scapula. There is an organic affinity for outward humeral rotation and upward scapular rotation and for inward humeral rotation and downward scapular rotation. Resisting these organically accommodating functions results in immobilizing tensions in the whole upper body.
c   In upward scapular rotation, the lowest part of the shoulder blade (the inferior angle) slides around the side of the rib cage as the arm moves forward and/or upward. In downward scapular rotation, the inferior angle slides back to its starting place. There will be no elevation of the scapula in this process, and therefore no need to press the shoulder down.
d   We can steer proximal rotation by activating and leading with the distal ends of each independently-functioning finger and thumb as we carve pathways in the kinesphere. When each phalange has its own independent life, rather than being part of a hand held in a fixed position, the mobility of the whole upper body is enhanced. Each fingertip and thumb tip has its own kinetic chain to a different point on the scapula, but we can focus on the relationship of the *little finger to the inferior angle* of the scapula when we experience outward humeral/upward scapular rotation and the relationship of the *thumb to the coracoid process* of the scapula when we inwardly/downwardly rotate.
e   The clavicle will also move as the arm rises, with rotation, a little retraction and distal elevation in accommodation to the changes in the humerus and scapula. These accommodations reverse themselves as the arm returns to neutral.
f   There is rotation in the forearm as well, as the radius pronates and supinates around the ulna.

FOR YOUR CONSIDERATION:

I invite you to "flip" the rotation in one arm as you reach it upward and then to Carve with your fingers to gradually rotate the other arm to the same high level. What differences do you sense in the two sides of your shoulder girdle?

I invite you to play with arm circles in the Door Plane (which has more up-down, less side-side and no front-back). Could you tune in, one at a time, to each of the accommodating anatomical experiences described in a. through f. above? (Although they occur simultaneously, we can only fully focus on one of these experiences at a time.) Which came most easily? Did your body struggle with one or more of them?

73 Arm Circles with Shape Qualities

If we explore standing Arm Circles in the vertical, sagittal, horizontal and diagonal planes while following the fingertips with the gaze, we can allow and savor continuous reorganization of the shoulder girdle, spine and rib cage, particularly, and the rest of the body, generally, as everything changes in accommodation to our attention on the leading hand. We can provide opportunities for *myofascial* sliding, gliding, enlivening and release. That is, we can encourage motion in the fascia surrounding and separating muscle tissue.

In L/BMS, these integrated total body changes are referred to as *Shape Qualities*, with underlying *Shape Flow Support*. Shape Qualities can be thought of as cellular-level changes defined in relationship to the Three Cardinal Dimensions: *Rising* and *Sinking* in the vertical; *Spreading* and *Enclosing* in the horizontal; and *Retreating* and *Advancing* in the sagittal.

Note: Please consult Appendix E for more information on these Shape concepts.

In two-dimensional/planar Arm Circles, we can invite students to:

a   Spread, Rise, Enclose and then Sink in the Door Plane, cycling from Side Middle Open to Place High to Side Middle Across to Place Low; or

b Advance, Rise, Retreat and then Sink in the Wheel Plane, cycling from Forward Middle to Place High to Back Middle to Place Low; or
c Advance, Enclose, Retreat and then Spread in the Table Plane, cycling from Forward Middle to Side Middle Across to Back Middle to Side Middle Open.
d In three-dimensional Diagonals in the Cube, I can invite them to: Advance/Sink/Spread, then Rise, then Retreat/Enclose then Sink, cycling from Right Forward Low to Right Forward High to Left Back High to Left Back Low. They could then explore Left Forward Low-Left Forward High-Right Back High-Right Back Low.

Shape Flow Support refers to breath-related changes in the thoracic and abdominal cavities that support gestures and postural movements. They are called *Lengthening-Shortening* (vertical dimension), *Widening-Narrowing* (horizontal dimension) and *Bulging-Hollowing*

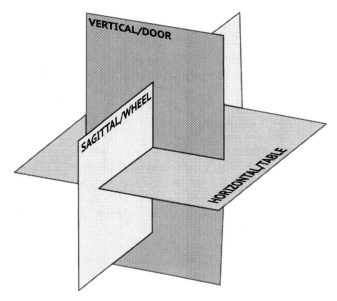

Intersection of the Three Cardinal Planes

Figure 7.11 Intersection of the Three Cardinal Planes.

120 *Anatomical Imagery*

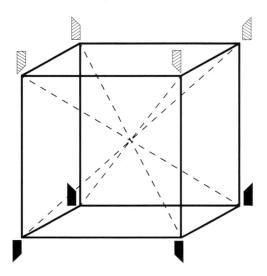

Figure 7.12 L/BMS Diagonals of the Cube.

(sagittal dimension). These actions pour in and out of each other gradually as we cycle in the planes. As we inscribe Arm Circles in the vertical plane, we can Widen, Lengthen upward, Narrow and then Shorten downward. In the sagittal plane, we can Bulge, Lengthen upward, Hollow and then Shorten downward. In the horizontal plane, we can Widen, Bulge, Narrow and then Hollow. In the Diagonals of the Cube, we can Bulge/Shorten downward/Widen, Lengthen upward, Hollow/Narrow and then Shorten downward.

Guiding the exploration of Arms Circles with gradated humeroscapular rotation and eye-tracking in different spatial sequences while also encouraging the activation of Shape Qualities and Shape Flow Support is one of my favorite ways of eliciting total body participation and integration. The specialized meanings of these words in L/BMS stimulate cellular-level expressive change throughout the body.

When we explore these multi-dimensional Arm Circles, we are facilitating myofascial release (enlivening of the fascia surrounding and separating muscle tissue). Fascia is a sheet (or "stocking") of connective tissue, primarily collagen, beneath the skin that attaches to, stabilizes, encloses and separates muscles and other internal organs. Different muscles are contracting in different directions as they slide over one another and press against their fascial coverings. We image

Anatomical Imagery 121

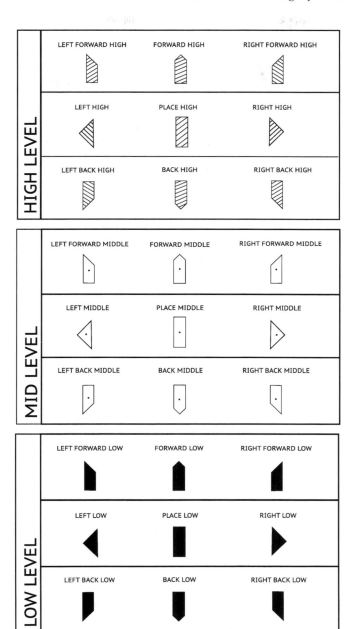

Figure 7.13 L/BMS Directional Symbols.

muscle filaments sliding together and apart and fascial wrappings gliding and reconfiguring as they respond to the bulging and flattening of the muscles they surround. Fascia recoil happens when we move at the speed or rhythm that allows fibers to rebound elastically. If we move too slowly or too quickly, we rely entirely on muscle. At the speed or rhythm known as "resonant frequency," the fascia assists in returning the bones closer to the body's center. When we inscribe our arm circles in rhythms that allow for fascial recoil and rebound, we are mobilizing and smoothing our myofascial components so that our bodies will function at an optimal level.

FOR YOUR CONSIDERATION:

I encourage you to ask students to improvise Carving Arm Circles with eye-tracking in any pathways they choose throughout the kinesphere and ask them to notice how readily total body reorganization comes alive as they do so.

I encourage you to define the Shape Qualities for students and then use those concepts to guide both gestural and postural journeys through their personal space.

Could you ask students to notice their bodies before and then after an exploration of three-dimensional Arm Circles and comment on changes they experience in their muscles and fascia?

---

74 A Few Samples of Inner Speech

I often model for students the kind of self-talk they might engage in as they explore our movement investigations. I like to share samples of inner dialogues that have helped me become a more mindful mover. For example, as we explore Arm Circles, we might say the following encouraging words to ourselves:

a   "Could you enjoy the luscious warmth of synovial fluid bathing the head of the humerus as it gradually rotates and collaborates in continuous liquid reorganization with the scapula and clavicle."

b   "I invite you to notice the independent life of each finger and the thumb as they carve the space and steer mid-limb and proximal rotation."

c   "Can you savor the independent but coordinated engagement of each phalange enlivening its own kinetic chain to a different point on the scapula—especially the thumb to the coracoid process and the little finger to the scapula's lowest point, its inferior angle."
d   "I invite you to imagine that your synovial fluid has the consistency of olive oil as it bathes the articulation of each phalange, metacarpal, carpal and the radius and ulna."
e   "Please sense the volume and texture of the space in your kinesphere as if you are swimming, penetrating the water's surface with your fingertips and feeling the gentle resistance of the water to the movement of your arms and torso. Can you tune in to the accommodating, three-dimensional changes occurring throughout your body?"

Anatomically-based guiding images bring us efficient functioning. Over time, the images we feed ourselves will manifest in new body-mind connections that will serve us as efficient new habits.

> **FOR YOUR CONSIDERATION:**
>
> I invite you to compose some language you would like to speak to yourself as you explore one of more of your favorite standing-in-place technique class explorations. Could you write four self-encouraging sentences concerning the spine and/or shoulder girdle and four focused on the pelvis, legs and/or feet?

75 Axes of Rotation/Spreading the Workload

It is crucial that students know the prime-mover muscles of femoral and humeral rotation, which are located near the iliofemoral and glenohumeral joints. It is also important for them to understand that rotation takes place *around an axis* from the proximal head of the femur or the humerus all the way through a distal toe tip or a fingertip. By sensing the primary actions near the proximal joints *and* the appropriate involvement of muscles through the whole length of the axis, they can create synergistic muscle balance that will *spread the workload throughout the leg or arm*, rather than overloading the muscles closest to the trunk and underutilizing the rest of the limb.

Sometimes students hold so much tension in the pelvis that they immobilize the hip joint and try to force outward rotation at the knee and foot. Sometimes students hold so much tension in the shoulders

124   *Anatomical Imagery*

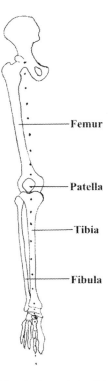

Figure 7.14 Simulation of the Right Pelvic Half, Leg and Foot as Seen from the Front.

that they block the motion of the sternoclavicular and scapulothoracic joints; rather than allowing rotation in both the glenohumeral and mid-limb joints, they diminish the actions of the humeral ball in the scapular socket and rely primarily on the rotary pronation and supination of the radius and ulna at the elbow.

I like to sense the axis in the arm and hand as extending from the humeral head through the third finger, and to notice that my little finger can steer outward rotation of the humerus and my thumb its inward rotation. I like to sense the axis in the leg and foot as extending from the femoral head through the second toe and to notice that the small toe can steer outward rotation of the femur and that the big toe can guide its inward rotation.

As I articulate an arm or leg, I can sense the web of connective tissue that connects all the muscles from proximal to distal ends. (This web is *fascia*, and it surrounds blood vessels and nerves as well as muscles and groups of muscles, to both separate and connect throughout the body.) As muscles bulge in concentric contractions, they press against their fascial coverings. As they contract in different directions, they slide over one another inside their slippery fascial wrappings.

We can distinguish between primary and auxiliary functions in all parts of ourselves and activate muscles responsible for each of them appropriately, to distribute the movement workload synergistically, with each muscle responsible for its proportional share and none doing more than required. It is important not to overwork any parts of ourselves, because when one part does more than its share, other parts check out, creating overuse/underuse imbalances and eventual injuries.

In BF, we access multiple inroads into *total body organization, connectivity, coordination* or *integration*. Integrative imagery (mental pictures that incorporate the whole body) will help us balance the workload, but thinking of any body part as separate from or more important than the rest might create imbalances. There is a time to focus on component parts (as in the *differentiation* stage of knowledge generation), but after attending to one part, it is important to focus on total body coordination (the *integration* stage of learning) to function at our best.

Any chain is as strong as its weakest link; therefore, we must make sure that the links of all the kinetic chains from the core to the distal ends of our bodies are recruited and enlivened to the necessary degree. When we are alive throughout the neuromusculoskeletal system, tuning into relationships within the body-mind so that each part of us does its fair share of rotation or any of our other physical tasks, we can dance with connectivity and efficiency.

> **FOR YOUR CONSIDERATION:**
>
> I invite you to outwardly rotate in one hip by focusing exclusively on the action of the prime movers of outward rotation, the six deep-lateral rotators. Then, I invite you to repeat the process with modification: initiate the turn-out once more in the deep rotators but allow a sensation of outward spiraling to immediately pour from the proximal end through the length of the limb and out the distal ends. Could you describe each experience?
>
> I invite you to borrow or craft three statements that would help students balance the workload throughout their bodies in an exploration that interests you and would be relevant to them.

Notes

1. Eric Franklin (born in 1957) is a Swiss dancer, movement educator, university lecturer, writer and founder of the Franklin Method, which combines creative visualization, embodied anatomy, physical and mental exercises and educational skills. He has written many books, but I particularly recommend *Dynamic Alignment through Imagery: Edition 2*. It contains a wealth of detailed information on what Franklin calls "bone rhythms" and images for improving functional anatomy. In 2018, Mr. Franklin accepted my invitation to serve as a keynote presenter in the Somatic Dance Conference and Performance Festival at Hobart and William Smith Colleges in Geneva, New York, which I founded and co-direct with Cynthia Williams. In May, 2021, I became a level one Certified Franklin Method Teacher.
2. Nora Reynolds Daniel, an exquisite dancer, served as a treasured adjunct professor when I headed the University of New Mexico Dance Program. Since her mother, the powerhouse modern dance icon Bella Lewitzky, visited Nora and her family frequently, I had many stimulating interactions with both of them. In 1997, Bella gave the Bill Evans Dance Company permission to reconstruct her work *Ceremony for Three*. I believe it was the first time any company but her own had performed her work.
3. A few years ago, Nancy and Allegra Romita, another empowered mother and daughter team, served as guest teachers in the Bill Evans Summer Institute of Dance at Hobart and William Smith Colleges in Geneva, New York. In several enlightening workshops, they shared highlights of their approach to embodied anatomy, which they call Functional Awareness. I recommend their book, *Functional Awareness: Anatomy in Action for Dancers*.
4. Sondra Horton Fraleigh and I were undergraduate modern dance students together at the University of Utah in the late '50s/early '60s, and we have remained friends ever since. She authored *Dance and the Lived Body* and many other widely-read books on dance and movement and is the founder of the Eastwest Somatics organization. We were reunited in 2004, when I became a professor of dance at SUNY Brockport and Sondra (who had just retired) was still teaching one course a semester. Our offices were side by side, and we had many lingering conversations about our respective, decades-long journeys in the realm of somatic investigation. We last saw each other in July, 2019, when she accepted my invitation to deliver a keynote presentation in our seventh annual Somatic Dance Conference and Performance Festival in Geneva, New York.

References

Franklin, Eric. *Dynamic Alignment through Imagery*. 2nd ed., Human Kinetics, 2012.

VIII Converting Theory into Action

Note: Words with specialized meanings in the Laban/Bartenieff Movement System, are capitalized in this chapter (e.g., Light Weight, Center of Gravity, Effort Affinities).

76 Riding the Dynamic Pelvis through Space

Dancing through space in upright body forms depends on different variations of walking or running, which have evolved over more than four million years as humans' primary modes of locomotion. In efficient walking, the center of gravity in the pelvis travels freely through space as the two pelvic halves contribute fluid spirals and counter-spirals. I like to imagine that I am riding my dynamic pelvis through space as I find the pace and rhythms that maximize fascial recoil and rebound so that I travel with minimal exertion.

The basic *walking reconfigurations* of the myofascial and skeletal systems are amplified when dance steps move us in multiple directions and levels. Each time we shift the center of weight in any direction to travel in space, the changes in the hip joints initiate significant reorganizations throughout the body. If efficient bone and myofascial rhythms are not fully available to us in walking and running, we will struggle inordinately with the more complex traveling movement of dancing.

As the leading femur flexes, the lowest part of the pelvic half on that side wheels forward, to increase the range of the stride. The lowest part of the pelvic half on the pushing side counterwheels backward. The longitudinal spiraling actions through the feet (the back one in propulsive lever mode and the forward one in foundation mode) are crucial, of course, but they are part of a complex chain of events triggered by the desire to move the center of gravity in space. The spine is also spiraling, the lumbar vertebrae and sacrum rotating to support

DOI: 10.4324/9781003290209-9

128 *Converting Theory into Action*

the wheeling of the pelvic halves, and the thoracic spine counterrotating to enable cross-lateral reaching of the shoulder girdle and arm opposite the leading foot.

Allowing the lowest part of the pelvis to carry them freely through space as it continuously reorganizes is vital to students' success. Because efficient dancing is built on well-coordinated walking and running rhythms, I sometimes invite dancers to "take a hike" and tune in to all I've described in the paragraphs above for a few minutes, either near the beginning of class or as recuperation from complex investigations later on.

FOR YOUR CONSIDERATION:

Do you tend to talk more about the feet than the center of weight when describing traveling movement?

In what language could you stress the importance of allowing organic bone rhythms and rhythmic fascial recoil to move the center of gravity efficiently through space?

---

77 Undercurves

"Undercurves" are found in abundance in most dance styles, even though many teachers may not use that particular word. By about 20 minutes into a typical class, I ask students to explore standing undercurve pelvic shifts. I invite them to *Yield* into their weight through one foot and *Push* against the earth. As the energy of that Push radiates through the center of gravity, they will *Reach* through the other foot and *Pull* themselves to a new point in space. This particular sequence of *Yield and Push to Reach and Pull* allows students to be both grounded and fluid as they Sink and Rise to move in different directions. In these actions, the spiraling and counter-spiraling pelvic diamond inscribes a U-shaped curve through space with each transfer of weight, as one pelvic half wheels in the direction of the reaching femur and the other toward the pushing leg.

Undercurves are dynamic. As in a pendular swing of the arm or leg, there is an acceleration of the pelvis as it freely rides momentum on its way down and forward at the beginning and a deceleration on its way up to neutral weight at the end. From the perspective of L/BMS *Efforts,* or movement qualities, undercurves have affinities for Strong-into-Neutral Weight, Free-into-Controlled Flow and Sudden-into-Sustained time.

I design sequences that move sagittally, laterally and diagonally. I point out and encourage fulfillment of undercurve transitions throughout our dancing-through-space investigations. In most of the instances in which our weight is transferred from one foot to the other while dancing, the pelvis will inscribe either an undercurve or an overcurve. The down-and-under shifting in the undercurve is the organic preparation for up-and-over shifting in the overcurve. This cycle is found in such common steps as *piqué, temps lié, jeté* and *chassé* (to borrow the terminology of ballet that is used in many dance styles).

Note: See essay 80 for more thoughts on overcurves.

FOR YOUR CONSIDERATION:

I invite you to look for pelvic undercurves in one or more of the modern, contemporary, ballet or jazz dance styles you draw on in your teaching.

Could you choose a favorite dance sequence from any of the codified techniques you have studied and repeat it a few times while noticing and amplifying its undercurves?

Could you play with undercurves, first thinking that the whole pelvis moves in the same direction and then thinking of contrasting motions of the two pelvic halves? How is your experience of these two approaches to the undercurve different? Which one is more congruent with organic bone rhythms?

---

78 Upper-Body Strengthening

Today's contemporary and hip-hop dancers execute a variety of maneuvers in which the body's weight is supported by the hands, arms and shoulder girdle, with the crown of the head reaching or hanging downward and the tail and (usually) the legs and feet reaching upward. To prepare students for such *inversions*, we can offer upper-body strengthening opportunities in the early portions of our classes.

I encourage students to build both upper-body and core strength through explorations of what is called the "plank" pose in yoga. Some weight remains on the feet while the rest is shifted into the arms and hands. They play with variations of the basic plank, such as yielding to weight on both *forearms* and both feet. I often ask dancers to linger (while moving only gently in small ways) in one of these variations for about 30 seconds. It is crucial to breathe so fully that the deep abdominal wall is engaged.

After experiencing success with the weight on both hands or forearms and both feet, students are ready to develop *Cross-Lateral* strength. They bear weight through the forearms and then reach one hand and then the other away from the floor for about 15 seconds. Next, they reach one leg and then the other until the foot leaves the floor for about 15 seconds. *Total body* cross-lateral variations of the plank are fun and useful challenges, and as they gain more coordination and strength, I ask students to shift their weight into a plank with one arm and the opposite leg Arcing immediately off the floor for about 15 seconds.

It is important to incorporate such strength-building plank explorations into longer movement sequences with a focus on dynamic phrasing to musical accompaniment, so that students experience them as "dancing" rather than just "exercises." I usually invite dancers to play with the Growing and Shrinking of the Shape Flow Mode of Shape Change and Shape Flow Support within their investigations, rather than remaining completely still.

Note: You can read more about Modes of Shape Change, and Shape Flow Support in Appendix E.

FOR YOUR CONSIDERATION:

How do you include opportunities for upper-body strengthening in the early portions of your classes?

I invite you to add explorations of two or more variations of the plank to patterns you teach in the early portion of a class and then weave them into your culminating combination.

How could you encourage continuous movement within such explorations?

---

79 Undercurve-Inversion Dance

In the early 2000s, Kristin Torok[1] shared with me an exercise she had designed to prepare students for the many inversions that had entered the vocabulary of dancers in the Bay Area of California where she lives and teaches. Immediately, I recognized that I was not methodically preparing students to work upside down, even though I had included inversions in my culminating dances and my choreography for decades. As a result, I started playing with inversion investigations just a few weeks later.

Early in each class, I invite students to become as small as possible, while paying particular attention to the necessity of full hip flexion in that process. Soon after, I introduce *homologous* weight shifting, from feet to hands and hands back to feet. (Homologous is a term used in Body-Mind Centering and elsewhere to describe locomotion—moving from one place to another—in which the weight is shifted from both hands to both feet or from both feet to both hands. Babies evolve through a stage of homologous body organization as their primary mode of locomotion. In BF this pattern stage is called Upper-Lower/Lower-Upper, and we are sometimes asked to think of ourselves as frogs or rabbits to access it.

Initially, these successive weight shifts are small-range, with the spine remaining flexed and *Ball-Like*. Eventually, they become full-range, going from a condensed ball to an elongated *Pin-Like* plank with extended legs and spine. In both variations, they return to a low-standing Ball-Like form. Next, to explore the Cross-Laterality they will utilize in most inversions, they shift weight from one foot to the other as they go from feet to hands, reaching the non-weight-bearing leg away from the earth.

Later in class, they might explore the *undercurve-inversion dance*, which is appropriate for dancers at experienced-beginner through advanced levels. In this dance, they first play with "upright" undercurves, shifting their weight forward-back, diagonally forward-diagonally

Figure 8.1 Ball-Like and Pin-Like "Planks".

132 *Converting Theory into Action*

back and then one side-other side. As they do so, I emphasize total body integration by evoking *Shape Qualities: Rising-Sinking, Advancing-Retreating, Spreading-Enclosing.*

Inversions

Figure 8.2 Inversions.

Next, they explore "inverted" undercurves. They add *condensing* while shifting the weight from one foot to the other and *inverting* while transferring the weight to their hands, so that both feet leave the floor when they have traveled away from the starting location in the space. They transfer the weight from their hands back to one foot as they return to the starting location, while also returning the spine Successively to vertical.

They explore three different directional variations:

a   traveling forward/back (with both legs Arcing on the inversion, one reaching upward and the other at 90 degrees toward the back);
b   traveling diagonally forward/diagonally back (with the leading leg flexing at the knee and the other leg Arcing upward on the inversion); and
c   traveling to the side (with the hands on the earth, the tail reaching upward and both feet reaching downward—a "pike" position—on the inversion).

It is important to explore the different directional pelvic shifts (sagittal, diagonal and lateral) because each requires unique body organization. I point out that the head usually reaches upward with Lightness when we are standing, but that it changes its relationship to gravity and hangs or reaches downward with Heaviness when we invert. To prevent shoulder-girdle injuries, I encourage dancers to Yield elastically to the earth through their hands and avoid locking the midlimbs. By condensing fully, they discover that their hands are so close to the floor by the time they shift from lower to upper that there is little strain or harsh impact in their upper bodies. Over a few weeks, most dancers develop increased strength and coordination and start to feel confident being upside down.

The final phrase of the dance begins with a descending spiral into a sitting Ball, that rolls on the sitz bones before the weight returns to both feet in a small standing Ball, and ends with a Successive return to a vertical Pin. (The descent begins with a quarter turn toward the "side" of the space as they shift into the spiral. In the sitting/rolling Ball, they fold the back leg under the front. For the standing return from Ball into Pin, they face the original direction.)

By the end of the whole undercurve-inversion dance, students have experienced going from foot to hands, hands to foot, foot to sitz bones and sitz bones to feet. Once they feel comfortable in this investigation, I invite them to improvise different versions of it and play spontaneously with various kinds of undercurves, inversions and rolls.

134 *Converting Theory into Action*

> **FOR YOUR CONSIDERATION:**
>
> If you try to condense your whole body without fully flexing your hip joints, are you able to become really small?
>
> If inversions are part of your classroom or choreographic movement language, how do you prepare students to explore them safely and knowledgeably?

80 Overcurves

Often, the Strong and Free momentum of an undercurve morphs or into the Light, Bound Sustainment of an overcurve. Overcurve weight shifts take us up-and-over through *relevé-piqué* or through *jeté, sauté, pas de chat* or other kinds of traveling leaps and hops. At the top of each of these arcs, we can experience delicacy or buoyancy, which emanates from the *Center of Levity*, the volume of internal space behind the sternum in the upper thorax.

We transition from Strong Weight, through Neutral Weight, through Light Weight and then back to grounded Weight, as we go

Figure 8.3 Undercurve-Overcurve Cycle.

down-and-under to prepare for and complete the up-and-over. Each undercurve-overcurve cycle develops muscular strength in the feet, ankles and legs and continuity in level changes. Each cycle involves a sequence of plié-undercurve weight shift-relevé-overcurve-weight shift-piqué-plié; or plié-undercurve weight shift-leap or hop-airborne overcurve-weight shift-plié.

If the undercurve-overcurve cycle is efficient and supported by breath and organic Weight Affinities, energy rises from the pelvis through the abdomen to the Center of Lightness, from which it radiates upward as the mover lingers buoyantly. It then continues back through the abdomen and returns to the Center of Gravity in the lowest part of the pelvis as the dancer returns to a grounded plié.

In my classes, we regularly explore full undercurve-overcurve pelvic cycles in the Wheel plane (e.g., forward-up-back-down or back-up-forward-down), Door plane (e.g., side-up-side-down), and through the Diagonals of the Cube (e.g., low corner-up-high corner-down). We savor the independent rotations and counterrotations of the pelvic halves as we transfer the weight from one foot to the other in both undercurves and overcurves.

FOR YOUR CONSIDERATION:

I invite you to play with dance "steps" that take you through space as overcurves. Could you describe the role of undercurves in preparing for and transitioning out of such movements?

I invite you to perform overcurves without letting yourself experience Light Weight coming from behind the sternum at the top of the arc, and then to repeat them with an emphasis on energy pouring out from the Center of Lightness as you reach the top. Can you compare and contrast your experiences?

---

81 Playing with Possibilities/Improvising to Learn Technique

I try to notice and validate the unique strengths, dispositions and expressive qualities of each individual, while also helping all students develop a deeper understanding of the anatomy, kinesiology and movement possibilities that unite us all. The combination of self-knowledge and scientific/theoretical movement knowledge can be empowering because it prepares dancers to adapt to the styles of movement that interest them. Such adaptability enables dancers to bring their unique selves to the phrase-work given in auditions, and many of today's choreographers seek dancers who can combine and blend accuracy and spontaneity, who can reveal personal uniqueness during the process of learning and performing specific choreography.

One strategy I have developed to help dancers bring themselves to other peoples' movement is including several opportunities for *improvisation* around set phrases in each technique class. Thoughtfully-guided and playful improvisation can facilitate the development of personal expressivity, which I consider an important aspect of dance technique. It can be convenient to think of technique and expressivity as two separate things, but I am convinced that learning to dance means developing expressive skills as well as purely physical abilities. I suggest that we think of everything we investigate in our classes as "technique," including efficient body function, muscular strength, endurance, flexibility, aerobic fitness, expressivity, musicality, phrasing and revelation of personal attributes.

After modeling a new movement pattern, I invite students to move with me as I explain the expressive, theoretical and/or kinesiological concepts I investigated in composing it. I encourage dancers to learn the material I design for them as accurately and clearly as possible (modifying it if necessary to accommodate personal needs). Then I invite them to spontaneously reorganize it and have serious fun by spontaneously enlivening the pattern with their individual gifts, aptitudes, body attitudes and phrasing preferences.

Usually, I begin by asking dancers to change the timing of a phrase, then the Effort/movement qualities, then the sequence, then to leave portions out and repeat others, and finally to improvise freely around whatever they find most satisfying and/or challenging in the pattern I taught them. I encourage approaching these improvisations in a spirit of play, rather than judging themselves or trying to be interesting or "right." Through such improvisations, most students learn to more deeply understand the challenges and nuances of my underlying movement patterns, while also discovering something special about themselves.

By freely exploring the ideas embedded in choreographed phrases, students begin to understand that movement concepts can be investigated in many different frameworks, and that they can take ownership of their application of such ideas in innumerable ways. As they recognize the personal relevance of movement concepts beyond the structure of my investigations, they become empowered to participate more fully in the generation of new knowledge throughout their structured and unstructured experiences, and to more fully become co-creators of the material they explore in other technique classes and rehearsals.

> **FOR YOUR CONSIDERATION:**
>
> How would you define the term "technique" in dance?
> If you recall the first time a teacher asked you to improvise in technique class, what were your reactions?
> How could or do you offer improvisational explorations to students as a way of developing technique and personal agency?

82 Exploring Polar Opposites

By including a range of possibilities in each topic I introduce, I offer *variety* to those participating in my classes. It seems to me that Laban, Bartenieff, Mabel Todd, Margaret H'Doubler, Lulu Sweigard, Moshe Feldenkrais, Frederick Matthias Alexander and other somatic pioneers all came to the conclusion that people need variety. Variety offers the possibility of proportional balance, and balance can foster efficient function and physical, emotional and spiritual well-being.

In L/BMS, we often frame movement inquiries as *explorations of opposites*, recognizing that things are at least partially defined by what they are not. In rehearsals, I frequently ask dancers to explore an opposite quality or image of one they might be struggling to embody because by figuring out what it is not, they are more likely to understand what it is. I point out that there are always many possibilities along the spectrum between any two dualities. We can explore several options between two (or among three) contrasting extremes to better understand some of the multitude of choices available to us.

I enjoy designing classes that include polar opposites (and at least some of the many possibilities between them) including: function-expression, exertion-recuperation, mobility-stability, Coping Efforts-Indulging Efforts, inner-outer, contents-container, Growing-Shrinking, expanding-condensing, small-large, outward rotation-inward rotation, strength-flexibility, strong force-gentle force, set phrases-improvisation, evocative imagery-analytical imagery, fast tempi-slow tempi, musical rhythms-breath rhythms, part-whole, individual-group, simple-complex, amorphous-crystalline, activities-experiences and many more.

138 *Converting Theory into Action*

Three-fold possibilities include: inner space-kinespheric space-general space, near space-mid-space-far space, front-back-side kinespheric space, Central-Peripheral-Transverse Approaches to the Kinesphere and one-, two-, and three-dimensional pathways in space.

FOR YOUR CONSIDERATION:

I invite you to make your own list of opposites that you encourage students to explore. How could you emphasize that there are many possibilities along the spectrum from one end of such dualities to the other?

I invite you to choose five dualities or three-fold possibilities and focus on each as the theme for a lesson plan.

---

83 Playing with Weight Centers

To help students find dynamic variation and movement efficiency, I guide them into explorations of three different centers in the body, from which they can move actively or passively.

Note: Please see Appendix F, Movement Qualities, for more information on this topic.

In L/BMS we refer to the lowest part of the pelvis as the *Center of Gravity* or the *Center of Strength*. Qualitative Strength has an Affinity for downward or Sinking movement. When we move actively from the pelvic floor, we access our power, groundedness and/or forcefulness. When we move passively from this center, we become Heavy or weighed down.

L/BMS considers the upper thorax, the area behind the sternum, to be the *Center of Levity or Lightness*. Lightness has an affinity for upward or Rising movement. When we move actively from this center, we access our delicacy, gentleness or buoyancy. When we move passively from this center, we become Limp, wilted or lifeless.

I consider the area behind the navel to be the *Center of Neutral Weight*, neither forceful nor gentle. Moving from this center diminishes both Strength and Lightness, and allows other expressive qualities (Free-Bound, Indirect-Direct, Sustained-Sudden) to resonate more fully.

Moving with organic *Effort and Shape affinities* makes movement efficient and coherent with the laws of physics, satisfying expectations. To do so, we can play with simultaneously embodying the following: Rising with Lightness, Sinking with Strength; Spreading with Indirectness, Enclosing with Directness; Retreating with Suddenness, Advancing with Sustainment.

Moving with *Effort and Shape disaffinities* makes movement more surprising or startling, awakening curiosity. To do so, we can play with embodying the following: Rising with Strength, Sinking with Lightness; Spreading with Directness, Enclosing with Indirectness; Retreating with Sustainment, Advancing with Suddenness. Even simple movements can become surprisingly vibrant and compelling when explored through unexpected combinations of Weight and Shape Qualities.

To find variety for our students, we need not always create entirely new movement patterns; instead, we might play with the qualities of Strength, Lightness or Weight Neutrality, or with passive rather than active weight, and with affined or dis-affined Shape Qualities within a pattern we have already shared with our students. An existing dance can take on a whole new life when explored through different attitudes toward Effort and Shape.

> **FOR YOUR CONSIDERATION:**
>
> I invite you to select an excerpt from a dance you have choreographed or performed and then consciously add a variety of inner attitudes toward your investment of Weight as you perform it. If weight qualities are already important in your dance, could you change them to contrasting Efforts? Could you consciously pair both affined and dis-affined Weight and Shape Qualities and then describe your experience?

84 Shrinking Is as Important as Growing

I often hear teachers tell their students to be "longer, bigger or taller," but I seldom hear requests to "condense or become smaller." L/BMS tells us that all human movement is basically Growing and Shrinking, and that, as I mentioned in essay 82, we can often understand something more clearly by investigating its polar opposite.

What is more important, inhalation or exhalation? Would we continuously ask our students to inhale and never exhale? That, in effect, is what we are saying if we only ask students to become longer or make their movement larger. The filling and emptying cycle of the lungs is the support for expanding and condensing throughout the whole body. Clearly, our well-being depends equally on both Shrinking and Growing.

By encouraging students to become as small as possible, we can help balance the one-sided messages they receive elsewhere in their training. They can explore full breath support and discover and replace tension-holding patterns that might have resulted from a continuous focus on being long and could be prohibiting their ability to fully condense. Such blockages cause diminished mobility, lack of force absorption and possible injury. By becoming as small as possible, they can access the deeper, smaller muscles, closer to the bone, which might be unavailable if they always focus on the larger, more superficial muscles that we use to expand. By encouraging them to Shrink or condense as well as to expand or Grow, we are inviting students to explore and experience more of themselves. We gain greater access to our largest range of movement when we also explore our smallest.

FOR YOUR CONSIDERATION:

Could you watch a video of a dance work that significantly includes both Growing/expanding and Shrinking/condensing material and ask yourself which, if either, you aesthetically or kinesthetically prefer? If you have a preference, how do you think it came about?

Does the movement material you ask your students to explore include opportunities for becoming small as well as large?

---

85 The Interdependence of Mobility and Stability

One of our primary tasks is helping students embody both specificity and ease. Clarity of form without adaptability leads to brittleness and limited expressivity, while mobility without control produces amorphousness. Both could lead to injuries. A primary theme in L/BMS is *mobility and stability*. We needn't choose only one or the other; there is a lively interplay between these two interdependent conditions, which are equally important to humans moving. Since we change continuously throughout the organism, power is only truly useful to us if it is malleable.

Converting Theory into Action 141

When we notice our breath on a cellular level and connect to gravity with the sense of an open body wall, we claim our stability without sacrificing mobility. Bonding to the earth with full breath support, while imaging a permeable outer surface, makes us resilient as we move through fluid inner pathways of connectivity into clear spatial lines and forms. We become alternately or simultaneously mobile and stable.

The lower body-half in humans is constructed primarily for stability, and the upper body-half for mobility. That characteristic distinguishes us from other animals and accounts for the fact that we have been able to interact with one another and with the environment in such a variety of ways. Lower stability clearly supports upper mobility but upper stability can also support lower mobility. Modern, contemporary and hip-hop dancers often develop more lower-body mobility and more upper-body stability than the normal population. That means that we can experience overuse or misuse injuries more frequently than others, and that we must be particularly aware of maintaining healthy functioning as we push ourselves beyond ordinary capacities.

In L/BMS, we investigate *Mobile and Stable States*. It is believed that a person can access stability through a combination of clear attitudes toward Space and Weight. That is, I could experience a Stable State through the dual qualities of Direct-Strong, Direct-Light, Indirect-Strong or Indirect-Light. A person can access a Mobile State through a combination of clear attitudes toward Flow and Time, through the dual qualities of Free-Sudden, Free-Sustained, Bound-Sudden or Bound-Sustained. We can fluctuate between these two States seamlessly or embody them at the same time in different parts of ourselves.

Note: Please see Appendix F, Movement Qualities, for more information.

FOR YOUR CONSIDERATION:

When have you sensed simultaneous stability and mobility within your body? Have you ever experienced one but felt unable to access the other?

Could you formulate three sentences you could say to help a student develop a balance of mobility and stability?

86 Quantitative or Qualitative Strength and Flexibility

There is an important distinction between *quantitative strength*, which might be measured by how many pounds a person can lift, and the *quality of Strength*, which is determined by how grounded, forceful and adaptable a person can be. There is an equally important distinction between how passively flexible a person might be (*static range of motion*) and the amount of flexibility they can control and use (*functional range of motion*).

Many teachers make strengthening and stretching primary training goals. However, strong muscles, slippery fascia and flexible joints are only the beginning of a dancer's quest. Other factors are more important than either quantitative strength or flexibility to our success as movers. It is through focused inner awareness, appropriate intent, efficient anatomical functioning, total body coordination and effective phrasing of myofascial sequencing that dancers are able to fully utilize their power and range of motion.

Dancers are able to maximize mobility/flexibility and stability/strength by releasing excess tension, establishing a reciprocal energy relationship with the earth, allowing breath to flow freely throughout the body and permitting organic bone and muscle rhythms to happen without interruption. When stabilizing ourselves by connecting fluidly to gravity or levity, and mobilizing ourselves by riding our breath and balancing the workload among our small and large muscles, we become integrated and high-functioning humans moving.

FOR YOUR CONSIDERATION:

Can you remember an instance when efficiency and rhythmic coordination were more important that sheer strength in helping you or another dancer accomplish a movement task?

Can you remember an instance where a highly-coordinated person lacked the quantitative strength or flexibility to accomplish a movement task?

When you reflect on your own pedagogical practice, what ideas and language concerning quantitative and qualitative strength and flexibility do you share with students?

87 Recuperating without Stopping

I usually feel refreshed and regenerated rather than exhausted after a vigorous movement session. For more than five decades, I have tried to balance *Coping Efforts* (Bound, Strong, Sudden and Direct) and *Indulging* movement qualities (Free, Light, Sustained and Indirect) in my dancing. *Balancing exertion and recuperation* is a primary L/BMS theme. When our movement choices include a *variety* of the ways in which we change the body's form, express inner attitudes, relate to space and embody Patterns of Total Body Organization, we give ourselves the ability to keep going for long periods of time without feeling spent or worn-out.

Performing is the primary reason I have stayed in dance. I feel fully alive when on stage in a way that I experience at no other time. From my early 30s through my early 70s, I toured through many parts of the world performing more than a thousand solo concerts, which usually included eight or nine different works. I was onstage for as long as two hours, dancing and then talking to the audience during costume changes. I am beyond grateful that the built-in recuperations resulting from the way I liked to design and phrase movement allowed me to enjoy an unusually long performing career.

My friend Annie Dwyer[2] recently sent me this note:

> I often reflect on the realization you shared that you can recuperate by doing something different and not just by stopping. This continues to be a key component of how I frame my life flow. You see, you are providing a framework for dancing and for living.

People often remark that I am unusually active and vigorous for a person of my age. As Annie says, the knowledge that I can recuperate by changing the kind and quality of exertion, not necessarily by "resting" or stopping, pervades my life as well as my dancing and has allowed me to still do what I love as I enjoy my 83rd journey around the sun.

A practice of "going in to go out" balances the Shrinking and Growing aspects of dancing and provides ongoing recovery from the hard work of dancing. When choreographic phrases include frequent *condensing* moments, during which dancers can check into breath, core aliveness and inner sensation, they are able to move vigorously without experiencing undue fatigue. These going-in moments can transition into *expanding* moments, during which dancers connect through the edges of the kinesphere into the larger space.

Of course, there are times when actual physical rest will serve us better than anything else, and it is wise to honor the body's requests for such cessation of physical exertion. At such times, I practice what Eric Franklin calls "mental simulation of movement." The area of the cerebral cortex involved in execution of voluntary movement is activated when we imagine ourselves doing something at about 30% of the level observed during actual performance. We can improve physical skill and coordination by seeing ourselves move fully and efficiently in the mind's eye.

> **FOR YOUR CONSIDERATION:**
>
> How could you provide recuperation through movement in your classes?
> How could you balance exertion and recuperation in your non-dancing life?
> Do you encourage students to employ mental simulation of movement?

88 Spatial Imagery—Tensions, Pulls and Intents

I like to differentiate between *Spatial Tension* and *muscle tension*. Spatial Tension is created by moving in such a way that lines, arcs or volumes are felt by the dancer (and perceived by the observer) to exist in the space beyond the body. When embodying Spatial Tensions, we can distribute the workload throughout our kinetic chains with a resilient balance of concentric and eccentric muscle contractions.[3] Muscle tension is created when muscles continue to shorten (or hold) longer than the mover intended. Such isometric contractions, which generate force without movement, can diminish mobility, resilience and Flow. When we offer clear *spatial imagery* to students, they can imagine and experience Spatial Tensions and Pulls and embody *Spatial Intents* that provide visual clarity without sacrificing muscular resilience.

A *Spatial Pull* has two ends: a reach and a counter-reach. If I invite students to reach a part of their bodies toward Right Forward Middle, for example, I can also ask that they sense the counter-reach of one or more other body parts toward the equal-opposite direction in the kinesphere, which in this instance would be Left Back Middle. Encouraging students to discover vibrant Pulls and Counter-Pulls will help them connect their inner pathways of Flow and connectivity to points in their kinesphere and the general space beyond. This *inner-outer* integration enables both spatial clarity and muscular aliveness.

Note: Please consult Figure 7.13. L/BMS Directional Symbols.

Converting Theory into Action 145

Spatial Intent can organize the neuromusculoskeletal system for integrated movement in which all body parts contribute to the clarity of the whole organism. If we give instructions that are *action-oriented*, rather than position-oriented, students can embody continuously changing processes rather than assume static shapes. For example, "reaching," "being pulled," and "dropping" are thoughts that can dynamically integrate the whole body into a process through which Spatial Pulls are experienced and Spatial Tensions are revealed.

Directional Matrix

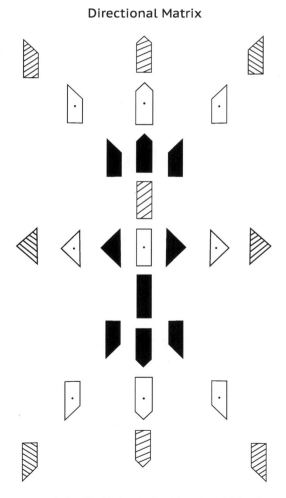

Figure 8.4 L/BMS Symbols, Directional Matrix.

146   *Converting Theory into Action*

To provide biomechanical and expressive variety, I consciously select a balance of one-, two- and three-dimensional pathways through the kinesphere when creating the several movement explorations I plan to include in each class. I give students clear guidance regarding the body's relationship to the kinesphere to streamline the coordination and efficiency of their dancing. L/BMS gives us the *Directional Matrix*, an identification of 26 directions radiating from the center (Place Middle). I find it a profoundly useful tool for spatial specificity and clarity.

For example, I might say:

a   "The right hand is being pulled toward Right Side Middle and the left hand is being pulled toward Left Side Middle" (one-dimensional or linear);
b   then, I might say that "The top of the head and both arms are reaching toward Right Side High, while the left foot is counter-reaching toward Left Side High" (two-dimensional or planar);
c   next, I might say that "The tail bone is dropping toward Place Low as the spine and arms create a descending spiral around the vertical axis" (three-dimensional); and
d   finally, I could say that "The right arm and top of the head are reaching toward Right Back High as the left arm, left foot and tail bone counter-reach to Left Forward Low" (three-dimensional or true diagonal).

Note: Please see Directional Matrix/One, Two or Three-Dimensional Pathways through the Kinesphere in Appendix G (2).

FOR YOUR CONSIDERATION:

I invite you to select a movement phrase you enjoy dancing and teaching. As you unpack it, can you find at least four moments where you could call attention to an existing or potential Spatial Pull-Counter Pull? How does revealing existing or potential Spatial Pulls alter your experience of the phrase?

I invite you to create a short dance around the idea of clear Spatial Intent, including one-, two- and three-dimensional spatial journeys. Then, without losing the clarity of Spatial Intent, I invite you to unpack, refine and enrich your dance by adding Free or Bound Flow, Light, Strong or Neutral Weight and/or Sustained or Sudden Time. What did you learn from those explorations?

89 Changing It up Spatially

The Space area of L/BMS theoretical inquiry is also known as *Space Harmony*. That name was inspired by Plato, who hypothesized in one of his dialogues that the classical elements of earth, water, air and fire are composed of five polyhedral crystalline forms. We refer to these forms as *Platonic Solids: Tetrahedron, Hexahedron (or Cube), Octahedron, Icosahedron* or *Dodecahedron*. When we move while imaging and sensing our relationship to one or more of these solids, we can understand Plato's belief that human beings are part of a universal order.

To help humans move fully and harmoniously with the natural world, Laban created different "Scales." A Scale is a movement progression through a sequence of locations in the kinesphere that we can practice to explore a variety of possibilities and gain enhanced mindbody potential. Each Scale requires us to visualize and kinesthetically sense our personal space as dimensions, planes or one of the Platonic Solids. In the planes and solids, each of the *vertices* or corners exerts a unique Spatial Pull. Each Scale responds to a different sequence of those Pulls and takes us on a unique journey through the kinesphere.

Note: To learn more about these scales, please read Space Harmony: Basic Terms (Revised Edition), by Cecily Dell and Aileen Crow.

The most basic Scale is called Dimensional or Defense. It invites us to explore one-dimensional or linear movement in the *Three Cardinal Dimensions* (vertical, horizontal and sagittal), what Laban called the Dimensional Cross of Axes. We explore the dimensions one at a time with Spoke-Like reaches. Starting in Place Middle (right hand leading), the sequence is:

a   Place High (Place Middle), Place Low (Place Middle)—vertical dimension,
b   Side Across (Place Middle), Side Open (Place Middle)—horizontal dimension,
c   Back Middle (Place Middle), Forward Middle—sagittal dimension.
    We can also notice the Effort and Shape Qualities that come alive (are affined) to this journey through space, and we can explore the scale through these words and thoughts:
d   Rising with Lightness-Sinking with Strength—vertical dimension,
e   Enclosing with Directness-Spreading with Indirectness—horizontal dimension,
f   Retreating with Suddenness-Advancing with Sustainment—sagittal dimension.

I have explored all the Laban-designed Scales, and they have brought me a cherished variety of movement experiences that have helped me get out of my personal movement ruts, enrich my movement vocabulary and awaken and embody more of my movement potential than I would have otherwise.

I expect that one of Laban's motivations for creating his Scales, particularly those that explore the Icosahedron (which has 20 triangular faces or surfaces and 12 vertices or corners) and the Cube (which has six square surfaces and eight corners), was the realization that the theatre dance of his time had a pronounced preference for one- and two-dimensional movement (lines and planes). When I observe the full access to space seen in children playing or in adults engaged in many sports (soccer, tennis or frisbee for example), I am reminded that formally-trained dancers in many traditional styles seldom have structured opportunities to venture into the dynamic realm of three-dimensional and off-vertical movement that can be explored in Laban's Icosahedral and Diagonal Scales.

I am now learning that we create healthy fascia by moving our whole bodies regularly in many different directions or pathways. The one-, two- and three-dimensional pathways of the multiple sequences of directions through the kinesphere we can experience when exploring Laban's Scales provide the kinds and variety of movement that well-functioning fascia requires. Without realizing it until recently, I have been conditioning my fascia in this manner for the past several decades. This realization helps explain the relative youthfulness of my body as an octogenarian. Franklin Method training includes a series of multi-directional movement patterns performed in rhythms that maximize myofascial recoil (or rebound) called "fasciasize." When I try it, I feel right at home.

It is easy for us teachers to get stuck in our favorite spatial sequences because they make us feel at home and reassure us that we are accomplished dancers. However, if we change things up spatially, if we leave our comfort zones and explore spatial sequences and pathways unfamiliar to us, we might be able to help ourselves and the students we teach create new synapses in our neuromuscular systems and, I believe, provide new possibilities in other aspects of our lives as well. I encourage every movement teacher to consider including a variety of one- (linear), two- (planar, diametral) and three-dimensional (spiral, diagonal, off-vertical) experiences in every class, for every student population.

Note: Please see Directional Matrix/One, Two or Three-Dimensional Pathways through the Kinesphere, in Appendix G (2).

> **FOR YOUR CONSIDERATION:**
>
> I invite you to mentally rewind and replay a class you recently taught or took. As you travel through it in your mind's eye, what different relationships to the space of your kinesphere do you notice? Can you pinpoint one-, two- and three-dimensional pathways (lines, planes, three-dimensional diagonals and spirals) through the kinesphere?

Notes

1 Kristin Torok, MFA, CET, is a former member of Bellingham, Washington's Dance Gallery, a Certified Laban Movement Analyst and a dance, Pilates and Gyrotonic teacher who has studied with me almost every summer for the last quarter century. In 2003, she joined the first cohort of Certified Evans Teacher candidates for four summers of workshops in Port Townsend, Washington. She was a dancer in a full-length version of my work *Velorio* to the complete *Requiem* by Gabriel Fauré, a major choreographic and performance project in Seattle in 1994, with live orchestra and chorus in Meany Hall at the University of Washington. I thank Kristin for the many ways in which she has inspired me and others.
2 Annie Dwyer, director of dance at Carolina Friends School in Durham, North Carolina, was the first artist/educator to be named an Honorary Certified Evans Teacher, in 2014. She weaves dancing, somatics, writing, and community-building creative processes in her classes for lower, middle and upper school students and provides transformative experiences for nearly everyone she teaches.
3 In concentric contractions, agonist muscle filaments slide closer together and muscles bulge, as they generate force. In eccentric contractions, antagonist muscle filaments slide apart, as the lengthening muscle responds to a greater force of the agonist.

Reference

Franklin, Eric. *Dynamic Alignment through Imagery*. 2nd ed., Human Kinetics, 2012.

IX Assessment and Variety

90 Formative and Summative Feedback

More than 25 years ago, to better serve the individual needs and interests of the people enrolled in my university dance major courses, I decided to learn more about their backgrounds and personal experiences in the classes I was offering. So, I started asking them to write me several informal letters each semester. I have continued the practice. I read each letter within a day or two of receiving it, answer questions, offer suggestions and return it as soon as possible.

In the first letter, they share what they consider pertinent biographical information and their reasons for enrolling. In the second letter, they identify at least three personal goals for our course and explain why they are significant. In the third, they chart their progress toward their goals, ask me questions about issues that have emerged and perhaps identify one or more additional goals. In the final letter, they reflect on changes they have made and describe any short- or long-range goals for the future that have become meaningful.

The first three letters give me opportunities to provide *formative feedback*. That is, students can consider my comments and respond to them while there is still course-time ahead of us and they are still in the process of generating knowledge based on our shared investigations. My response to the final letter contains *summative feedback*. That is, I sum up my perceptions of a student's overall achievements during the semester just ended and also make suggestions for possible future goals. Both formative and summative assessment are useful, but sometimes busy teachers forget to offer evaluative feedback while the student still has time to consider and act on it before the course has ended.

Michael Scriven is a British-born Australian academic philosopher, best known for his contributions to the theory and practice of evaluation. He coined the terms "formative and summative assessment" in a 1967 journal article titled, *The Methodology of Evaluation*. Since that time, those useful concepts have been embraced by numerous educators, including Don Halquist, who shared them in one of his BETI (Bill Evans Teachers Intensive) pedagogy courses many years ago.

Responding to the letters is a time-consuming task, but it is worth it. Because students are reflecting on their explorations and interactions, and wrapping words around them, the letters help them *write their way to understanding* their processes and discoveries. I learn more about who they are, how they are interpreting what I have shared with them, and the meanings they derive from our experiences.

I find that I sometimes make assumptions about students based on my misreading of outward appearances. By understanding what thoughts and feelings are behind their body language, I can offer learning strategies and opportunities that are suited to particular needs or challenges. Most significantly, the insights I gain by reading the letters enable me to structure more relevant classes and give more meaningful group and individual feedback than would otherwise be possible.

FOR YOUR CONSIDERATION:

How do you find out who students are and what they want and need from your teaching?

Could you describe examples of how you might provide both formative and summative feedback?

---

91 Assessment Dialogues

Inspired by experiences I enjoyed in the 1996-97 Integrated Movement Studies Certification Program conducted by Peggy Hackney, Janice Meaden and Pam Schick, I almost always ask students to select a course-long "study-buddy" with whom they work in and out of class to support progress toward and accomplishment of personal goals. For me, a significant component of the study-buddy process is a *three-person dialogue or conference* that takes place just after mid-term.

For this conversation, we sit in a triangular formation. Each buddy answers question one, then each answers question two, and then I respond to those questions. Then each answers question three, after which I respond:

a   Question 1: "What specific skills and aptitudes that help your buddy succeed did you notice at the beginning of the semester?"
b   Question 2: "What specific positive changes have you observed your buddy make toward personal goals in this course?"
c   Question 3: "What specific goals do you suggest your buddy might consider for the remainder of the semester, and/or beyond?"

I find that most students are surprised by what their buddy and I affirm as skills and aptitudes they brought with them. This information usually elicits the most discussion, and it almost always heightens the described student's self-confidence and engagement in subsequent classes. We often take our gifts and skills for granted, and it can be a powerful boost to self-esteem and self-awareness when someone we trust recognizes and validates our personal dispositions and abilities.

I don't share the questions in advance, nor do I plan ahead of time what I will say. Instead, I give each student my undivided attention while they speak, and memories of their participation in our classes come pouring into my consciousness, along with affirmations and suggestions I can honestly share. The give-and-take of these dialogues helps participants *talk their way to understanding* thoughts and feelings that had previously been amorphous or had escaped their conscious awareness.

I have discovered that students will say things in a confidential letter they would not to say in person, and also that realizations come up spontaneously in the face-to-face conversations that we would not have known about otherwise. I find that the combination of the letters referred to in the essay above and this mid-course conference enhances communication between students and their learning partners and between students and me.

FOR YOUR CONSIDERATION:

How could you organize assessment dialogues or conferences with students in a current or future teaching situation?

What might you hope to accomplish in such a face-to-face conversation?

If you have participated in such a conference yourself, as either a student or a teacher, could you describe its impact?

92 Study-Buddy Choreography

The culmination of the study-buddy process occurs in the final "exam," which involves the performance by each student of a solo choreographed by their learning partner. The piece is not assessed on choreographic inventiveness or originality; it is successful if it provides a vehicle for the performer to reach toward relevant goals as well as reveal existing gifts and strengths.

When the piece is shared with classmates, the choreographer introduces it, pointing out goals that guided its creation and sharing highlights of the process. The dancer speaks after performing, describing how she/he/they confronted and made progress toward personal goals and the knowledge generated by doing so.

We can't get better at something we refuse to confront, and it can be exciting to enter unknown territory and begin to feel at home within it. Both buddies learn that growth takes place only when a person leaves her/his/their comfort zone. They come to understand that the benefit of this project comes from meeting a challenge they may have been avoiding. They are able to reflect on the fact that technique class is not an end in itself; rather, it is a laboratory where meaningful knowledge can be pursued and accomplishments celebrated.

> **FOR YOUR CONSIDERATION:**
>
> I invite you to create a short choreographic study for yourself in which you confront one technical/expressive challenge that will force you out of your comfort zone, surrounded by movement material that you feel you already perform well. Perhaps you could repeat that process several times in the coming year.

93 Assessment Improvisations across the Floor

The letters, conferences and culminating solos described above serve as assessment instruments. Without resorting to standardized questionnaires, which I sometimes find minimally valuable, I can gain significant insights into what students are deriving from my classes, and what progress they have made toward relevant goals from these projects. Another form of authentic assessment I like to use is the *across-the-floor improv*.

A few times a semester, instead of designing a movement investigation for the dancing-through-space portion of the lesson, I will ask students to spontaneously reflect on what we've explored that day (or perhaps that week), select a few of those concepts or movement phrases, and improvise freely on their choices as they move across the floor of the studio.

Most dancers feel more at ease if I ask them to go two at a time, rather than all by themselves. They usually move with music, which they can respond to or ignore as they wish. I ordinarily invite them to cross the floor several times, revisiting the same material each time or adding or subtracting material in each crossing.

This can be a form of non-verbal evaluation of my teaching and their learning. It is fascinating and instructive to see which of the patterns and concepts we've explored rise to the top of each student's consciousness. I learn significantly by seeing what people retain from what I shared, how they interpret it and how they can make it their own. If they struggle with material or its underlying concepts, I know that I need to unpack it more clearly in future classes. If they are able to embody a pattern or underlying concept fully, I know that my teaching strategies were probably successful. If no one chooses some of the investigations I shared, I will try to figure out why. Did I not reveal their relevance sufficiently? Did I spend too little time on them? Or, for what other reason did those parts of my class have less aliveness for students than those they selected? These questions provide useful food for thought as I reflect on my teaching and try to make it more relevant to students' needs and interests.

FOR YOUR CONSIDERATION:

If you were required to create a course-evaluation questionnaire, what might you ask?

Besides standardized questionnaires, what forms of assessment have you found (or imagine you might find) useful?

94 The Spice of Life

"Variety's the very spice of life, that gives it all its flavour," wrote 18th century English poet William Cowper. I agree more wholeheartedly with that sentiment as each year passes. People need variety to be well and satisfied, to be fully alive. By offering multiple or diverse inroads to the explorations we undertake in each class, each week of classes and each semester, we can help students embrace their curiosity to develop or refine skills through which they might enjoy healthy and meaningful lives.

It is important to begin by guiding students toward recognition of the fact that they are OK just as they are. They deserve to know that they are not broken and don't need to be fixed, that they have already developed skills and generated knowledge that will serve them throughout their lives. It is equally important that we encourage them to build on who they are and to savor the excitement of exploring a multitude of new ideas and experiences. If I, their teacher, show a willingness to leave my own realm of comfort, rather than always indulging in the safety of things I like to do and feel I do well, I will model a kind of risk-taking through which they might discover new possibilities for themselves.

So, two large goals I try always to keep in mind are:

a   first, that students will learn to more deeply understand, appreciate and share their unique selves—the inherited aptitudes and already-acquired skills that make them who they are; and

b   second, that they will develop an appetite for risk-taking, uncertainty and new experiences through which they could potentially learn something that calls out to them or they don't yet even know exists.

As Irmgard Bartenieff is famous for saying, "There are many possibilities." If you look back through these essays, you will see suggestions for approaching your teaching through a variety of strategies or inroads. I hope you will consider and perhaps try out these ideas as I have presented them. Of course, you might disagree with some or many of my points of view. If so, you might use the ideas I have shared as food for thought or jumping-off points from which you could explore your own teaching methods, materials and guidelines.

FOR YOUR CONSIDERATION:

How do you encourage students to recognize positive attributes they already possess?

When were you last willing to leave your comfort zone and let students or peers see you struggle?

Could you describe at least four ways in which you could offer multiple inroads to movement explorations to current or future students, or to yourself?

Reference

Scriven, Michael. *The Methodology of Evaluation*. Purdue Univ., 1966.

X Teaching Dance through The Multiple Intelligences
Don Halquist, guest author

> Don Halquist, PhD, CET, is a specialist in early childhood education, a former professor and chair of Education at SUNY Brockport, a former professor and dean of Education at Rhode Island College, a member of the Bill Evans Dance Company since 1985, a long-time teacher in the Bill Evans Teachers Intensives and currently a second-grade teacher at Salish Coast Elementary School in Port Townsend, Washington. Don met Evans when he took a workshop in Evans Technique at Allegheny College in Meadville, Pennsylvania in 1984. They have been life partners since 1985 and legal spouses since 2009. Don first learned of the Multiple Intelligences as a master's student at the University of New Mexico. He first brought MI Theory to the Bill Evans Teachers Intensives in 1999.

The Theory of Multiple Intelligences was developed in 1983 by Dr. Howard Gardner, an American developmental psychologist and professor of cognition and education at Harvard University. It suggests that the traditional notion of intelligence based on I.Q. testing is far too limited. Instead, Dr. Gardner proposed eight different intelligences to account for a broader range of human potential in children and adults. These intelligences are: Linguistic Intelligence ("word smart"), Logical-Mathematical Intelligence ("number/reasoning smart"), Spatial Intelligence ("picture smart"), Bodily-Kinesthetic Intelligence ("movement smart"), Musical-Rhythmic Intelligence ("music smart"), Interpersonal Intelligence ("people smart"), Intrapersonal Intelligence ("self smart") and Naturalist Intelligence ("nature smart").

My work with Gardner's theory began in 1993 when I was teaching second grade. The theory resonated with me due to my background in art (my first degree is in graphic design) and dance (I had danced with Bill Evans for a number of years by this time) as well as my frustration with my own educational experiences, which often placed a higher premium on the verbal-linguistic and logical-mathematical ways of knowing.

For the next six years, I explored the work of Howard Gardner (1993, 1999), Thomas Armstrong (1994), David Lazear (1999), Bruce and Linda Campbell (1994) and others, with the intent of recognizing and honoring the "wholeness" of each of my students. I believe that each child's unique gifts, often overlooked in the craze of standardized testing, should be acknowledged and celebrated.

We esteem the highly articulate or logical people of our culture, and Dr. Gardner posits that our schools focus most of their attention on linguistic and logical-mathematical intelligences. However, he says that we should place equal attention on individuals who show gifts in the other intelligences: visual artists, architects, musicians, naturalists, designers, dancers, therapists, entrepreneurs and others who enrich the world in which we live. Unfortunately, many children who have these other gifts don't receive much reinforcement for them in school. Many of these kids, in fact, end up being labeled "learning disabled," "ADD (attention deficit disorder)" or simply underachievers when their unique ways of thinking and learning aren't addressed by a heavily linguistic or logical-mathematical focused classroom.

The Theory of Multiple Intelligences signals a need for a major transformation in the way our schools are run. It suggests that teachers should be trained to present their lessons in a wide variety of ways—using music, cooperative learning, art activities, role playing, multimedia, field trips, inner reflection and much more. MI Theory grabbed the attention of educators around the country, and hundreds of schools are currently using its philosophy to redesign the way it educates children.

The overview of each intelligence below draws intensively on the work of Gardner, Armstrong, Lazear, and the Campbells. The assessment ideas are designed to enable dance educators to explore dance concepts and vocabulary through a multiple intelligences framework.

1 Bodily-Kinesthetic Intelligence

The bodily-kinesthetic intelligence is the ability to use the body to express thoughts and feelings (as in dance and body language), to play a game (as in sports) or to create a new product (as in devising an invention). Learning by doing has long been recognized as an important part of education.

The elements of this intelligence are the abilities to control body movements with expertise, manipulate objects in a skillful way and create an attunement between the body and the mind, to create harmony between the two.

When we walk into a room or are talking to another person and have a "gut feeling" of what is really going on, our kinesthetic intelligence is at work. When we pick up a piece of clay or a paint brush and let our hands "speak" for us, that is kinesthesia. Often, we are not aware of what we are thinking or feeling or what we really know until we externalize it in some way. This external manifestation might take the form of painting, sketching, sculpture, manipulating objects, dance, mime, role-playing or some type of athletic expression. All of these are examples of the bodily-kinesthetic intelligence in action.

The bodily-kinesthetic intelligence is awakened through physical movement, as in various sports and physical exercises, as well as by the expression of oneself through the body, such as dance, drama and body language.

ASSESSMENT IDEAS:

Execute a variety of dance steps and movements.

Demonstrate musical concepts and forms with the body.

Show the physical embodiment of various choreographers' styles.

Create human tableaux and sculptures that show the meaning of a piece of poetry.

Choreograph an original dance to communicate an idea, belief, opinion or emotion.

---

2 Visual-Spatial Intelligence

The visual-spatial intelligence encapsulates the visual arts (including painting, drawing and sculpture); navigation, map-making and architecture (which involves the use of space and knowing how to get around in it); and games such as chess (which requires the ability to visualize objects from different perspectives and angles). The key sensory base of this intelligence is the sense of sight, but this intelligence is not limited to the ability to perceive things visually. According to Gardner (1983), a person who is blind can have a high level of visual-spatial intelligence, especially since the ability to create mental imagery is the other key element of this intelligence. There is evidence that the brain stores most information as holographic images. Having the ability to think in images, therefore, greatly enhances all of our other forms of intelligence.

The brain responds to a mental image just as if what is being imagined actually happened. Many world-class athletes and performing artists utilize this knowledge by rehearsing the perfect broad jump or dance routine over and over in their imaginations to augment their physical training. Imagined activities are invaluable tools in incorporating the multiple intelligences in the dance studio because such activities can include all eight intelligences easily.

The aesthetics of art is traditionally associated with the visual-spatial intelligence. These are things like the use of line, shape, balance, color, pattern, shading and space or the absence of space.

The visual-spatial intelligence is triggered by presenting the mind with or creating unusual delightful and colorful designs, patterns, shapes and pictures and engaging in visualization, guided imagery or pretending exercises.

ASSESSMENT IDEAS:

Express dance technique/choreographic motifs through drawing, painting and sculpture.

Recognize, reproduce and understand the artistic styles of a variety of choreographers.

Create an original composition using colors, patterns, designs and images to enhance its message.

---

3 The Musical-Rhythmic Intelligence

The musical-rhythmic intelligence includes the recognition and use of rhythmic and tonal patterns and sensitivity to sounds from the environment, the human voice and musical instruments. Gardner (1983) recognizes that of all forms of intelligence identified thus far, the "consciousness altering" effects of music and rhythm on the brain are the greatest. Music can calm us when we're stressed, stimulate us when we're bored and help us maintain a steady pulse in activities such as exercising. It has been used to inspire religious beliefs, intensify national loyalties and express loss or joy. The two core aspects of this intelligence are sensitivity to the basic elements of music (pitch, rhythm and timbre) and responsiveness to music, sounds and silences in one's environment. Pitch refers to melody, rhythm to placement of sounds in time, and timbre to quality of tone.

Music has a direct impact on the limbic brain, which is the area where feeling, motivation and memory reside. Because of this, music can be used to: stimulate a positive emotional environment in the classroom; focus attention and assist concentration; relax students and reduce stress; arouse interest and enthusiasm for a lesson; enhance the content of a lesson and inspire creativity in many aspects of the curriculum.

The musical-rhythmic intelligence is enlivened by the resonance or vibrational effect of music and rhythm on the brain, including such things as sounds from nature, musical instruments, the voice and other humanly-produced sounds.

ASSESSMENT IDEAS:

Compose a musical or rhythmic piece to express various feelings, emotions or ideas.

Research a particular musician or composer.

Identify various rhythms, instruments and techniques used in music.

Choreograph a movement sequence based on music (waltz, cha-cha or two-step).

Recognize rhythmic patterns, musical expressions and vocal inflections of different cultures.

---

4 Interpersonal Intelligence

The interpersonal intelligence involves the ability to work cooperatively in a group as well as the ability to communicate verbally and non-verbally with others. Specific abilities of the interpersonal intelligence are: distinguishing moods, temperaments, motivations and intentions of others; acting upon this knowledge; responding in an appropriate manner; getting along with, motivating, persuading and influencing others.

This intelligence also helps us appreciate that not all cultures value the same things or express their values in the same way. This awareness is fundamental to working together in a multi-ethnic work force and a multi-national society.

Gardner (1983) observes that there is vital interaction between the interpersonal and intrapersonal intelligences. These are the only two MIs that have receptor sites in both the limbic brain and the frontal lobes of the neocortex. Thus, they are responsible for controlling our emotions and motivations (limbic brain) and providing the possibility for foresight, insight and creative problem-solving (neocortex). Together these two intelligences form our sense of self.

Students with a strong interpersonal intelligence learn best in a social setting. Their success is strengthened by activities that involve interacting with others. They also may need to talk things over with you more often than other students tend to do. They are drawn to participation in school activities and to service projects in the classroom, school and community. Students with strong interpersonal intelligence thrive on appreciation and acknowledgment.

ASSESSMENT IDEAS:

Demonstrate ability to blend individual performance skills with a group.

Create a dance in collaboration with a partner or partners.

Evaluate and coach improvement of a partner's movement patterns.

Use group problem-solving skills to address a movement problem.

---

5 Intrapersonal Intelligence

The intrapersonal intelligence involves knowledge of the internal aspects of the self, such as knowledge of feelings, a range of emotional responses, thinking processes (metacognition—thinking about thinking), self-reflection and a sense of—or intuition about—spiritual practices. Gardner (1983) suggests that the intrapersonal intelligence allows us to be self-reflective, that is, to step back from ourselves and watch ourselves as an "outside observer." The development of this intelligence is a basic life-long survival skill. It impacts one's ability to set goals, to work independently, to understand motivations, to make appropriate choices, to be emotionally healthy and to be able to step back from a situation and accurately reflect on it.

The intrapersonal intelligence is essential to the full development of its counterpart, the interpersonal intelligence. A person can only discern

Dance through The Multiple Intelligences 163

and appropriately respond to the moods, temperaments and intentions of others to the extent that he/she/they is able to recognize them.

The intrapersonal intelligence is awakened when we are in situations that cause introspection and require knowledge of the internal aspects of the self. A challenge for the teacher is to create an environment and provide opportunities that allow students time for inner reflection and self-awareness.

ASSESSMENT IDEAS:

Demonstrate knowledge of key movement concepts by explaining how they are useful in everyday life.

Develop a movement phrase that expresses what was meaningful about a personal experience.

Create a dance to celebrate your values, philosophy and beliefs.

Assess your performance of a piece of choreography.

Assess your creation of a piece of choreography.

Create a dance or movement phrase by drawing on your response to visual art, music, other dances, sculpture, poetry and/or drama.

---

6 Verbal-Linguistic Intelligence

The verbal-linguistic intelligence is responsible for the production of language and all the complex possibilities that follow, including poetry, humor, storytelling, grammar, metaphors, similes, abstract reasoning and, of course, the written word. The verbal-linguistic intelligence is awakened by the spoken word, by reading someone's ideas or poetry, by writing one's own ideas, thoughts or poetry and by various kinds of humor, such as puns, jokes and twists of language.

According to Gardner (1983), areas of the verbal-linguistic intelligence include:

a Phonology—Sound. Phonology means an awareness of the sounds of words. It includes a sense of the rhythm of words, the inflection of a poetic meter, the use of puns, rap, rhymes and alliteration. It also includes the mnemonic potential of language, that is, the ability to use language to help remember.

b Syntax—Structure. Syntax has to do with the structure of language. It includes rules of grammar and the inflection and ordering of words.

c Semantics—Meaning. Semantics is the branch of linguistics concerned with the meaning of words, using language as a tool to communicate precisely what one wants to say. It includes denotation, connotation, definition, explanation and interpretation in written and oral language.

d Pragmatics—Purpose. Pragmatics means the ability to use language to achieve a purpose—to explain, convince, challenge, inspire, encourage or any of the other purposes for which language can be used. When the emphasis is on pragmatics, a person is not concerned so much with language structure or whether exactly the right choice of words is being made; the goal is to successfully communicate with others.

ASSESSMENT IDEAS:

Keep a dance journal or corrections notebook.

Write an essay about a particular topic or genre of dance, dance history or a choreographer.

Give an oral presentation to the class on a topic of special interest.

Write poetry to express an idea, opinion, feeling or belief.

Write the directions for recreating/performing a movement phrase.

Combine text and movement.

Create a dance that communicates the ideas and feelings evoked by a piece of literature.

---

7 Logical-Mathematical Intelligence

The logical-mathematical intelligence is most often associated with "scientific thinking." Logical-mathematical intelligence is activated in situations requiring problem-solving or meeting a new challenge. This intelligence likewise involves the capacity to: recognize patterns, work with abstract symbols such as numbers and geometric shapes and discern relationships among separate and distinct pieces of information.

It is important to note that most students are not purely logical-mathematical thinkers. For many, the logical-mathematical intelligence is supported by activities that also engage their visual-spatial and bodily-kinesthetic intelligences. This would suggest that "hands-on" logical-mathematical activities are important and necessary, even after a student has matured to the stage where formal operational thinking is possible.

> **ASSESSMENT IDEAS:**
>
> Show recognition of key patterns of a choreographer's style/vocabulary.
> Demonstrate understanding of the basic language of dance.
> Reveal geometric forms through movement pathways and sequences.

8 Naturalist Intelligence

The naturalist intelligence is related to the ability to recognize, appreciate and understand the natural world. A naturalist demonstrates expertise in the recognition and classification of the numerous species—flora and fauna—of his/her/their environment.

Every culture places a premium on those individuals who can recognize members of a species that are especially valuable or notably dangerous and can appropriately categorize new or unfamiliar organisms. Gardner posits that in cultures without formal science, the naturalist is the individual most skilled in the application of the current "folk taxonomies." In cultures with a scientific orientation, the naturalist is a biologist who recognizes and categorizes specimens in terms of current formal taxonomies, such as those devised in the 1700s by the Swedish scientist Carolus Linnaeus.

A naturalist is comfortable in the world of organisms and may well possess the talent of caring for, taming or interacting subtly with various living creatures. Potential roles range from hunters to farmers to gardeners to cooks.

According to Gardner (1999), "Even apparently remote capacities—such as recognizing automobiles for the sounds of the engines, or detecting novel patterns in a scientific laboratory, or discerning artistic styles—may exploit mechanisms that originally evolved because of their efficacy in distinguishing between, say toxic and nontoxic ivies, snakes or berries. Thus, it is possible that the pattern-recognizing talents of artists, poets, social scientists and natural scientists are all built on the fundamental perceptual skills of the naturalist intelligence." (p. 50)

The naturalist intelligence is triggered by immersing the self in the full sensory experience of the natural world, including plants, animals, weather conditions, water, forests and inorganic matter from

166 *Dance through The Multiple Intelligences*

the microscopic world to what can be perceived with the senses of sight, taste, touch, smell, hearing and the inner senses of the human spirit (i.e., being moved, touched, and evoked by nature).

> **ASSESSMENT IDEAS:**
>
> Perform role-plays of cycles in nature, animal behavior.
>   Identify characteristics of a particular genre of dance.
>   Identify characteristics of a particular choreographer.
>   Order, rank, separate or group movement phases.

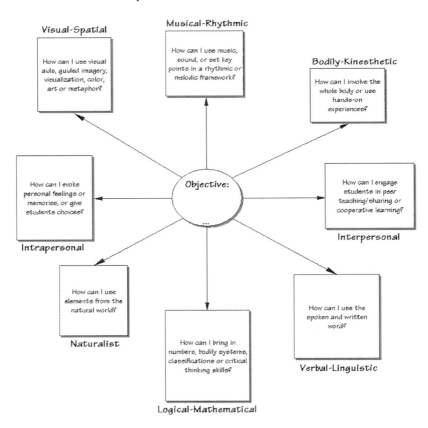

Figure 10.1 Multiple Intelligences and Dance.

Multiple Intelligences and Dance Reference List, prepared by Don Halquist

Armstrong, T. (1994). *Multiple Intelligences in the Classroom.* Alexandria, VA: Association for Supervision and Curriculum Development.

Campbell, B. (1994). *The Multiple Intelligences Handbook: Lesson Plans and More....* Stanwood, WA: Campbell & Associates.

Gardner, H. (1983). *Frames of Mind: The Theory of Multiple Intelligences.* New York: Basic Books.

Gardner, H. (1993). *Multiple Intelligences: The Theory in Practice.* New York: Basic Books.

Gardner, H. (1999). *Intelligence Reframed: Multiple Intelligences for the 21st Century.* New York: Basic Books.

Lazear, D. (1999). *Eight Ways of Knowing: Teaching for Multiple Intelligences.* Arlington Heights, IL: Skylight.

Appendix A
Resource Texts

For the Reader Not Immersed in Laban/Bartenieff Theories:

Bartenieff, Irmgard, and Dori Lewis. *Body Movement: Coping with the Environment*. Routledge, 1980.

Dell, Cecily, and Aileen Crow. *Space Harmony: Basic Terms*. Princeton Book Co Pub, 1977.

Hackney, Peggy. *Making Connections: Total Body Integration through Bartenieff Fundamentals*. Routledge, 2001.

Studd, Karen, and Laura Cox. *Everybody is a Body*. Outskirts Press, 2020.

Wahl, Colleen. *Laban/Bartenieff Movement Studies: Contemporary Applications*. Human Kinetics, 2018.

For Those Wanting to Know More About Functional Anatomy:

Clippinger, Karen. *Dance Anatomy and Kinesiology*. 2nd ed., Human Kinetics, 2015.

Franklin, Eric. *Dynamic Alignment through Imagery*. 2nd ed., Human Kinetics, 2012.

Olsen, Andrea. *Body Stories: A Guide to Experiential Anatomy*. Wesleyan University Press, 2020.

Romita, Nancy, and Allegra Romita. *Functional Awareness: Anatomy in Action for Dancers*. Oxford University Press, 2016.

For Those Wanting to Know More About Body-Mind Centering or Ideokinesis:

Hartley, Linda. *Wisdom of the Body Moving: An Introduction to Body-Mind Centering*. North Atlantic Books, 1995.

Sweigard, Lulu. *Human Movement Potential: Its Ideokinetic Facilitation*. Allegro Editions, 2013.

For Those Wanting to Know More About Dance Pedagogy:

Davis, Cristal U. "Tendus and Tenancy: Black Dancers and the White Landscape of Dance Education." *Palgrave Handbook of Race and Arts in Education*, edited by Amelia Kraehe, Palgrave Macmillan, 2018.

Davis, Cristal U. "Laying New Ground: Uprooting White Privilege and Planting Seeds of Equity and Inclusion." *Dance Education and Responsible Citizenship: Promoting Civic Engagement through Effective Dance Pedagogies*, edited by Karen Schupp, Routledge, 2019.

Erkert, Jan. *Harnessing the Wind: The Art of Teaching Modern Dance*. Human Kinetics, 2003.

McCarthy-Brown, Nyama. *Dance Pedagogy for a Diverse World: Culturally Relevant Teaching in Theory, Research and Practice*. Illustrated ed., McFarland & Co., 2017.

Vissicaro, Pegge. *Studying Dance Cultures around the World: An Introduction to Multicultural Dance Education*. Kendall Hunt Pub., 2004.

Whittier, Cadence. *Creative Ballet Teaching: Technique and Artistry for the 21st Century Ballet Dancer*. Routledge, 2017.

Other Books and Articles Referred to in the Essays, Listed Alphabetically:

Bateson, Gregory. *Mind and Nature: A Necessary Unity (Advances in Systems Theory, Complexity, and the Human Sciences)*. Hampton Press, 2002.

Bloom, Benjamin, Max D. Engelhart, Edward J. Furst, Walker H. Hill, and David R. Krathwohl *Taxonomy of Educational Objectives: The Classification of Educational Goals*. David McKay Co., 1968.

Caine, Renate Nummela and Geoffrey Caine. *Unleashing the Power of Perceptual Change: The Potential of Brain-Based Teaching*. Assn. for Supervision & Curriculum Development, 1997.

Jackson, Robyn R. *Never Work Harder Than Your Students and Other Principles of Great Teaching*. 2nd ed., ASCD, 2018.

MacRae-Campbell, Linda. "Whole Person Education: Nurturing the Compassionate Genius in Each of Us." *IN CONTEXT: A Quarterly of Humane Sustainable Culture #18*, edited by Robert Gilman, Context Institute, 1988.

McTighe, Jay, and Grant Wiggins. *Understanding by Design*. 2nd ed., Assn. for Supervision & Curriculum Development, 2005.

Scriven, Michael. *The Methodology of Evaluation*. Perdue Univ., 1966.

For Those Wanting to Know More About Sondra Fraleigh, I Recommend Starting with These Two of Her Many Books:

Fraleigh, Sondra Horton. *Dance and the Lived Body.* Univ. of Pittsburgh Press, 1996.

Fraleigh, Sondra, editor. *Moving Consciously: Somatic Transformations through Dance, Yoga, and Touch.* Univ. of Illinois Press, 2015.

Multiple Intelligences and Dance Reference List, prepared by Don Halquist:

Armstrong, T. (1994). *Multiple Intelligences in the Classroom.* Alexandria, VA: Association for Supervision and Curriculum Development.

Campbell, B. (1994). *The Multiple Intelligences Handbook: Lesson Plans and More...* Stanwood, WA: Campbell & Associates.

Gardner, H. (1983). *Frames of Mind: The Theory of Multiple Intelligences.* New York: Basic Books.

Gardner, H. (1993). *Multiple Intelligences: The Theory in Practice.* New York: Basic Books.

Gardner, H. (1999). *Intelligence Reframed: Multiple Intelligences for the 21st Century.* New York: Basic Books.

Glock, J., S. Wertz, and M. Meyer (1999). *Discovering the Naturalist Intelligence: Science in the School Yard.* Tucson, AZ: Zephyr Press.

Lazear, D. (1999). *Eight Ways of Knowing: Teaching for Multiple Intelligences.* Arlington Heights, IL: Skylight.

Appendix B
Embracing Non-Eurocentric and Multicultural Perspectives

I have wanted to be a teacher since age eight, when I rounded up neighborhood kids to attend the "school" I set up in the family laundry room and taught spelling, history and geography. I started teaching professionally at age 13, in the Irene J. Earl School of Dance in American Fork, Utah, and established the Bill Evans School of Dance at age 16, first in Lehi and later in Draper and Sandy as well, teaching tap and freestyle ballet classes to 225 children per week to fund my undergraduate studies at the University of Utah.

Even though I studied classical ballet as a child and early teen, I was more passionate about rhythm tap dance and swing-style jazz. I felt innately connected to bodily wisdom in those forms and was able to learn quickly, dance expressively and find deep satisfaction in moving.

When I entered a pre-college ballet program and later became an undergraduate at the University of Utah, however, I was told "we don't tap dance here" by my ballet professors in the Department of Speech and Theatre and "jazz is so commercial" by my modern dance professors in the Department of Women's Physical Education. Like thousands of other students, I found that the dance forms associated with Black culture I had loved as a child, in which I had developed significant skills, were looked down upon as "mere entertainment" in academia. Today, this phenomenon is recognized as an aspect of the "colonization" of higher education in North America.

As I shifted my concentration from the forms I had most loved to the "privileged" styles of ballet and classic modern dance, I gradually became consumed by my body's limitations, as pointed out for me by well-meaning teachers. I tried to overcome those perceived deficiencies, and please my teachers, from the outside in, through muscular force and hard work.

I became a professional dancer in my early 20s, and I approached every class and rehearsal in the Eurocentric styles of ballet, modern and musical theatre dance in which I was working with full emotional and physical commitment. However, as a result of what many of my teachers and directors told me (and how I interpreted what they were saying), I became chronically injured. I suffered unrelenting pain in my sacrum and lumbar spine, after years of trying to reduce their curves and keep my pelvis "square." I endured chronic and painful *chondromalacia*, softening of the patellar cartilage, resulting from forcing outward rotation of the tibia at the knee joint and from lateral-medial muscle imbalance in my quadriceps.

I consciously started to embrace the pedagogical values I share in this book in 1969. Fearing that my dancing years might already be behind me, I resolved not to take more technique classes until I figured out for myself what my body needed. I decided to "start over," and to discover from the inside what movement patterns would be safe, healthful and regenerative to invite back into my neuromuscular system.

I had been given a hiatus from the Repertory Dance Theatre (RDT), the professional company of which I was then a full-time member, to travel to West Berlin to create a new work for the Deutsche Oper Ballet. While there, I spent daily hours alone in a huge, empty opera house studio, exploring simple gestures, postures and shifts of weight. I tried to recapture the instinctive gifts that had enabled me to be such a successful tap and jazz dancer as a child and figure out how I could apply them to my work as an adult professional modern dancer. I came to realize that I had learned to hate my body for what it was not, and I started a process of accepting myself just as I was. I started respecting my body's messages to my mind, and discovered that my body would tell my mind what I needed if I would just pay attention to it. I was encouraged by early breakthroughs in the process of looking inside and acknowledging and validating what I discovered there.

I began to see that I could unpack my years of training and differentiate those ideas about dancing that had been toxic (many of which, it seemed, were emphasized in Eurocentric traditions) from those that could be healing (which, it appeared, were often from non-Eurocentric attitudes and practices). For example, I became aware that my early tap and jazz dancing had included liberal use of what the Laban/Bartenieff system describes as "shape flow support" (breath-related changes in the size and shape of the abdominal and thoracic cavities to support postural and gestural activities). Rhythm tap dance and swing-style jazz were created over decades by mostly Black artists, and the African dance values embedded within them are based on function (creating music with your feet and body) and personal mojo (expressing individual style), rather than on duplicating external form.

I began to understand that static positions and designs are usually not important in the African-based forms I cherished as a child. The body attitude of those forms encourages a releasing of the superficial muscles surrounding the hip joint, creating a balanced use of the whole leg and foot by establishing what I eventually learned was a harmonious rhythm between the iliopsoas and hamstrings as major initiators of femoral flexion and extension. I discovered that by replacing the over-reliance on the quadriceps and gluteal muscles I had developed as a ballet and modern dancer with a fuller use of the smaller and deeper muscles closer to the bone, I could find the joint mobility and qualities of Lightness and Free Flow that had characterized my early tap and jazz dancing.

I began to incorporate the relaxed and natural qualities I had embodied as a boy and early teen into my modern dance exercises and choreography. In the early '70s, that was a radical permutation of the movement languages that had been developed by an earnest generation of pioneering artists struggling to have movement taken seriously as profound communication, not mere entertainment.

I reflected on the teaching of Janet Collins and Percival Borde, Black artists with whom I had studied as a scholarship student/apprentice at Harkness House for Ballet Arts in New York City. Collins, the first Black ballerina at the Metropolitan Opera House, offered my first experience of somatic exploration. She would ask us to interrupt the eight hours of vigorous technique training we were undergoing each day to lie on our backs with our feet up and resting on the wall, as she directed our attention to sensing our breath and the "bowl" of the pelvis. Borde, the personal and professional partner of the anthropologist, dancer and choreographer Pearl Primus, taught us traditional West Indian and West African dances. He embodied a light-hearted and humorous spirit, and he validated my sense of rhythm, which had not been noticed by most of my ballet teachers. Most significantly, he modeled for me how to move with ease, grounded strength, control and authority.

I revisited the Bharatanatyam *Swan Lake* I had learned from Jack Cole, also at Harkness House. He had been commissioned to choreograph for the Harkness Ballet but said, "First I need to teach them how to dance." In evening classes over several months, while spending his days choreographing a Broadway production of *Man of La Mancha,* he painstakingly coached us in Russell Meriwether's Hindu *Swan Lake,* and I learned to respect and savor the bodily wisdom embedded in those centuries-old Hindu dance traditions. Cole had studied with "La Meri," an anthropologist, scholar, dancer, choreographer and "ethnic dance" teacher, extensively in his early career and had drawn on what he had learned of grounding, centeredness, gestural specificity and refined phrasing in her East Indian dance classes to create his "jazz" technique. Even though his teaching methods were often harsh and humiliating, he had drilled complex but physically healthy coordination and integration patterns into my body-mind, and I found that I could call upon them in happier contexts to override unnatural ideas and practices I had forced onto my body from a concern for how I looked, rather than how I functioned.

I often describe myself as a slow learner and late bloomer, and it was a few years after I had studied with those artists in New York City that I was finally able to let their words sink in and recognize the importance of self-care, anatomical awareness, light-heartedness and grounding to my well-being as a professional dancer.

After completing my project in West Berlin and returning to RDT, I started teaching advanced teens in Virginia Tanner's Creative Dance Program, which was based in the Division of Continuing Education at the University of Utah, when my rehearsal day with RDT was over.

Tanner (1915–79) was a pioneering teacher of children's creative movement in Utah and a crusader for change in our culture's attitudes toward the arts. The iconic New York choreographer Anna Sokolow called Virginia the "Mormon Isadora Duncan," because both Duncan and Tanner proclaimed expansive visions in which every child would have the opportunity to dance freely and jubilantly.

For five years, whenever I was not touring, I worked with a remarkable group of Tanner students who had danced creatively from early childhood but had not previously experienced training in rigorous technique. They were nimble, passionate and courageous, and had not been subjected to the regimented training many similar young people endure in conventional studios, which tells them they must look and behave in circumscribed ways. Those evening classes with those extraordinary young people became a laboratory in which I started to develop a methodology and movement lexicon for teaching my own style of dance.

Just as I began my teaching in the Tanner program, RDT engaged Donald McKayle to be our guest teacher and choreographer for several weeks. "Donny" fused Eurocentric and Black West Indian influences in a way that I found liberating, and I shared what I experienced in his daytime classes and rehearsals with those young students in our evening sessions. I had previously studied Martha Graham Technique with sternly serious artists who had emphasized its heroic aspects, and I found it refreshing to experience that classic modern dance style combined with McKayle's freely outpouring joy. He grew up in East Harlem, in a Jamaican family, and he evolved a style that infused Graham's muscularly powerful movement language with effervescent West Indian rhythmic pulsations. He had a beautiful singing voice and his verbal directions were melodious, uplifting and encouraging. He taught us his piece *Nocturne*, a sensual West Indian celebration to excitingly rhythmic music by the NYC street musician Moondog, and we performed it all across the country for several years.

In the early '70s, RDT toured to New Mexico, and I was able to witness ceremonial dances in several of the Pueblos surrounding Albuquerque. Something deep within me moved when I observed whole communities—from the elders to the toddlers—dancing together to celebrate what they held sacred, mixing indigenous and European symbolism on the bare earth of the open-air dancing place. "This," I felt, "is what's been missing in my life." I knew then that someday I would live in New Mexico.

Elizabeth Waters served as a guest artist with RDT shortly before our first visit to Albuquerque, and she invited us to experience a blend of Eurocentric and non-Eurocentric perspectives that significantly influenced my teaching. In several weeks of classes and rehearsals, she planted seeds that grew within me over years, prepared me for my eventual embrace of Laban/Bartenieff concepts in 1976, and buttressed my decision to apply for and accept a job at the University of New Mexico in 1988.

Waters had been a member of the Hanya Holm Dance Group in New York City before relocating to Albuquerque in 1942. Holm had been a member of the Mary Wigman dance company in Germany, and Wigman had collaborated with Rudolf Laban before they parted in anger and disavowed each other's work. Despite the rupture of their professional relationship, the Wigman pedagogy included theories that have become known as "Laban" throughout the world. Elizabeth brought Laban/Wigman/Holm concepts to New Mexico, where she fused them with perspectives, values and practices she absorbed from the ceremonial dances of the Zuni Pueblo community in western New Mexico. Extraordinarily, she was welcomed as an "honorary member" of the Zuni nation, and she lived there for an extended period of time before establishing a dance program at the University of New Mexico in 1946.

In her classes and rehearsals, we would "tread with reverence on the sacred ground, and serve as vessels of energy from Mother Earth to Father Sky." We would ceremoniously address and honor both "Grandmother Moon and Grandfather Sun." I embodied for the first time a conviction that humans are part of the life cycles of the natural world, organically connected to our brother and sister animals. She introduced me to what I later learned was Laban's *Directional Matrix* while asking me to see myself dancing within an eight-sided Navajo hogan. She invited me to imagine and explore palpably clear surfaces, forms and pathways in space, with Flow, Strength, economy of movement and clarity of intention. She guided me into creating "sacred" music with percussive hand and body sounds and vocal chants to accompany my own dancing.

I found Elizabeth's fusion of Eurocentric (Laban/Wigman/Holm) and Indigenous American (Zuni/Navajo) traditions captivating and inspiring, and I resolved to explore my own ways of moving harmoniously with nature, of going deep inside and honoring the life force I discover there before connecting to the larger world. I came to embody and share with students a view that dance can be a spiritual practice in which we celebrate our oneness with the natural world. As I explored Waters' words and practices, I invited students to form *learning circles* (which characterize both Native American and African cultures), and I asked each student to hold an imagined (Native-American-inspired) "talking stick" as they wrapped words around their thoughts and feelings without interruption from me or peers. I guided young dancers in the creation of "incantations" in which they simultaneously performed their own sacred sound and movement scores.

As a professor at the University of New Mexico, I studied flamenco from 1988 through 2002 with Eva Encinias, my colleague on the dance faculty, who became a long-time member of the Bill Evans Dance Company. We fused and combined rhythm tap and flamenco rhythms in many pieces, celebrating what they share and how each is a unique expressive entity.

Both times I produced American College Dance Festivals at the University of New Mexico, I included "world dance" concerts. *World Dance* was a term used at that time to indicate that forms other than white-centric ballet and modern dance would be performed. ACDFA—now ACDA—had primarily been a modern dance-focused organization, and those multicultural dance events gained widespread notice. I dedicated the first of those festivals to Ms. Waters, and the UNM Contemporary Dance Ensemble, which I directed, opened that gathering with my work based on her pedagogical and compositional methods, *Incantations for Elizabeth*. My UNM dance faculty colleagues and I developed World Dance and Flamenco Minors in the late 1990s, and there has been a Flamenco Major there for many years, both at the BA and MFA levels.

When I organized and co-directed the National Dance Education Organization Conference at UNM in 2003, the opening event was a panel entitled *Ethical and Artistic Issues Surrounding the Teaching and Performing of Indigenous Dance Forms in Schools and Colleges*, which was followed by a performance of the Navajo Pollen Trail Dancers from Window Rock, Arizona and the Buen Viaje VSA Dance Company of Albuquerque. A "world dance" concert included Native American dances performed by member of New Mexico's San Juan and Taos Pueblos, as well as flamenco, Mexican *bailé folklorico*, traditional dances from Zimbabwe, hip-hop and rhythm tap.

I profoundly cherish the Eurocentric dance forms in which I was immersed in my early professional study and career. However, I discovered a need to balance my interpretation of what I heard my mentors tell me within those forms that were so privileged in my university study with ideas embedded within the non-Eurocentric forms I have also been fortunate enough to experience. I draw on the tap/African, Bharatanatyam/Indian and flamenco/Spanish Gypsy rhythms that live within my body-mind and I fuse those influences with the ballet and modern dance movement languages I have also absorbed. I have understood since childhood that dance is a very big word, and I have possessed a life-long appetite for experiencing as many dance traditions as possible and for making new works based on the response of my inner voice to the multiple influences and traditions I have witnessed and embodied.

Appendix C
Applying Concepts from the Laban/Bartenieff Movement System and the Franklin Method of Dynamic Alignment through Imagery

The summer of 1976, when Peggy Hackney and I were among the resident teaching faculty in the American Dance Festival's six-week summer school at Connecticut College, was extraordinary for me in many ways. In addition to teaching three classes a day, I opened the Festival with a solo concert and premiered an ADF-commissioned new work in a Bill Evans Dance Company Concert several weeks later. I taught Evans Technique and repertory and Peggy taught Laban Effort/Shape and Bartenieff Fundamentals (BF). She took one of my classes daily, and we shared several of the same students. At the end of the summer, I was astonished to witness the quantum leaps of positive change achieved by the students who had taken courses from both of us. It seemed clear that our combined teaching supported student curiosity, agency and willingness to explore.

I realized that I was on a pathway of investigation that could be enhanced by an understanding of the theories and practices in which Peggy was so profoundly immersed. She had studied and collaborated extensively with Irmgard Bartenieff, who brought Rudolf Laban's theories to New York and then evolved and disseminated them as she developed her own approach to learning from the living body. I wanted to know more, and Peggy, a skilled and expressive dancer, was interested in performing as a member of my professional company. So, we joined forces. She performed in my touring ensemble for several years, and generously shared Bartenieff's somatic explorations and approach to Laban theory with me, members of my company and students in the Bill Evans Dance Seattle School.

As I began to explore Laban/Bartenieff ideas, I gained access to a theoretical framework for the myriad choices available to us as humans moving. By looking at my own work through L/B lenses, I was able to continue my personal journey while also developing insights and verbal language to relate it to the larger world, wrapping words around what I was trying to achieve as an artist and educator.

I started to integrate theoretical concepts from the Laban/Bartenieff Movement System (L/BMS) into my teaching in 1977, and I am now both a CLMA, Certified Laban Movement Analyst (through Integrated Movement Studies) and CMA, Certified Movement Analyst (through the Laban/Bartenieff Institute of Movement Studies).

In her incomparable book, *Making Connections: Total Body Integration Through Bartenieff Fundamentals,* published in 2001, Peggy explains that the Laban/Bartenieff framework

> ...provides a rich overview of the scope of movement possibilities.... [Its] basic elements can be used for generating movement or for describing movement. They provide an inroad to understanding movement and for developing movement efficiency and expressiveness. Each human being combines these movement factors in his/her own unique way and organizes them to create phrases and relationships which reveal personal, artistic, or cultural style.

I do not believe that one needs to investigate Laban/Bartenieff concepts (or to consider and explore the suggestions I make in this book) to be an effective dance and movement teacher. There are many possible routes to any destination, and there are numerous superb teachers who use other frameworks to convey their ideas and practices. I have found L/BMS to be enormously useful to me, however, and I share the story of how that came to be in the hope that those who read it may be better able to contextualize my thoughts and feelings.

Rudolf Laban was an ethnic Hungarian born in Bratislava (now the capital of Slovakia) in 1879. He became a scientist, teacher, artist, social activist, philosopher and creator of theoretical frameworks that help people understand more deeply the scope and magnitude of human movement from his Eurocentric perspective. Most of his groundbreaking work took place in Germany between the two World Wars, but he relocated to England in 1938. He continued his work in the United Kingdom for two decades and passed away in 1958.

Like many geniuses, Laban was complex and multifaceted. Despite many human flaws, he was a brilliant and visionary thinker and a catalyst for making dance and movement understood by and relevant to scholars and practitioners of other disciplines. He was capable of sincere compassion and shared his theories liberally with many artists and scholars who documented, codified and elaborated upon them.

Applying Concepts through Imagery 181

He was not a trained dancer and worked in collaboration with mostly female dancers to develop his work. Although he was a true Renaissance man, I like to think of Laban as "the father of modern dance in Europe." Modern dance was simultaneously developing in America, of course, where its "parents" included Martha Graham, Doris Humphrey and Charles Weidman. Hanya Holm was among the first to bring Laban-based theories to America (as they were embedded, though uncredited, in the pedagogy of Mary Wigman). I gratefully acknowledge that I have benefited from the combined legacies of all these brilliant (though humanly-flawed) pioneers.

Laban's work is preserved and disseminated through several different streams. Some Laban scholars and practitioners believe that "it is only Laban if he himself said it." Others, including those who mentored me, have used Laban's germinal ideas as starting points for continued investigation, and they have augmented them with other forms of somatic wisdom to evolve approaches that are more diverse and inclusive than what existed when Laban was alive.

He was a product of this time and place and, of course, his work was not culturally neutral. His reputation is controversial at this time, when de-colonizing the teaching of dance is important to many educators and artists. Some discredit him as a womanizer and distrust him as part of the white patriarchy responsible for so much that is problematic in our world today. Because he worked primarily in Germany and was employed for a while by the Nazi regime, and because he expressed uninformed disparagement of Black dancing in America in a few comments in his autobiography, *A Life for Dance*, he and his work are currently depreciated by several dance scholars.

I believe that no system can be culturally neutral, but I am encouraged by the fact that those who provide leadership for the Laban/Bartenieff Movement System in North America are continuously questioning and reassessing its theoretical underpinnings and trying to make them and their application more inclusive and socially just. They recognize that there is still work to be done, and they are not afraid of that challenge. I do what I can in my small corner of the L/B world to continue its evolution toward increased cultural inclusiveness and social justice.

Some activists claim that L/BMS is a reflection of Laban's personal shortcomings. I believe absolutely that we must be wary of personal and cultural biases, but I don't find that claim to be accurate. It is not perfect, and I struggle with some of its pat theoretical constructions and its historic, Eurocentric white privilege, but I find that L/BMS as it is practiced in twenty-first century North America is becoming increasingly compatible with an encompassing and equitable worldview.

I am a gay man who experienced severe marginalization and overt oppression in my early decades. Because of my own past suffering, I draw on many influences to create an inclusive and just world for those I teach. When I choose to draw on L/BMS, it offers me inroads to becoming more inclusive, empathetic and compassionate, and to effectively supporting the growth of the widely diverse individuals with whom I interact.

Irmgard Bartenieff was born in Berlin in 1900. She was already an accomplished dancer when she studied with Laban, but she modified her approach based on his theories before co-founding her own dance company with her husband Michael. Because he was Jewish, they were forced to shut down their successful troupe in 1933, and they fled to New York City in 1936. In the U.S. she continued her work as a dancer and choreographer and also became a physical therapist, a pioneer in the development of dance movement therapy and the founder of the Laban/Bartenieff Institute of Movement Studies. She passed away in 1981.

Peggy Hackney says that Bartenieff's frequent answer to questions from students was, "There are many possibilities. Let's return to the body." Her book, *Body Movement: Coping with the Environment*, was published in 1980. In it, she wrote of her applications of Laban theories, group interaction, dance therapy and her own therapeutic movement fundamentals. She also included a few cross-cultural movement studies, which she approached objectively and non-judgmentally. Though brief, these studies reveal an intellectual curiosity about Native American, African-American, Caucasian-American, Japanese, North African and East Indian cultures.

I perceive L/BMS to be a living practice that continues to adapt, evolve and grow. It is led by many (mostly white, female, North American) artists, scholars and teachers who continue to question its historic assumptions as well as to embrace and incorporate concepts and practices from other somatic, scientific and educational disciplines. In my lifetime, I have witnessed an infusion of ideas and language from educational theorist Howard Gardner; psychiatrist Charles Johnston; other somatic practices, including Ideokinesis, Body-Mind Centering, the Alexander Technique and the Feldenkrais Method, and ancient movement practices from East Indian, Chinese, African and Indigenous American cultures into the work of L/BMS practitioners.

I have personally shared my approach to this work with many BIPOC (Black, Indigenous and people of color) artists and teachers who

Applying Concepts through Imagery 183

have told me that they find it compatible with beliefs drawn from non-Eurocentric traditions and valuable in their individual movement practices. Students and collaborators who have affirmed to me the significance of L/BMS-based investigations in their movement lives include people of many skin tones and backgrounds from North America, Central America, Europe, India, Japan, China, South Korea, Zimbabwe, New Zealand and Australia.

I became a professor and head of the Dance Program at the University of New Mexico in 1988, and for 16 years I had the pleasure of teaching and collaborating with numerous graduate and undergraduate students from several Indigenous American Nations: Jicarilla Apache, Blackfoot, Navajo, Isleta, Jemez, Laguna, Sandia, Santo Domingo and Taos. My interactions with those mostly young people convinced me that when members of the human race go inside, to sense, feel and explore fundamental movement patterns, we discover that we are all in many essential ways the same, despite our different cultural backgrounds and superficial variations in skin tones and physical characteristics.

As I wrote this book, I was also a student again. Since February of 2020, I have studied Eric Franklin's Method of Dynamic Alignment through Imagery. I am a level one Certified Teacher of the Franklin Method (FM) and am pursuing certification as a level two educator. As I complete this book, I am in the process of integrating Franklin language, which is still new to me, with the Laban/Bartenieff language I have spoken for decades. It has been doubly challenging to both crystallize ideas and language I formulated over decades and integrate new and often more detailed body knowledge at the same time. Nonetheless, I am happy that I investigated Mr. Franklin's ideas before this book was complete because the specificity of the anatomical information I have gained from this study has enabled me to describe movement more clearly.

Eric Franklin is a dancer who was influenced by Lulu Sweigard's Ideokinesis and other somatic systems and developed a highly accessible approach to fostering understanding and embodiment of functional anatomy. He is a prolific author of books for dancers and other movement specialists and he travels widely, sharing his work and encouraging people of all walks of life to learn more about their bodies and—above all—nourish them with embodied movement.

I am gaining new insights from my FM study through which I am developing an increasingly refined and satisfying relationship with my own body. I have included as many of those insights as possible in this book. What I have learned of FM so far is harmoniously compatible with BF. One significant difference is that "fascia" was not frequently mentioned in my BF studies, but—in the second level of my FM training—we are focusing on fascia in every lesson. Happily, as I am learning the FM approach to enlivening and lubricating connective tissue through myofascial "sponging," and "training" it through multi-directional movement in rhythms that maximize elastic rebound, I am realizing that my Laban/Bartenieff-based training has already taken me on a very similar journey, but without the use of the word "fascia." I am savoring the opportunity to bring the BF and FM worlds together in my body-mind.

Appendix D
My Take on Bartenieff Fundamentals

1 Body-Part Phrasing and Other Foundational Concepts

Unlike her contemporary Joseph Pilates, for example, who established and codified procedures and "rules" for his incredibly popular approach to physical conditioning, Irmgard Bartenieff was interested in exploring the movement life of each unique individual, and in a lifelong journey of investigation. Since her passing, numerous followers have contributed to the evolution and dissemination of her work. I am intensely grateful that Peggy Hackney brought Bartenieff Fundamentals into my life, and that many others have continued to evolve and share this life-enhancing work.

Areas of investigation in Bartenieff Fundamentals include:

a *Body-Part Phrasing*, which describes how movement spreads through the body— Simultaneous: All active body parts move at once. Successive: Adjacent body parts move one after the other. Sequential: Non-adjacent body parts move one after the other.
b *Body Attitude*, which can be described as persistent habitual stances or constellations of body parts from which we customarily move and to which we usually return.
c *Active/Held Body Parts*, a look at what parts of ourselves move freely and which parts are braced against movement.
d *Phrasing, or Initiation to Follow-Through*: Where does the movement initiate? In what routes does it travel through the body? Where does it arrive? Where do we send it in space?

2 Basic Six

Bartenieff began to formulate her "correctives," which evolved into her **Fundamentals**, while helping polio patients regain lost mobility in

186   *My Take on Bartenieff Fundamentals*

the 1950s. Dancers in her sphere of influence found that the increased awareness and efficiency provided by the correctives work were of enormous value to them, supporting body-level discoveries and repatterning of inefficient movement habits. By now, her ideas have swept through many corners of the dance world across the globe, and I see Bartenieff-inspired material taught in dance classes wherever I go.

Bartenieff left us with her *Basic Six* areas of exploration. Peggy Hackney writes comprehensively of them in *Making Connections: Total Body Integration Through Bartenieff Fundamentals*, and Bartenieff wrote of them in *Body Movement: Coping with the Environment*. I will not go into detail here, and I strongly recommend Peggy's book to anyone who would like to know more about them.

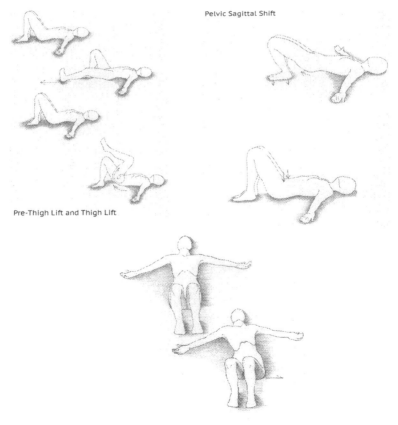

Pelvic Sagittal Shift

Pre-Thigh Lift and Thigh Lift

Pelvic Lateral Shift

My Take on Bartenieff Fundamentals 187

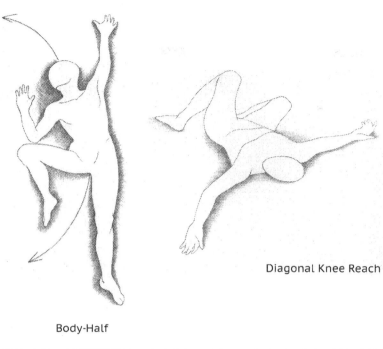

Diagonal Knee Reach

Body-Half

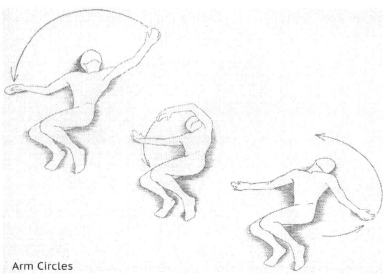

Arm Circles

Figure D.1 a-f Basic Six. (a) Pre-Thigh Lift and Thigh Lift. (b) Pelvic Sagittal Shift. (c) Pelvic Lateral Shift. (d) Body-Half. (e) Diagonal Knee Reach. (f) Arm Circles.

The Basic Six:

a *Pre-Thigh Lift and Thigh Lift, or Femoral Flexion.* I visit this Fundamental to explore such neuromusculoskeletal functions as pelvic-femoral rhythm, engagement of the hamstrings as prime movers for extension of the hip and flexion of the knee, and engagement of the iliopsoas complex as the prime mover for flexion of the hip.

b *Pelvic Sagittal Shift.* I play with this Fundamental to heighten my awareness of the kinetic chains between the tripods in the feet and the tripods at the hip (discussed in essay 67) and efficient successive homologous transfer of weight from upper to lower and lower to upper.

c *Pelvic Lateral Shift.* Explorations of this Fundamental allow us to tune in to the changes in the lowest part of the pelvis that support efficient sideways weight shift, our awareness of the motion in the pelvic diamond (including the transfer of weight through the pubic symphysis), our sensing of the lesser and greater trochanters of the femur and our savoring of the fluid accommodations of each pelvic half to the actions of each femoral head in its acetabulum.

d *Body-Half.* This Fundamental focuses on lateral body side and allows us to explore how the Yield and Push in the stable body-half supports the Reach and Pull in the mobile one and how the body sides frequently trade the lead within a single phrase of movement.

e *Diagonal Knee Reach.* This Fundamental brings rotation into the organism as we explore internal and external diagonals, spirals and cross-lateral total body organization.

f *Arm Circles.* This is the only Fundamental focusing primarily on the upper body (which reveals Bartenieff's profound concern for mobilizing the hip joint to help polio patients walk again). In this pattern, we can explore gradated scapulohumeral rhythm, eye-tracking and inner torso shaping.

g *Preparatory Exercises.* In addition to the Basic Six, Bartenieff designed "preparatory exercises," such as heel rocks (which I think of as "sloshing" of our fluids to open pathways of flow from feet to head) and vocal soundings (to bring reverberations to and heightened awareness of our inner cavities). I share both these explorations with students and practice them myself regularly.

h *Other foundational explorations.* She also designed many other explorations, such as the X-roll (which allows us to deeply explore cross-laterality and internal diagonals) and propulsion excises to explore and enhance changing levels from sitting or kneeling to standing.

3 Patterns of Total Body Organization

Bonnie Bainbridge Cohen, creator of the somatic system known as Body-Mind Centering, was once Bartenieff's student. She has researched human developmental patterns over several decades and has disseminated her groundbreaking findings widely. She created a framework for understanding how humans develop through instinctive, progressive movement patterns in utero and the early months of life. These patterns are the foundation for everything that follows throughout our lives.

In her book, *Making Connections*, Peggy Hackney unpacks what she considers the six most fundamental of these developmental movement patterns and shares them in conceptual frameworks and language congruent with the work Bartenieff accomplished before her passing in 1981. Peggy calls these six stages *Patterns of Total Body Organization* or PTBOs (also Patterns of Total Body Coordination, Integration and/or Connectivity). She tells us that these patterns develop in overlapping waves, each stage incorporating and building on the previous one. As adults, we can use the lenses of these patterns to notice how the total body is coordinated or organized as we learn new movement phrases or skills from the outside, or we can consciously embody them as images to integrate the whole of ourselves from the inside in the accomplishment of movement tasks.

The great teacher of creative movement for children, and my friend and former collaborator, Anne Green Gilbert, has combined this sequence of patterns, with *Tactile* at the beginning and *Vestibular* at the end, to create the *Brain Dance*. Anne is the founder of the Creative

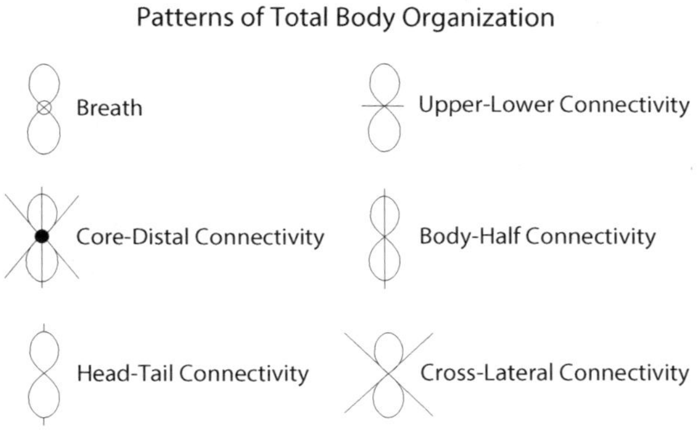

Patterns of Total Body Organization

- Breath
- Upper-Lower Connectivity
- Core-Distal Connectivity
- Body-Half Connectivity
- Head-Tail Connectivity
- Cross-Lateral Connectivity

Figure D.2 L/BMS Symbols, Patterns of Totally Body Organization.

Dance Center and Kaleidoscope Dance Company in Seattle. She has shared her brain dances generously throughout the world, and thousands of teachers of dance and other subjects gratefully and enthusiastically use a brain dance to prepare their students for learning. When I first relocated my dance company from Salt Lake City to Seattle, in 1976, Anne was president of our board of directors. Her children's creative dance program was originally based at Dance Theatre Seattle, the Bill Evans Company school. She has been a mentor and source of inspiration to me for four decades.

Here are examples of how I think about the PTBOs in my practice:

a   *Breath* begins with cellular respiration shortly after conception. The semi-permeable cell wall allows fluid to pour in to nurture life and fluid to pour out to get rid of what is no longer needed. (Useful image: an amoeba.) Cohen said that "Cellular breathing forms the building blocks of our life process. Where it is not taking place, the cells are dead, where there is difficulty, the cells are struggling; and where it is occurring freely, the cells are alive and healthy."[1] Lung respiration kicks in at birth to feed cellular respiration throughout our lives. Bartenieff said, "Where there is breath, there is the possibility of efficient functioning."[2]

b   *Core-Distal*, or navel radiation, begins with the development of the umbilical cord. Energy radiates from the navel to the distal ends of all six limbs (head, tail, arms and legs). (Like a sea star.) Hackney said, "The whole body is connected; all parts are in relationship. Each limb finds its connection into core and through core to the other limbs."[3]

c   *Head-Tail*, or spinal, begins with the development of the spinal cord. Eventually, the head communicates to the tail through the length of the spine, and a change in the head creates a change in the tail, and vice versa. (Like a fish or an inchworm.) This pattern generates a sense of becoming an individual, through compression of the spine into itself (Yield and Push Patterning), followed by spinal elongation (Reach and Pull Patterning).

d   *Upper-Lower*, or homologous, is the first of our locomotor patterns. Babies, lying on their bellies, Yield and Push from the upper half of the body to Reach and Pull to the lower half, and then vice versa. Energy travels from two hands and the head to two legs and the tail or the reverse. (Like a frog.) Yield and Push patterns provide grounding, and Reach and Pull patterns provide access to space.

e   *Body-Half,* or homo-lateral, is our second locomotor pattern. We Yield and Push from one body side to Reach and Pull to the other. (Like a lizard or alligator.) By doing so, we move more efficiently than in Upper-Lower. Mobility-Stability becomes the major functional body issue. This pattern facilitates hand-to-mouth and eye-hand coordination.

f   *Cross-Lateral,* or contra-lateral, is our third locomotor pattern. By Yielding and Pushing from one upper limb and the opposite lower limb, our energy crosses the mid-line, as we Reach and Pull to the other two limbs. This brings rotation into the musculoskeletal system and allows us to move with greater efficiency and satisfaction. This is the pattern we employ in creeping on our hands and knees and later in walking. (Like primates and humans.) Cross-laterality supports complexity, rapid locomotion and level change, a commitment to action in the world.

Notes

1   From an unpublished document prepared by Peggy Hackney for participants in the 1996–97 Integrated Movement Studies Certification Program.
2   See note above.
3   See notes above.

Appendix E
How The Body Changes Its Form

1 Modes of Shape Change

"Shape" can be thought of as the bridge between Body and Space; that is, the body relates to space through its ability to alter its size and form. In the Shape area of L/BMS, we identify four different ways (or modes) in which the body reconfigures itself. The body's shape changes continuously with each breath throughout our lives, and the lens of these modes brings us clarity concerning that ever-present process. I introduce the *Modes of Shape Change* in the very first class with new students because I find them cognitively accessible and enormously useful to even beginning dancers.

The different modes are *Shape Flow, Directional* and *Carving*.

a   *Shape Flow.* When we move only in relationship to ourselves (self to self), we are noticing or responding to inner sensation and/or feeling. When we "squirm" to find a comfortable body position, for example, we are experiencing *Shape Flow*.
b   *Directional.* When we move in relationship to the environment, we make bridges to points in the personal sphere of space. A *Spoke-like Directional* reach creates a bridge with a straight line. Spokes travel from, to and/or through the body/center of the kinesphere. Examples would be pressing an elevator button or giving someone a "high five." An *Arc-like Directional* reach inscribes the edge of a circular pathway, and never approaches center. An example would be shaking hands with someone.
c   *Carving.* If one follows the three-dimensional contours of an imagined volume, they are *Carving* the space of the kinesphere. This mode activates rotation in the musculoskeletal system. Examples are kneading bread dough or sculpting clay (real or imagined).

How the Body Changes Its Form   193

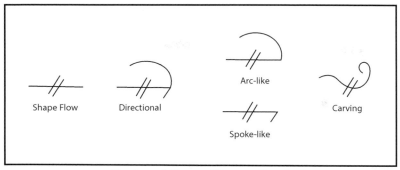

Modes of Shape Change Symbols

Figure E.1 L/BMS Symbols, Modes of Shape Change.

2 Still Forms

Teachers of creative movement often ask students to "make shapes" (e.g., symmetrical, asymmetrical, angular, curved, happy, sad, etc.) because doing so allows students to reorganize the whole of themselves quickly and easily around one unifying image. If I am teaching people new to dance, I will ask them to explore L/BMS *Still Forms*. I find them accessible to almost everyone, and I have noticed that most people enjoy creating forms or "shapes" with their whole bodies.

Sometimes, the whole body is in one of the following Still Forms. At other times, we might see one form in the lower body and another in the upper, or one form in one lateral body-half and another form in the other body-half. We can understand aspects of a person's movement life by noting which of these total body forms they prefer to pass through or move within (descriptive use) or we can ask students to create one or more of these forms (prescriptive use).

If we were to ask a moving person to "freeze," we would see one or a combination of some of the five Still Forms. They are:

a   *Pin*—elongated, a line;
b   *Wall*—planar, a surface;
c   *Ball*—spherical, symmetrically voluminous with rounded edges;
d   *Spiral*—twisted;
e   *Tetrahedron or Pyramid*—angularly voluminous with jagged edges.

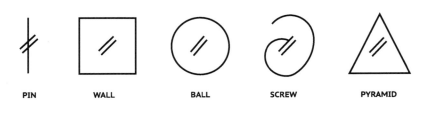

Still Form Symbols

Figure E.2 L/BMS Symbols, Still Forms.

3 Shape Flow Support

Shape Flow Support (SFS) is the growing and shrinking of the *internal kinesphere* that supports the architecture of the body in space. It is related to lung respiration, which feeds the expanding and condensing of the torso.

The general terms for this experience are:

a *Growing-Shrinking.*
   Directionally specific terms are:
b *Lengthening-Shortening*, SFS in the Vertical Dimension;
c *Widening-Narrowing*, SFS in the Horizontal Dimension;
d *Bulging-Hollowing*, SFS in the Sagittal Dimension.

> Movement goes out into space and creates shapes. But also there is inner space, and breath is an inner shaping experience. The body shrinks and grows with each breath. Inner breath changes can be supported by sound. Posture is not built by muscles but by the whole way you breathe.
> —Irmgard Bartenieff[1]

The support for gestures of the arms and legs provided by inner shaping in the torso (which I now call Shape Flow Support) became important to me in 1968 (when I had no specific terms to describe it). It began when 15-year-old Debbie Poulsen became my student of modern dance in Virginia Tanner's Creative Dance Program at the University of Utah Extension Division.

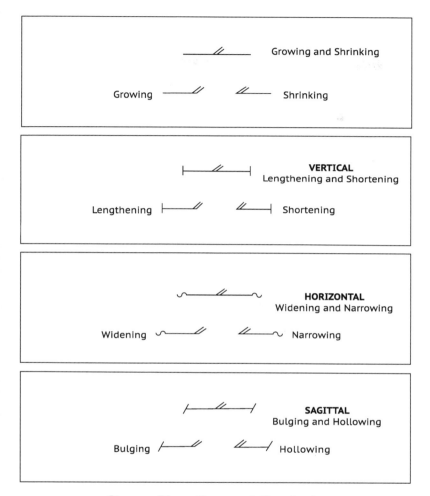

Shape Flow Support Symbols

Figure E.3 L/BMS Symbols, Shape Flow Support.

I would ask Debbie (who later became a member of my company and danced with me for over 15 years) to "lift an arm," for example, but what she did was inhale, expand the corresponding lung and let the inner shaping of her torso send and support her arm into the high space. As I witnessed her instinctive use of inner breath support to expand her reach space in her kinesphere and move with total body involvement, I started to experiment with that process on my own.

I soon incorporated this practice into the developing Evans Dance Technique. My students would call my way of moving "breath dancing." When Peggy Hackney and I entered each other's orbits in 1975-76, I suspect that my use of inner shaping to support almost everything I did was one of the reasons she joined my dance company and the faculty of my school. Inner shaping was not popular in the post-modern downtown dance scene of New York City by which Peggy was surrounded before she moved to Seattle to dance with the Bill Evans Dance Company. However, it was extraordinarily important to Peggy (who pioneered the development of Shape Flow Support theory within L/BMS) and to me. It has been a hallmark of my work for more than 50 years.

4 Shape Qualities

Shape Qualities (SQ) reveal the mover's attitude toward the body's forming or shape-change process. We talk about these aspects of shape change in relationship to the spatial direction in which the form is changing, and they have an expressive component.

The generic terms for this process are:

a *Opening-Closing.*
   Directionally specific terms are:
b *Rising-Sinking*, SQ in the Vertical Dimension/Upward and Downward;
c *Spreading-Enclosing*, SQ in the Horizontal Dimension/Side Open/Side Across;
d *Advancing-Retreating*, SQ in the Sagittal Dimension/Forward and Backward.

My friend, former member of the Evans Dance Company and my teaching colleague for 35 years, Debra Wright Knapp, has found this shape quality language to be of immense value. She uses the SQ terminology continuously throughout technique and creative movement classes. She speaks with qualitative vocal inflections and conveys extensive amounts of information succinctly while evoking total body participation.

I find these words to be integrative because they are action words that encourage students to notice the whole (rather than parts) of themselves. I frequently use these terms to describe movement that is continually changing dimensions. If I am changing in two dimensions I can say "Spreading and Rising," or "Advancing and Rising," for example, rather than saying "circle your arm to the side and then

How the Body Changes Its Form 197

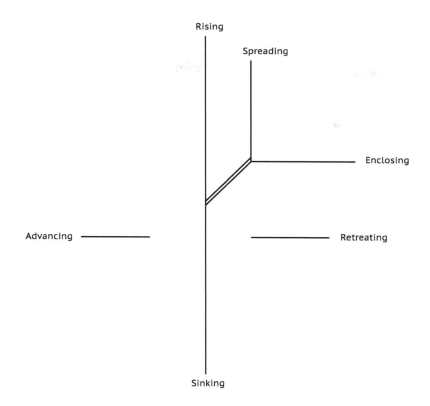

Shape Quality Graph

Figure E.4 L/BMS Symbols, Shape Quality Graph.

up," or "to the front and then up." If I am changing in three dimensions, I might say, "Advancing, Spreading and Rising," or "Retreating Enclosing and Sinking." Whether the change is one-, two- or three-dimensional, when students understand that I am inviting them to experience cellular-level, gradated change as they move through different directions, they reveal heightened integration and expressivity.

Note

1 From an unpublished document prepared by Peggy Hackney for participants in the 1996–97 Integrated Movement Studies Certification Program.

Appendix F
Movement Qualities

Laban and Bartenieff were interested in our non-verbal communication, which often conveys more information than our spoken words. In L/BMS we learn that we are always revealing inner attitudes toward our investments of energy. Sometimes, these different inner attitudes are subtle, but at other times they can be extreme or intense.

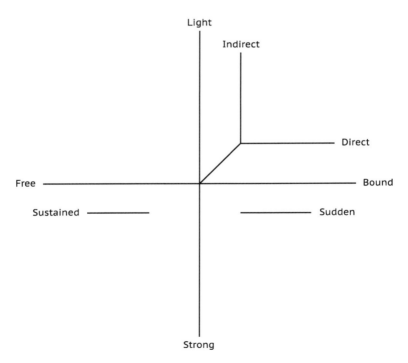

EFFORT GRAPH

Figure F.1 L/BMS Symbols, Effort Graph.

1 Motion Factors and Efforts

In L/BMS theory, there are four *Motion Factors: Weight, Space, Time* and *Flow*. One can think of Motion Factors as the physical properties of movement. Whenever we move, our attitudes toward some or all of those factors are expressed in subtle or pronounced ways. There are eight of those inner attitudes, which are called *Efforts*, one at each end of a bi-polar spectrum for each Motion Factor. The Efforts are:

a *Light* or *Strong* (active Weight) or *Limp* or *Heavy* (passive Weight),
b *Indirect* or *Direct* (Space),
c *Sustained* or *Sudden* (Time), and
d *Free* or *Bound* (Flow).

We can also think of Efforts as *movement qualities* or *energies*. There are many possible gradations from one Effort, along its Motion Factor spectrum, to its opposite.

Some Movement Analysts perceive that by expressing an attitude toward any of these factors we are manifesting a different function of the psyche, as defined by Carl Jung, founder of analytical psychology (1848–1923). In this framework, an attitude toward:

e Weight reveals *Sensing*;
f Space reveals *Thinking*;
g Time reveals *Intuition*; and an attitude toward
h Flow reveals *Feeling*.

This perception makes sense to me. When students access and reveal their inner attitudes and deeply invest in expressing a variety of movement qualities as they dance, I see them become fully alive. I believe that we involve more of the brain (and therefore the whole body) by moving with rich qualitative intent, and I encourage all participants in the classes I teach to move expressively (or "Effortfully").

2 States and Drives

Efforts or movement qualities almost always crystallize in twos, threes or fours, almost never just one at a time. A constellation of two Efforts is called a *State*. A constellation of three Efforts is called a *Drive*. Each of us possesses what Laban called a *Movement Signature*, individual configurations of movement preferences, habits or fallback responses in which a person feels at home, and which define a person to others. A prime component of a person's Movement Signature is their *Effort Life,* the States and Drives of movement qualities in which they feel most themselves.

The different States are:

a   *Dream*—Weight and Flow;
b   *Awake*—Space and Time;
c   *Remote*—Space and Flow;
d   *Near* (or *Rhythm*)—Weight and Time;
e   *Mobile*—Time and Flow; and
f   *Stable*—Weight and Space.

The different Drives are:

g   *Action*—Time, Weight and Space:
h   *Vision*—Time, Space and Flow;
i   *Spell*—Weight, Space and Flow; and
j   *Passion*—Time, Weight and Flow.

A constellation of four Efforts is called a *Complete Effort Action*—attitudes toward Weight, Space, Time and Flow all crystallizing simultaneously.

When I first became aware of the concept of *Effort Life,* I noticed that my preferences are Mobile State (Free and Sudden), Remote State (Indirect and Bound) and Passion Drive (Sudden, Free and Light). I also embody the other Effort constellations, of course, but I know as a performing artist or teacher that when I wish to be most compelling, I can draw on and amplify these preferred (and most-practiced) aspects of my movement lexicon.

I enjoy giving dancers opportunities to reveal what I perceive as special aspects of their movement signatures, emphasizing as a choreographer the expressive qualities that are already fully alive within them. For example, I loved creating phrases for Debbie Poulsen that allowed her to reveal her powerful Strong Weight and Free Flow. For Peggy Hackney, it was her effervescent Light Indirectness. For Gregg Lizenbery, his animalistic fluctuations from Free to Bound Flow and his virtuosic embodiments of Direct Space and Quick Time. For Don Halquist, his calligraphic Direct Space and Bound Flow. For Shirley Jenkins, her riveting Bound, Strong Sustainment.

When a second cast learns one of my existing pieces, they have the challenge of fitting themselves into the Effort Life of the dancer on whom a role was originally created. As a dancer, I love the challenge of recreating a role designed for someone else, because it forces me to discover new possibilities in my own expressive life.

There are early post-modern styles of choreography in which the Efforts are mostly neutralized, so that it is the outer form and sequential organization of movement that is emphasized rather than the inner/expressive intent. When I view such work, I find myself seeing dancers as if they were mostly inanimate art objects rather than living, breathing human beings. I often find such work intellectually fascinating and visually compelling, but it has seldom held much richness for me as a creative artist. In many current post-modern or contemporary styles, Flow is of such high intensity that it often subsumes all the other potential expressive aspects of the dancing. Such work can be mesmerizing and kinesthetically satisfying in the moment, but it often leaves the viewer with few visual after-images or infectious rhythms that can be savored in retrospect.

In 1975, I had opportunities to witness several early contact improv performances by Steve Paxton, an iconic figure in the development of post-modern dance. His performances were full of dynamism and extreme changes in attitudes toward Space, Time, Weight and Flow. We lived in the same house during a summer intensive workshop sponsored by American University and the Wolf Trap Performing Arts Foundation, and we had many spirited late-night kitchen-table talks about how he and I were both pursuing extreme and risk-taking movement qualities (what he called "flung dancing") in dance styles that were aesthetically worlds apart.

3 Eight Basic Effort Actions

Many students who know nothing else about L/BMS theory have heard of *Float, Punch, Glide, Slash, Dab, Wring, Flick* and *Press*. These are the eight three-effort combinations of the Action Drive, which we often use to accomplish work tasks. They are also called the eight Basic Effort Actions. These configurations have become popular among those who teach movement for actors because they convey copious amounts of information efficiently and because they are words that evoke a wide variety of expressive qualities in our students.

The configurations are:

a   *Float*—Sustained, Light and Indirect (all indulging efforts);
b   *Punch*—Sudden, Strong and Direct (all coping efforts);
c   *Glide*—Sustained, Light and Direct;
d   *Slash*—Sudden, Strong and Indirect;
e   *Dab*—Sudden, Light and Direct;

f   *Wring*—Sustained, Strong and Indirect;
g   *Flick*—Sudden, Light and Indirect;
h   *Press*—Sustained, Strong and Direct.

In L/BMS theory, the Action Drive is Flowless (meaning to me that it is not primarily about feeling or emotion), but when I use these words while teaching technique classes (which I do often), I also incorporate Flow in my embodied demonstrations, making them the *Action Drive with Flow*, or *Complete Effort Actions*. I try to embody the expressive qualities in my vocal inflections when teaching them, so that my sounding, as well as my moving, is conveying qualitative intent.

Appendix G
The Geometry of Movement

1 Basic Spatial Terms and Concepts

L/BMS gives us many ways of understanding movement as it relates to Space, geometry or architecture. Some basic terms in this area of the system are:

a   *Kinesphere:* One's personal movement sphere. The three-dimensional volume of space I can access with my body without changing my location. Psychologically, the space I can intimately attend to.
b   *Levels:* High, Medium or Low Zones in the kinesphere.
c   *General Space:* The larger space in which my kinesphere exists and through which it travels.
d   *Pathways:* Gestural routes through my kinesphere or Postural routes through the general space.
e   *Approach to kinesphere:* How my kinesphere is revealed through Spatial Tension.
f   *Central approach to the kinesphere:* A spatial tension between the center and the edge of my kinesphere, traveling from, to or through the center (affined to the Spoke-like Directional Mode of Shape Change).
g   *Peripheral approach to the kinesphere:* A Spatial Tension along the edge of my kinesphere, maintaining a sense of distance between the center and edge (affined to the Arc-like Directional Mode of Shape Change).
h   *Transverse approach to the kinesphere:* A Spatial Tension between the center and the edge, revealed by Carving or molding the volume of the kinesphere (affined to the Carving Mode of Shape Change).

204 *The Geometry of Movement*

i *Directions:* Rays that radiate out from the body's center into space. Locations in my kinesphere.
   Note: See figures 7.13, L/BMS Directional Symbols, and 8.4, L/BMS Symbols, Directional Matrix.

j *Spatial Pull:* An invisible line of potential energy that can be revealed in movement.

k *Scale:* A sequence of directions (or locations) within the kinesphere that can be phrased in different ways and led by different parts of the body.

l *Cardinal Dimensions:* The three most important dimensions, or lines—Vertical (up-down), Sagittal (front-back) and Horizontal (side to side). Each dimension has two directions and one Spatial Pull.

m *Cross of Axes:* The intersection of the three cardinal dimensions. Also known as the Dimensional Cross. Laban created the Defense Scale in this spatial form. It is the internal support for the Octahedron.

n *Plane:* A flat surface that contains two dimensions and can be dissected by a Diameter.

o *Diameter:* A line from one corner of a plane to its two-dimensional opposite corner.

p *Cardinal Planes:* The three most important surfaces, or planes—Vertical (up-down and side-side), Sagittal (front-back and up-down) and Horizontal (side-side and front-back).

q *Diametral Cross:* An intersection of the three cardinal rectangular planes. It is the internal support for an Icosahedron.

r *Rectangular Planes:* Door Plane—a vertical plane with more up-down than side-side. Wheel Plane—a sagittal plane with more front-back than up-down. Table Plane—a horizontal plane with more side-side than front-back.
   Note: See Figure 7.11, Intersection of the Three Cardinal Planes.

s *Diametral Scales:* Laban created several scales, each with two unequal Spatial Pulls, within the three rectangular planes. When peripheral, such scales are called cycles through a plane.

t *Transverse Spiraling:* A twisting journey through the kinesphere with three unequal spatial pulls.

u *Platonic Solids:* Crystalline or polyhedral forms whose vertices, or corners, serve as road maps for Spatial Pulls. Laban created numerous Scales in these different polyhedral, voluminous forms (v. through z. below).

v   *Tetrahedron:* Four faces or surfaces. Laban made numerous drawings of human figures responding to the Spatial Pulls of the tetrahedron.
w   *Octahedron:* Eight faces. Many classical dance styles (which began as court dances) prefer the one- and two-dimensional pathways or Spatial Pulls of this form. It feels stable and emphasizes the status quo.
x   *Hexahedron* or *Cube*: Six faces. Laban created the Diagonal Scale within this form. That scale sequences alternately from three even spatial pulls to two even spatial pulls. It feels dynamic, like flying or falling, upsetting the status quo.
y   *Icosahedron:* 20 faces. Laban created many scales within this form. Some are Peripheral and are called Girdles or Primary Scales. Others are Transverse and are called Axis, A or B Scales. By exploring the unequal, always off-center pathways of these scales, dancers are able to find new journeys through both the kinesphere and within their bodies, creating new neuromuscular synapses, and, I believe, new possibilities in all aspects of their lives.
z   *Dodecahedron:* 12 faces. Laban explored this form less than the others, but some of his successors are investigating possible scales within this form.

Note: *For more information on Scales, read* Space Harmony: Basic Terms *[Revised Edition], by Cecily Dell and Aileen Crow.*

2 Directional Matrix/One-, Two- or Three-Dimensional Pathways through the Kinesphere

In L/BMS, we identify 27 significant directions (or locations) in the kinesphere. Together, they are known as the *Directional Matrix*. From the body's center, Place Middle, there are eight directions (or points in the kinesphere) radiating out at the middle level and nine directions at both the high and low levels.

Note: *Please see Figures 7.13, Directional Symbols, and 8.4, Directional Matrix.*

By exploring all 27 points in the kinesphere and as many as possible of the pathways from point to point, you could give yourself and students a rich variety of spatial journeys. I suggest that you try to introduce a few new pathways through the kinesphere each week, with the goal of having offered most or all of them to your students by the end of a semester or extended series of classes. Each movement phrase you compose with different spatial sequences will enliven different Body co-ordination patterns, different Effort affinities and different Shape affinities in the mover.

Below is a template I have organized for remembering the different pathways from one direction to another one might travel within the kinesphere.

Thirteen of the pathways from one direction to its opposite are *Central* and travel through *Place Middle*.

a   The *one-dimensional central pathways* are:
    Place High to Place Low or reverse (vertical dimension);
    Forward Middle to Back Middle or reverse (sagittal dimension);
    Right Side Middle to Left Side Middle or reverse (horizontal dimension).

b   The *two-dimensional central pathways* are:
    Right Side High to Left Side Low or reverse, or
    Left Side High to Right Side Low or reverse (vertical plane);
    Forward High to Back Low or reverse, or
    Forward Low to Back High or reverse (sagittal plane);
    Right Forward Middle to Left Back Middle or reverse, or
    Left Forward Middle to Right Back Middle or reverse (horizontal plane).

c   The *primary three-dimensional central pathways* (or *True Diagonals)* are:
    Right Forward High to Left Backward Low or reverse;
    Left Forward High to Right Backward Low or reverse;
    Right Forward Low to Left Backward High or reverse, and
    Left Forward Low to Right Backward High or reverse.

Twenty-four other pathways are *Peripheral* and travel from one direction to its opposite along the edge of the kinesphere.

d   The *one-dimensional peripheral pathways* are:
    Vertical—
    Right Forward High to Right Forward Low or reverse;
    Left Forward High to Left Forward Low or reverse;
    Right Back High to Right Back Low or reverse;
    Left Back High to Left Back Low or reverse.
    Horizontal—
    Right Forward High to Left Forward High or reverse;
    Right Forward Middle to Left Forward Middle or reverse;
    Right Forward Low to Left Forward Low or reverse;
    Right Back High to Left Back High or reverse;

Right Back Middle to Left Back Middle or reverse;
Right Back Low to Left Back Low or reverse.
Sagittal—
Right Forward High to Right Back High or reverse;
Right Forward Middle to Right Back Middle or reverse;
Right Forward Low to Right Back Low or reverse;
Left Forward High to Left Back High or reverse;
Left Forward Middle to Left Back Middle or reverse;
Left Forward Low to Left Back Low or reverse.

e   The *two-dimensional peripheral pathways* are:
Front—
Right Forward High to Left Forward Low or reverse;
Left Forward High to Right Forward Low or reverse.
Right Side—
Right Forward High to Right Back Low or reverse;
Right Back High to Right Forward Low or reverse.
Left Side—
Left Forward High to Left Back Low or reverse;
Left Back High to Left Forward Low or reverse.
Back—
Right Back High to Left Back Low or reverse;
Left Back High to Right Back Low or reverse.

Many other pathways from one direction to another are *Transverse*, and travel with uneven spatial pulls through the volume of the kinesphere, between the center and the edge.

f   One example of these transverse pathways is the *Icosahedral A Scale*, right hand lead:
Right Side High-Back Low-Left Forward Middle;
Right Side Low-Back High-Right Forward Middle;
Left Side Low-Forward High-Right Back Middle;
Left Side High-Forward Low-Left Back Middle.

g   The phrases through three-points-in-space described above visit 12 of the corners (or *Vertices*) of the Icosahedron. To visit the other 12 corners, lead with the left hand in the following sequence:
Left Side High-Back Low-Right Forward Middle;
Left Side Low-Back High-Left Forward Middle;
Right Side Low-Forward High-Left Back Middle;
Right Side High-Forward Low-Right Back Middle.

Index

Acomb, Heather 8
active/held body parts 185
African American *see* Black American
Albuquerque 7, 18, 33, 176, 178
alignment 3, 49–50, 79–80, 88–89, 126, 149, 169, 179, 183
American Dance Festival (ADF) 18, 67, 89, 179
American Dance Guild 7
arm circles 71, 93, 110, 113, 115–20, 122, 187–88
Armstrong, Thomas 158

backward design 68
Bailie, Jolene 8
Bainbridge Cohen, Bonnie 50, 53, 115, 189
Ballet West 6
Bartenieff, Irmgard 33, 46, 53, 79, 155, 169, 179, 182, 185, 194
Bartenieff Fundamentals (BF) 21, 33, 46–49, 53, 65–66, 75, 77–80, 89, 92, 102, 106, 113, 116, 125, 131, 169, 179, 180, 184–86
Basic Six 93, 106, 185–88
Bateson, Gregory 38, 53, 170
Bennett, Colette 38, 52
big dance 68–69, 88
Bill Evans Dance Company (BEDCO) 7, 9, 16, 18, 33, 53, 60, 89, 126, 157, 177, 179, 196
Bill Evans Summer Institute of Dance 7, 21, 126
Bill Evans Teachers Intensive (BETI) 21, 32–33, 60, 151, 157

BIPOC (Black, Indigenous and other people of color) 2, 182
Black American 1, 2, 9, 38–40, 52, 61, 72, 75, 170, 173–74, 177–78, 182
Bloom's Taxonomy 28, 32
body attitude 40, 174, 185
body-half 56, 93, 141, 187–89, 191, 193
Body-Mind Centering (BMC) 51, 53, 108, 131, 169, 182, 189
body-mind/mind-body 6, 28, 38–39, 46–47, 57–58, 73, 125, 175, 178, 184
Body-part Phrasings: Sequential 80–81, 113, 185, 201; Simultaneous 80–81, 113, 185; Successive 80-1, 88, 90, 100-102, 111-13, 131, 133, 185
bones and discs: acetabulum 85–86, 92, 188; ankle 58, 82–83, 100–103, 105, 135; anterior superior iliac spine (hip bone) 91; appendicular skeleton 114; atlanto-occipital joint 87; axial skeleton 85, 114; bone rhythms 72, 91, 97–98, 102, 126, 128–29; calcaneus 58, 82, 101, 103–106; cervical spine 81, 106–107, 109–12; clavicle 72, 99, 113, 115-17, 122; coccyx 80, 90, 92–93; cuboid 101, 104; cuneiform 101; facets 107, 111-13; femoral condyles 98; femoral head 85–87, 92, 124, 188; femoral joints 91; femur 83, 85, 91, 93, 96, 98,

123–24, 127–28, 188; fibula 82, 101–103; glenohumeral joint 113, 115, 123; humerus 72, 113-14, 116–17, 122–24; iliac crest 96; ilium 93; intervertebral discs 107; ischial tuberosity (sitz bones) 85–87, 90–91; ischium 93; lumbar spine 81–82, 96, 109-11, 173; malleoli 103–106; meniscus 98; metacarpal 115, 123; metatarsals 91, 100–106; navicular 101; patella 91, 98, 173; pelvic diamond/pelvic outlet 90–92, 97, 109, 128, 188; pelvic half 92–94, 96-97, 124, 127–28; phalange 115, 117, 123; planar joints 107, 111; pubic symphysis 90–91, 96-97, 188; pubis 83, 93; rib cage, ribs 72, 76–77, 110, 112-13, 115, 117–18; sacral spine 107–108; sacroiliac joints 93, 96; sacrum 83, 91–93, 97, 108, 111, 127, 173; scapula 72, 99, 110, 113–17, 122–23; scapulohumeral rhythm 71, 113, 188; scapulothoracic joint 115, 124; skull 88, 108–109; sternoclavicular joint 114–15, 124; sternum 114, 134–35, 138; talus 82, 101–102, 104; tarsals 82, 103; thoracic spine 107–13, 119, 128, 173; tibia 82–83, 91, 98, 101–103, 173; trochanter (greater/lesser) 85–87, 105-106, 188; ulna 99, 114-15, 117, 123–24
Borde, Percival 8, 38, 52, 75, 174
breath: dances 78; support 78, 79, 140–41, 195

Caine, Renate Nummela and Geoffrey 20, 33, 36, 53, 170
Campbell, Bruce and Linda 158
Carving 122, 192–93, 203
center of gravity 127–28, 135, 138
Center of Lightness 135
Center of Neutral Weight 138
Certified Evans Teacher (CET) 18, 21, 29, 32–33, 56, 60, 69, 149, 157
Certified Laban Movement Analyst (CLMA), Certified Movement Analyst (CMA) 149, 180

Chicago Moving Company 78
Christensen, Willam 6, 52
circumduction 92, 106, 115
Clippinger, Karen 8, 86, 89, 169
cognitive/cognitively 20, 27–28, 32, 47, 63, 67, 192
Cole, Jack 8, 13, 17, 88, 174
Coleman, Jim 8
Collins, Janet 8, 174
Complete Effort Action 200, 202
Connecticut College 179
Contact Quarterly 6
Cooper, KLee 23, 32
Core-Distal 189–90
Cornish College of the Arts 7, 60
COVID-19 (pandemic) 1, 64
cross-lateral 110, 128, 130–31, 188–89, 191
Cube 110, 119–20, 135, 147–48, 205

Dance Studio Life Magazine 1
dance styles/techniques: bailefolklorico 174; ballet 3, 6–7, 24, 55, 74, 86–87, 96, 98, 129, 172, 174, 177–78; Bharatanatyam 174; contemporary 3, 6, 18, 24, 70, 98–99, 129, 141, 201; Cunningham 66; flamenco 177–78; Hawkins 66; hip-hop 3, 6, 129, 141, 178; jazz 3, 6, 24, 40, 52, 66, 82, 88, 98, 129, 172–75; Limón 66; Luigi 66; Mattox 66; modern 6–8, 14, 17, 45, 52–53, 66, 75–76, 79, 88, 126, 172, 174–75, 177–78, 181, 194; post-modern 196, 201; rhythm tap 38–40, 52, 61, 172–73, 177–78; Simonson 66; swing-style jazz 172–73; tap 3, 6, 24, 38–40, 52, 61, 172–74, 177–78
Dance Teacher Magazine 7
Daniels, Kathryn (Kitty) 8, 21, 55, 60, 86, 115
Dapena, Dr. Jesus 99
DaPron, Louis 39, 52
Dean College 7, 69
Debenham, Kathie 63
Deutsche Oper Ballet 173
Dewey, John 22

Index

Diehl, Kathy 8
Directional Matrix 145–46, 148, 177, 204–205
Door Plane 111, 118, 135, 204
dopamine 41
Dowd, Irene 89
Duke University 67
Dwyer, Annie 143, 149

Effort Life 200
eight Basic Effort Actions 201
embodied, embodiment 6, 11, 24, 41, 46–47, 49, 60, 80, 113, 126, 159, 174, 176, 178, 183, 202
endorphin 15, 41
Eurocentric 173
The Evans Company School 7
Evans Dance Technique 3, 21, 79, 157, 196, 179
Evans Somatic Dance Certification Program 3
Evans Somatic Dance Technique 7, 9
eye-tracking 110, 113, 115, 120, 122, 188

fascia, fascial 59, 78, 81, 113, 115, 118, 120, 122, 124–25, 127–28, 142, 148, 184
Fitt, Sally 8
fluids: arterial blood 77; cerebrospinal fluid 77, 107; intracellular fluid 77; fat 77; lymph 77; synovial fluid 77, 81, 101, 107, 115, 122–23; venous blood 77
formative feedback 150–51
Fraleigh, Sondra 8, 106-107, 126, 171
Franklin, Eric 8, 80, 89–90, 92, 100, 110–11, 126, 144, 149, 169, 183
Franklin Method 3, 8, 109, 126, 148, 179, 183
Franklin Method Teacher 8, 126

Gardner, Howard 21, 157–58, 182
Gavers, Mattlyn 82
general space 66, 73, 138, 144, 203
Gisolo, Margaret 8
Graham, Martha 76, 175–76, 181
Green Gilbert, Anne 8, 189

Gregory, Cynthia 23
Guggenheim Foundation 7

Hackney, Peggy 8, 31, 33, 46, 48, 53, 63–64, 70, 75, 88–89, 93, 151, 169, 179, 180, 182, 185-86, 189, 191, 196–97, 200
Halquist, Don 3, 5, 8, 21, 32, 40, 60, 63, 151, 157, 167, 171, 200
Hamburg, Janet 8
Hansen, Anna 8
Harkness Ballet 7, 18, 38, 52, 88, 174
Hauschild-Mork, Melissa 8
Hayes, Dr. Elizabeth R. (Betty) 6, 8, 45, 53
H'Doubler, Margaret 8, 45, 52–53, 137
Head-Tail connection 107
Hobart and William Smith Colleges 5, 53, 126
Hollywood 17, 39, 88
Holm, Hanya 176, 181
homologous 131, 188, 190
human spirit 24, 67, 166
Humphrey, Doris 17, 76, 181
Hyatt, Janyce (Jan) 8, 16–18
hyperextension 98-99, 105

Icosahedron 147–48, 204–205, 207
ideokinesis 86, 88, 169, 182–83
Indiana University 7, 18, 69, 99
Indigenous Americans 2, 176–77, 182–83
Integrated Movement Studies (IMS) 33, 63, 151, 180, 191, 197
International Association of Dance Medicine and Science 7, 60
inversion 130–31, 133

Jackson, Robyn R. 42, 54, 170
Johnson, Linda 8
Johnston, Charles 182
Jung, Carl 199
Jones, Betty 8, 86
Jacob's Pillow 18, 23

kinesphere 66, 115, 117, 122–23, 138, 143–44, 146–49, 192, 194, 196, 203–207

212 Index

kinesthesia 45, 63, 159
kinesthetic 8, 21, 29, 39, 45–46, 57, 60, 65–66, 81, 111-12, 157–59, 164
kinetic chains 58, 80, 99, 105-106, 123, 125, 144, 188
Knapp, Debra (Debbi) Wright 16, 18, 32, 37

Laban, Rudolf 4, 46, 76, 137, 147–48, 176, 179–82, 198–99, 204–205
Laban/Bartenieff (L/B) 3, 14, 33–34, 42, 46, 53, 55, 90, 127, 169, 173, 176, 179, 180–84
Laban/Bartenieff Movement System (L/BMS) 3, 34, 42, 46, 49, 53, 55–56, 60, 90, 118, 120–21, 127–28, 137–41, 143–47, 179, 180–83, 189, 192–99, 201–202, 204–205
Lamont, Bette 8
Langstaff, Gretchen 88–89
Lazear, David 158
learning circles 61, 177
Lehi (Utah) 172
levels 203, 205
Lewitzky, Bella 103, 106, 126
Lifetime Achievement Award 7
Linnaeus, Carolus 165
Lizenbery, Gregg 8, 200
Lundgren, Suzie 8, 29

McKayle, Donald 8, 175–76
MacRae-Campbell, Linda 34, 54, 158, 170
McTighe, Jay and Grant Wiggins 68, 75, 170
Mattox, Matt 82, 88
Meaden, Janice 8, 33, 63, 151
Meriwether, Russell ("La Meri") 174
mind-body *see* body-mind
mind/body/spirit 28, 40, 47, 57, 79
Modes of Shape Change 130, 192–93
motion factors: weight, space, time, flow 199
movement signature 49, 199–200
[the] multiple intelligences: bodily-kinesthetic intelligence 21, 157–59, 164; interpersonal intelligence 157, 161–62; intrapersonal intelligence 162–63; logical-mathematical intelligence 21, 157–58, 164; musical-rhythmic intelligence 160–61; naturalist intelligence 157, 165, 171; Theory of Multiple Intelligences (MI) 3, 21–22, 33, 157–58, 167, 171; verbal-linguistic intelligence 158, 163; visual-spatial intelligence 159–60
muscles: abdominal muscles 76; concentric 125, 144, 149; eccentric 144, 149; gemellus inferior/superior 85; hamstring 95-96, 174, 188; iliopsoas 95-96, 174, 188; isometric contraction 76; lateral rotators 85–86, 125; muscle tension 144; obturator externus/internus 85; pelvic diaphragm 97; pelvic floor 85, 138; piriformis 85; quadratus femoris 85; respiratory diaphragm 76–78; sartorius 86; transversus abdominis/deep abdominal wall 76

National Dance Association (NDA) 6, 53
National Dance Education Organization (NDEO) 7, 178
National Endowment for the Arts (NEA) 7, 18
National High School Dance Festival 7
Navajo 177–78, 183
Nelson, Judith 79
neuromusculoskeletal 72, 84, 87, 125, 145, 188
New York City 13, 18, 38, 46, 52, 79, 88, 174–76, 182, 196
non-Eurocentric 173

objective language 55
organs 59, 78, 80, 120; heart 77; liver 76; lungs 76–78, 140, 190, 194–95; spleen 76; stomach 76
Ossola, Cheryl 1
overcurve 129, 134–35

(patterns of) total body organization 50, 66, 125, 143, 188–89
Paxton, Steve 201
pedagogy 3, 6, 14, 18, 34, 40, 42, 69, 142, 151, 170, 173, 176–77, 181

Pilates, Joseph 185
Plato 147
Platonic Solids 147, 204
plié 57, 83–84, 86, 91–92, 98, 102–103, 105, 135
Port Townsend, Washington 1, 18, 149, 157
Poulsen, Debbie 8, 194–95, 200
Primus, Pearl 38, 52, 67, 75, 174
proprioception 45
proximal 81, 106, 117, 122–25
Purrington Park, June 6, 8, 39, 52

Repertory Dance Theatre (RDT) 7, 18, 45, 52–53, 82, 86, 173, 175–76
Reynolds Daniel, Nora 126
Rhode Island College 157
Rice, Rebecca 79
Ririe, Shirley 6
ritual 74; closing 68, 74–75; opening 73–74
Romita, Nancy and Allegra 8, 103, 106, 126, 169
Royne, Lois 78
Ruth Page International Ballet 7

Salt Lake City 6, 39, 45, 52, 63, 78, 190
San Diego Union 82
Schick, Pam 8, 33, 63
Scriven, Michael 150
Seattle 7, 18, 23, 53, 60, 63, 86, 88–89, 149, 179, 190, 196
self-talk 20, 35, 92, 109, 122
Shape Flow Support 118-20, 130, 173, 194–96
Shape Qualities 71, 90, 118, 120, 122, 132, 139, 147, 196
Shineflug, Nana 78
Showalter, Jenny 8
Sokolow, Anna 175
Space Harmony 147, 169, 205
spatial: organization 63; pull, pulls 145–46, 204–205, 207; relationships 63; tension 144, 203
States and Drives 199–200
static alignment 79–80
Stepenberg, Tara 8
still forms: ball 131, 133, 193; pin 131, 133, 193; spiral 56, 193;

tetrahedron 147, 193, 205; wall 50, 141, 193
subjective language 55
summative feedback 150–51
SUNY Brockport 7, 42, 52, 69, 106, 126
Sweigard, Lulu 88–89, 137, 169, 183

Table Plane 119, 204
Tanner, Virginia 175, 194
Thies, Mariah-Jane 56
Three Cardinal Dimensions 118–19, 147, 204
Todd, Mabel Ellsworth 88–89, 137
Torok, Kristin 79, 149
tripod of balance 101, 103–106
turn-in 87–88
turn-out 84–88, 91, 102, 125

undercurve 128–135
University of New Mexico 7, 33, 69, 103, 126, 157, 176–77, 183
University of Utah 6, 7, 14, 39, 45, 53, 75, 82, 86, 126, 172, 175, 194
University of Wisconsin-Madison 45, 53
Upper-Lower 189–91, 131

Walker, Dianne 8, 38, 52
walking 48–49, 93, 97, 100-101, 127–28, 191
Wallace, Kyla 8
Wancier, Daniela 8
Waters, Elizabeth 8, 176–77
Weidman, Charles 17, 181
Welsh, Anne Marie 82
West Berlin 173
Wheel plane 111, 119, 135, 204
Wigman, Mary 176, 181
Wilde, Patricia 7, 52
Williams, Cynthia J. 8, 53, 126
Wilmerding, Ginny 8
Wilson, John M. 8
Woodbury, Joan 6
World, Courtney 8

Yield and Push to Reach and Pull 34, 50–51, 128

Zuni 176–77

Taylor & Francis eBooks

www.taylorfrancis.com

A single destination for eBooks from Taylor & Francis with increased functionality and an improved user experience to meet the needs of our customers.

90,000+ eBooks of award-winning academic content in Humanities, Social Science, Science, Technology, Engineering, and Medical written by a global network of editors and authors.

TAYLOR & FRANCIS EBOOKS OFFERS:

- A streamlined experience for our library customers
- A single point of discovery for all of our eBook content
- Improved search and discovery of content at both book and chapter level

REQUEST A FREE TRIAL
support@taylorfrancis.com

Printed in the United States
by Baker & Taylor Publisher Services